Mastering

C++ Programming

MACMILLAN MASTER SERIES

Accounting
Advanced English Language
Advanced Pure Mathematics
Arabic
Banking
Basic Management
Biology
British Politics
Business Administration
Business Communication
Business Law
C Programming
C++ Programming
Catering Theory
Chemistry
COBOL Programming
Communication
Databases
Economic and Social History
Economics
Electrical Engineering
Electronic and Electrical Calculations
Electronics
English as a Foreign Language
English Grammar
English Language
English Literature
French
French 2
German
German 2

Global Information Systems
Human Biology
Internet
Italian
Italian 2
Java
Manufacturing
Marketing
Mathematics
Mathematics for Electrical and
    Electronic Engineering
Microsoft Office
Modern British History
Modern European History
Modern World History
Pascal and Delphi Programming
Philosophy
Photography
Physics
Psychology
Science
Shakespeare
Social Welfare
Sociology
Spanish
Spanish 2
Statistics
Study Skills
Visual Basic
World Religions

Macmillan Master Series
Series Standing Order ISBN 0–333–69343–4
(outside North America only)

You can receive future titles in this series as they are published by placing a standing order.
Please contact your bookseller or, in case of difficulty, write to us at the address below with
your name and address, the title of the series and the ISBN quoted above.

Customer Services Department, Macmillan Distribution Ltd
Houndmills, Basingstoke, Hampshire RG21 6XS, England

Mastering

C++ Programming

W. Arthur Chapman, BSc (Hons), BA (Hons), PhD
Senior Lecturer
Edinburgh's Telford College
Edinburgh

Series Editor

William Buchanan, BSc (Hons), CEng, PhD
Senior Lecturer
Napier University
Edinburgh

MACMILLAN

Published in 1998 by
MACMILLAN PRESS LTD
Houndmills, Basingstoke, Hampshire RG21 6XS
and London
Companies and representatives
throughout the world

ISBN 0–333–73179–4

A catalogue record for this book is available
from the British Library.

This book is printed on paper suitable for recycling and
made from fully managed and sustained forest sources.

10   9   8   7   6   5   4   3   2   1
07   06   05   04   03   02   01   00   99   98

Typeset by W. Buchanan in Great Britain.

Printed by Biddles Ltd, Guildford and King's Lynn.

Contents

Preface

This book introduces the reader to the fundamental constructs of C++ and provides a gentle introduction to the ideas of object-oriented programming. It is an advantage to have some previous knowledge and experience of other programming language, such as Pascal or C. Languages such as Pascal, C and C++ are constructed out of a number of basic control structures (sequence, selection and iteration) and use well-defined blocks of code which perform particular tasks (procedures and functions in Pascal; functions in C and C++). In addition these languages require some basic data types and allow the creation of user-defined data types. For example, in Pascal the fundamental types are integer, real, char, Boolean and, in some implementations, string. In C and C++ we have int, float and char. Type qualifiers (short, long, signed and unsigned) in C and C++ provide extensions to the basic data types. Further extensions are introduced through the use of arrays to provide collections of a particular data type (in all three languages) and then through the use of record in Pascal, struct (and typedef) in C and C++ and through the use of class in C++ to allow for more complex user-defined data types.

The C++ language grew out of C (hence its name) and so is based on a functional approach to programming. In such languages a problem is broken down into modules, which perform a particular well-defined task. Each module is then created through a design process consisting of stages such as description, outline design, detail design, coding and testing. C++ can be thought of as an extension to C by, for example, introducing function and operator overloading or providing better ways of implementing abstract data types. However, it can also be thought of as a completely new language which allows for the use of a new approach to software design. This new approach – object-oriented design – is based on modelling a problem using objects. These objects are members of classes; they have various behaviours and they pass messages to other objects. Often such an approach to software design more closely models our everyday world, for example think of the interaction of a passenger getting on a bus and buying a ticket from the driver. The passenger and driver can be thought of as two separate objects with certain behaviours, who pass 'messages' between them.

The main aim of this book is to help you to learn the fundamental constructs of the C++ language. It is organised as follows:

- Chapters 1 and 2. Provides an introduction to the fundamental structure, semantics and syntax of C++ and illustrates some of the basic enhancements made to C.

- Chapter 3. This deals with pointers and their uses, including a look at dynamic memory management. Whilst pointers are not as necessary in C++ as they are in C they still have important uses and anyone programming in C++ needs to have some understanding of their use.
- Chapter 4. Provides a glimpse of the essentials of input and output in C++ as well as a short review of i/o in C.
- Chapter 5. Provides more detail of classes, why they are needed, how they are constructed and how they are used.
- Chapter 6. A detailed discussion of the many extended function facilities, where the central concepts of function overloading and operator overloading is discussed.
- Chapter 7. Looks at ways of manipulating objects using arrays and pointers.
- Chapter 8. Discusses inheritance, central to object oriented programming, and reusability.
- Chapter 9. Looks at the way classes can be used as containers for other classes and the extension to templates.

In a book of this length it is not possible to go deeply into the details of program design, although some examples of functional design and object-oriented design will be provided. It is important that you understand the basics of both of these approaches to program design. Contrary to some views not every problem can be squeezed into an object-model solution. However, providing another method of software design is a means of providing one more tool for the programmer and, as in any jobs it is important that the right tool is used for the right job. After working through this book you should be:

- More familiar with some of the more important details of C++.
- Familiar with both functional design and object-oriented design methods.
- Better able to choose when to use which method.

Once again I would like to thank my friend and colleague Noel Chidwick at Edinburgh's Telford College for the suggestion to publish this material – it has been used in various forms in normal 'face-to-face' classes and 'on-line' via Scotland's Virtual College (http://www.svc.org.uk) – and I am grateful for the help and feedback from staff and students during the gestation period. Thanks are also due to Suzannah Tipple at Macmillan for her help, encouragement and understanding throughout the lifetime of this project and, in particular, when I was trying to keep to, but missing deadlines. I am grateful also to Bill Buchanan for his help, understanding and perseverance in dealing with the text in its various unfinished forms and for his diligence in producing the final version. Finally, for their support, understanding and encouragement I would like to thank my wife Judy, and children Emma, Lucy and Donald. Emma, whilst not having to put up with the physical presence and inevitable household problems, provided the occasional 'How's the book going Dad?' either via e-mail or telephone which acted as a spur to carry on.

W. Arthur Chapman, June 1998 (`arthurc@ed-coll.ac.uk`)

Note from Series Editor:
The Macmillan Mastering IT and Computing series is expanding rapidly and this book is a key foundation book in the whole series. I have known and respected Arthur's work for many years. Many people around the world have used his excellent Mastering C Programming book and I myself used it when I first started to learn C. As we both currently live and work in Edinburgh, it has made the production of this book much easier than it usually is. I must thank Arthur for his constant commitment to the project and his patience in answering my questions.

It is amazing how programming has changed over the years. Initially it was simple Basic programs written on microcomputers or FORTRAN and COBOL programs running on massive, and expensive, main-frame computers. Nowadays most people can afford all the required development tools and produce software which is infinitely more complex than programs which were developed decades ago. There has also been a great change in the emphasis in electronic systems. At one time much development effort went into producing the hardware and less on the software. These days, in most cases, much of the development time goes into software development. Hardware, in many cases, is becoming less important and is often programmed by the software.

It can be said that software development has truly changed our modem life. Without software we could not have complex air traffic control systems, ATMs, computer games, the Internet, electronic mail and video conferencing. The application of software increases day-by-day, such as databases, electronic communications, graphics, satellite navigation systems, engine management systems, and so on.

At one time software development was done by one or two programmers who just 'hacked' programs together, now, much of it is written by large programming teams using object-oriented design, and implemented in languages such as C++. In job adverts for Software Engineers the most prevalent development language asked for is C++. This shows the importance of learning the language and especially in understanding object-oriented design.

Finally, as Arthur has done, I would personally like to thank Suzannah Tipple, Isobel Munday and Christopher Glennie at Macmillan for their hard work and their continued support for the Mastering IT and Computing series. Also, I would like to thank my family, Julie, Billy, Jamie and David for their love and understanding.

William Buchanan, June 1998 (`w.buchanan@napier.ac.uk`)

1 From C to C++

1.1 Introduction

In this first chapter you will be introduced to the *basic structure* of a C++ program and we will be looking at the various elements which go to make up such a program. Much of the content of this chapter will be familiar to you if you have already delved a little into C. However there are important elements in this chapter which are C++ specific, so even if you are a competent C programmer you should still read through these notes and try out the exercises.

Although this book is intended to be self-contained and suitable for anyone with a basic understanding, or previous knowledge, of at least one other programming language, this first chapter does cover a lot of ground in a fairly short space of time. If you require a more extended introduction to C then you should take a look at *Mastering C Programming* by the present author. The book introduces the C language at a rather more gentle pace and is suitable for anyone with no previous knowledge of programming.

1.2 C ++ program structure

The basic structure of a C++ program is very similar to that of a C program – it will generally consist of comments, preprocessor instructions (e.g. to allow library files to be included), function declarations (and definitions) and a main program function. The general structure is:

```
//:PROGNAME.CPP - what the program does additional information
//.explaining the purpose of the program, any special
//.requirements,etc., Author's name, date of writing and version.
#include <iostream.h> // includes the 'header file'
        // iostream.h plus any other header files that
        // may be required by the program

// function declarations - indicating the types,
// names and arguments of functions which will be
// defined later on in the program
// ................................................
void main()
```

```
{
    // main body of the program
}
// function definitions - which must match the
// declarations given earlier
/* alternatively the function definitions may be in other files,
   either in a header file (and then #included), or in a precompiled
   object file which is 'linked' to the main program during final
   compilation. */
// as you can see from the previous comment standard
// C comments can also be used in C++ programs
```

This translates into a traditional first program (HELLO.cpp) as given in Program 1.1.

📋 **Program 1.1**

```
//: HELLO.cpp - traditional first program, even in C++
//. no need for any further comments!
//.   Name:    Arthur Chapman
//.   Date:    12 May 1997
//.   Version:   1.0
#include <iostream.h>
// ..................................................
void main()
{
    cout << "Hello world\n";
    cout << "Welcome to C++\n";
}
```

The output when this program is compiled is shown in Test run 1.1.

🖥 **Test run 1.1**
```
Hello World
Welcome to C++

─
```

The _ indicates the position of the cursor after execution of the program. If you are already familiar with the C language then you will require very little further explanation concerning the structure of a C++ program. The key points concerning the basic program structure are given in the next sections.

1.2.1 Comments

In C++ comments can be included by using the double forward slash (//) – anything following the double slash will be ignored by the compiler but only to the end of the line. If a second, or third ... comment is required then another double slash must be used on each new line. The start of the comment can be anywhere on a line, even on a line containing a C++ statement, but its scope only lasts for the remainder of that line.

Note that in the first line of comments we have followed the opening slashes with a colon (:) and that in the following line(s) they have been followed with a full-stop (.). This is by no means obligatory but it can be helpful when cataloguing programs, functions etc. If you have access to the utility *grep* then you can use this to scan a number of files and extract lines which match certain criteria. So we can 'pull out' from our C++ files all the lines which begin //: and/or //. to produce a list of program names together with a brief explanation of the program.

C-style comments (/* ... */) can also be used in C++; where for example extended comments are required. However it is better to stick to one form of comment throughout rather than mix different styles.

1.2.2 Header file

The header file included in the basic C++ program is `iostream.h`, rather than `stdio.h` which would be used in a basic C program. The file `iostream.h` serves the same purpose as `stdio.h` in that it provides the fundamental input and output definitions and functions but specifically for C++. As with comments we will be using the specifically C++ I/O functions in this book, although occasionally we will be using some of the C I/O functions.

1.2.3 cout

Which brings us to `cout <<`. The two statements which do all the work in this program are simply output statements which direct output to the standard output stream (i.e. the screen). The statement `cout << "Hello World\n";` can be interpreted as 'send the string "Hello World" followed by a newline character, to the screen'. `cout` is the standard output stream and `<<` is the *overloaded* left shift operator which is used to send output to `cout`. (We will discuss I/O in more detail shortly.) You should already know that \n is an escape sequence which writes a newline character to the output device; other escape sequences, which can be useful for formatting output, are given in Table 1.1.

One of the most useful of the above is the double backslash. When dealing with file I/O we often need to specify the path for a DOS file, e.g. `a:\Chapter1\programs` which in C & C++ we would write as `a:\\Chapter1\\programs`. Another useful one is \" which must be used when we want to include in a string the double quote as a printable character. So if we wish to output:

```
This prints "Hello world"
```

we could write

```
cout << "This prints \"Hello world\" \n";
```

Table 1.1 Escape sequences

Type	Escape sequence	Type	Escape sequence
Backspace	\b	Carriage return	\r
Newline	\n	Vertical tab	\v
Tab	\t	Bell	\a
Form feed	\f	Question mark	\?
Backslash	\\	Double quote	\"
Single quote	\'	Octal number	\ooo, e.g. \253, \025
Hexadecimal number	\xhhh, e.g. \xAB		

or, to output,

```
Sophie's World
```

we would write

```
cout << "Sophie\'s World\n";
```

You should experiment with these escape sequences with some examples of your own.

1.2.4 void main()

This marks the start of the main part of the program. All programs will contain one and only one definition of a function called main. As with all functions in C and C++ if the function does not return a value then the type must be specified as void (the default return type of a function is int, not void as one might at first expect). Function definitions include, as well as their name (in this case main) a list of any arguments which may be required enclosed in brackets (). Even if there are no arguments the brackets must still be used.

1.2.5 {...}

The opening brace ({) and the closing brace (}) mark the beginning and the end of the program body. These serve the same purpose as BEGIN and END respectively in a Pascal program. Any code enclosed by the two braces is referred to as a block. Any variable, or function, defined in a block only has scope (i.e. is only available) within that block, or other blocks contained within its own block and following the definition. (We will be looking at the scope of variables and functions in more depth in later chapters.)

At this point it is worth noting that the physical layout of a C++ program (or for that matter a C program) is immaterial, barring the point concerning comments mentioned earlier. So, for example, the program HELLO.cpp could equally well be written as follows:

```
//:HELLO.CPP - traditional first program, even in C++
//.no need for any further comments!
#include <iostream.h>
// no functions!
void main(){cout << "Hello world\n";cout << "Welcome to C++\n";}
```

However, such a layout is not to be recommended! The earlier version is much better – it is easier to read and therefore easier to understand. Make sure that you stick to a well constructed layout for your programs, along the lines of our first basic program. Place one statement only to a line, use indentation to indicate block structure and use comments where necessary. (It is important though to remember that over-commenting can be as off-putting as under – or no-commenting – only use comments to explain obscure points or highlight important aspects of the code; don't state the obvious.)

1.3 Keywords and identifiers

1.3.1 Keywords

The keywords in C++ are built up from those already available in C – only a few additional words are required so C++ is still a reasonably compact language. During the later stages of writing discussions finally ended concerning the C++ standard (equivalent to the ANSI standard for C developed a few years ago). The previous draft standard has finally been approved and an ISO/ANSI standard agreed upon. However there will be variations between different C++ implementations. The list given here (Table 1.2) is based on that used in the Borland C++ implementation (Ver. 3.0) and includes only those keywords which are in both the new standard and the Borland C++ implementation. Table 1.3 lists the new keywords added to the final standard. The keywords available to you may vary and you should ensure that all the words in both lists are assumed to be keywords even if some of them are not implemented in your version. However the essential keywords will be common to all implementations and as we will not be concerned, at this stage, with very advanced applications or compiler dependent applications there should be no problems.

The main reason for given you this information at this time, is not for you to try to remember them all – although, as you can see there aren't that many (62 in all) – but to provide you with a feel for the language and give an easy reference at an early stage. Another important reason is that variable names, function names etc. cannot be given the same name as any keyword, so in order to avoid doing that it is as well to know which are the keywords.

Table 1.2 C and C++ keywords (additional words are in italics)

asm	auto	break	case	char
class	const	continue	default	*delete*
do	double	else	enum	extern
float	for	*friend*	goto	if
inline	int	long	*new*	*operator*
private	*protected*	*public*	register	return
short	signed	sizeof	static	struct
switch	*template*	*this*	typedef	union
unsigned	*virtual*	void	volatile	while

Table 1.3 Additional C++ keywords (included in final ISO/ANSI standard)

bool	catch	const_cast	dynamic_cast
explicit	false	mutable	namespace
reinterpret_cast		static_cast	throw true
try	typeid	typename	using
wchar_t			

1.3.2 Identifiers

In order to construct any program, in any language, we need to know the rules for making up new names (i.e. identifiers) which will be used to refer to variables, functions, classes, objects, user-defined data types and so on. The rules for constructing identifiers in C++ are the same as those in C i.e.:

An identifier must begin with:

An underscore (_) or a letter (upper- or lower-case)

which may be followed by

an underscore, a letter, or a digit (0..9)

using the BNF notation this can be written as

$$\text{Identifier} ::= \{\text{nondigit}\}_1 + \{\text{nondigit} \mid \text{digit}\}_{0+}$$

where nondigit is one of

```
a b c d e f g h i j k l m n o p q r s t u v w k y z
A B C D E F G H I J K L M N O P Q R S T U V W X Y Z _
```

and digit is one of:

```
0 1 2 3 4 5 6 7 8 9
```

There are a few rules and conventions which you should follow when constructing identifiers. These also apply to C and so you may already be familiar with them. It is advisable to start all identifiers with a letter (many system variables begin with an underscore and you lose very little flexibility if you avoid starting an identifier with an underscore but have the advantage of not producing a conflict with system variables). C++ (as with C) is case sensitive so that `incomeTax` is a different identifier from `Incometax`, so be careful how, and when, you use uppercase letters. As a rule you should keep to lowercase letters for variables, functions, classes etc. (use an uppercase letter if more than one word is included in the name, as with `incomeTax` or use an underscore, e.g. `income_tax`). Uppercase letters can then be used for symbolic constants (or identifiers defined as `const`), e.g.

```
#define BASIC_TAX_RATE 20.0   // symbolic constant
```

or

```
const float BASIC_TAX_RATE = 20.0;// constant
```

(We will be discussing the pros and cons of `#define` and `const` in Chapter 2) There is no practical limit to the length of an identifier but it makes obvious sense to keep them as short as possible whilst at the same time making them as descriptive as possible. So for example `incomeTax` is to be preferred over `personalIncomeTax` or it and `BASIC_TAX_RATE` preferred to `BTR`.

1.4 Data types

In order that any processing can be performed,, e.g. finding the average age of the students in the class or computing the volume a sphere; we need to have access to variables of different data types. There are three fundamental data types in C++: `int`, `char` and `float`. These basic data types together with a small number of modifiers (e.g. `short`, `long`, `unsigned`) are used to build up more complex data types. Rather than discuss all the ins and outs of data types in abstract terms we will introduce them, as well as some C++ syntax, by looking at some simple programs. Program 1.2 is a program which just adds together two integers.

Program 1.2

```
//: ADD.cpp - adding two integers
//. Illustrating the use of the int data type
#include <iostream.h>
// ...........................................................
void main()
{
int num1, num2;
```

```
    cout << "Enter your first integer > ";
    cin >> num1;
    cout << "Now the second > ";
    cin >> num2;
    cout << num1 << " + " << num2 << " = " << num1 +
    num2 <<endl;
}
```

1.4.1 Analysis of ADD.cpp

There is very little in this program which needs explanation, but we will look
at each new statement to aid revision and introduce a couple of new elements
of the language.
  As with C, the statement:

```
int num1, num2;
```

declares two variables num1 and num2 to be of type int – the compiler sets
aside storage for each of these variables (with most compilers this will be two
bytes) and thus determines the range of values that can be allocated to them
and, furthermore, defines the operations which can be performed on them
(such as add, multiply, subtract and divide).
  The statement:

```
cin >> num1;
```

is an equivalent to the scanf function which is frequently used for input in C
programs. As you will have realised cin is the converse of cout, it represents
the standard input device (normally the keyboard) and it is used with the right
shift operator (>>) to take input from the keyboard to whatever variable is to
its right.
  The final statement:

```
cout << num1 << " + " << num2 << " = " << num1 + num2 << endl;
```

prints out the original two integers and performs the arithmetic operation of
addition. (The usual arithmetic operators are used in C++ i.e. +, -, * and / for
the four basic arithmetic operations of addition, subtraction, multiplication
and division.) One other new element in this statement is endl. (Note that the
last character is the lower case letter L – not the digit 1 – this is an easy mis-
take to make so be warned!) This can be used, instead of \n, to move the cursor to a new line – sometimes this is more convenient than using the \n sequence, at other times not! Which method you choose, and when, is up to you.
Note however that the endl must follow the << operator and must itself be
followed by the semicolon (;), marking the end of the statement, or another <<
operator followed by another expression. So we might have:

```
cout << "num1 = " << num1 << endl << "num2 = " << num2 << endl;
```

which embeds one endl within the cout statement as well as terminating the output with an endl. This would produce the following output:

⌨ **Test run 1.2**
```
num1 = 24
num2 = 127
```

If you compile and run this program but use larger integers for num1 and num2 such as:

num1	num2
32765	1
32765	3
32768	32769

you may find that you get rather odd results. For example, the output I got when I ran this program was:

```
32765 + 1 = 32766
32765 + 3 = -32768
32768 + -32767 = 1
```

You will most likely have got the same. The reason for the output obtained is because the int data type has a range from -32768 to 32767 and any arithmetic value which results in a value outside this range will cause an overflow and therefore may be incorrect.

1.4.2 More stream I/O

Since we are discussing numbers and number bases this is an appropriate point to introduce a couple of further I/O stream manipulators. So far we have been outputting integers in their decimal form, which is the default version. However we occasionally wish to display integers in their octal or hexadecimal form. We can do this by means of the manipulators oct and hex. (Note this is not the same as using the escape sequences for octal and hexadecimal numbers which we introduced earlier. There we output a known octal or hexadecimal number, here we are converting a decimal number to its octal or hex equivalent.) Program 1.3 (NUMCONV.cpp) illustrates this in a very simple way.

📋 **Program 1.3**
```
//: NUMCONV.cpp - converts decimal to octal and hex
//. and illustrates input in C++
```

```
#include <iostream.h>
#include <conio.h>
// ...........................................................
void main() {
int   number;
   clrscr();
   cout << " NUMCONV -- Converts decimal to octal and hex "
      << endl;
   cout << "               and illustrates input in C++ " << endl
                     << endl;
   cout << "Enter an integer : ";
   cin >> number;
   // using some format manipulators
   cout << number << " in octal = " << oct << number << endl;
   cout << number << " in hex   = " << hex << number << endl;

   cout << " \nPress <ENTER> to Quit ";
   cin.get();   cin.get();
}
```

The important elements of the program for our present discussion are:

```
cout << "Enter an integer : ";
cin >> number;
// using some format manipulators
cout << number << " in octal = " << oct << number << endl;
cout << number << " in hex   = " << hex << number << endl;
```

In particular notice the way we have used the oct and hex manipulators.
These are placed in the output stream in a similar way to endl and once they
have been used the numbers following will be displayed in the new form. Test
run 1.3 shows a sample test run with an entered value of 78.

🖥 **Test run 1.3**
```
78 in octal = 116
116 in hex  = 4e
```

Once the number has been converted to octal it remains in that form until
overridden by the use of hex. One other manipulator which may be of use in
examples such as this is dec which, as you might expect, resets the output to
decimal format. The two statements used to output the number in its various
forms might be used in the following form so that the original decimal value is
displayed both times. Test run 1.4 shows the output with the changes.

```
// using some format manipulators
cout << number << " in octal = " << oct << number << endl;
cout << dec << number << " in hex   = " << hex << number << endl
```

There are a couple of other points to notice about the NUMCONV program. First notice the use of the function clrscr() near the beginning of the program. This is used, as you might suspect, to clear the output screen. As it is a function declared in the header file conio.h this file needs to be included so that the relevant library file can be located and the function therefore linked to the program.

Second notice the use of the cin.get() function at the end of the program. This is a (member) function of the (class) cin and is used to read a single character from the keyboard (similar to getch() in C). Such statements are often useful to enable the output screen to remain in view once the program as run – in some implementations this may not be required as the output screen remains in view until closed by the user – check your version and if it helps use it, if not ignore the cin.get() statement(s).

1.4.3 Basic arithmetic operators

As well as addition, which we have already looked at, there are three more standard arithmetic operators with which you will probably already be familiar:

- subtraction * multiplication / division

In addition, for int data types we have in C and C++ the modulo operator %. This produces the remainder after division of the first integer by the second. Thus 25 % 7 produces the result 4 (i.e. the remainder after dividing 25 by 7). If you are completely new to C and C++ then you should now try out all these operators in a program of your own. (See the exercises at the end of the chapter for an example to try.)

1.4.4 Data types float and char

The other two basic data types in C and C++ are *float* and *char*. *Float* allows real numbers to be used, i.e. those which are not exact integers whilst the *char* data type is used to represent single characters, e.g. 'a', 'B', '?', '8' etc. It is important to remember that '8' (i.e. as a character) is not the same as 8 (as an integer), or even as 8.0 (stored as a float). A character is normally stored in one byte (8 bits) of memory and has an integral value determined by a particular code (usually ASCII – American Standard Code for Information Interchange, although other codes may be used with different operating systems). Thus the digit 8 is represented in ASCII by the decimal integer 56. In my implementation of C++ the (float) number 8.0 is represented by four bytes (32 bits) such that bit 31 is the sign bit, bits 22–30 represent the 'biased exponent' and the remaining bits (0–21) are used to store the 'significand' – i.e. the significant part of the number, for example 2345 in 23.45.

As well as the three basic data types just mentioned there are a number of modifiers (or specifiers) which can be used to change the range of a particular data type. The short and long modifiers are used to alter the maximum and minimum values a data type can hold. The signed and unsigned modifiers specify how the sign bit is to be used (only allowed with the integral types – all floating-point data types always contain a sign).

This gives us, for example, a type short int which may take up less storage space than an int, an unsigned int (used for positive integers only) and long float (normally double the number of bytes of that of a float). (Also, since long floats are quite common another keyword has been set aside for such types – double.) Program 1.4 (DATATYPE.cpp) will list for the main data types their size for your version of C++.

This program uses one new function – the sizeof() function. This returns the number of bytes occupied by the data type of the argument.

Program 1.4

```
//: DATATYPE.cpp - illustrating the sizes of basic data types
//. using the sizeof() keyword
#include <conio.h>
#include <iostream.h>
// ...........................................................
void main()
{
    clrscr();
    cout << " DATATYPE " << endl;
    cout << " ======== " << endl << endl;
    cout << " \t Type \t Size (bytes) " << endl;
    cout << " \t ---- \t ------------ " << endl << endl;
    cout << " \t char \t\t " << sizeof(char) << endl;
    cout << " \t short \t\t " << sizeof(short) << endl;
    cout << " \t int \t\t " << sizeof(int) << endl;
    cout << " \t unsigned int \t " << sizeof(unsigned int) << endl;
    cout << " \t long \t\t " << sizeof(long) << endl;
    cout << " \t float \t\t " << sizeof(float) << endl;
    cout << " \t double \t " << sizeof(double) << endl;
    cout << " \t long double \t " << sizeof(long double) << endl;
}
```

1.5 Unary operators

There are a number of other operators in C++ in addition to the basic arithmetic operators we met earlier and before looking at control structures it is worth spending a few moments examining some of these new operators.

In C and C++ operators fall into two main groups (there is a ternary operator – with three operands, and we shall be looking at that later on in this chapter, but there is only one in this group so it can hardly be called a main one!). These two main groups are identified by the number of operands which are involved – one or two – hence unary and binary operators. The unary operators only operate on a single operand. These are:

&	Address operator	*	Indirection operator
+	Unary plus	–	Unary minus
~	Bitwise complement (1's complement)	++	Increment
!	Logical negation (not)	--	Decrement

Examples of how some of these operators might be used are given below.

```
pch = &ch; // pch is the address of ch
*pch = 'a'; // change value stored at ch to 'a'
n2 = -n2;  // n2 = minus n1
n = 29;    // assuming n is a 2-byte int
           // n = 0000 0000 0001 1101 (1D in hex)
ncomp = ~n; // ncomp =  1111 1111 1110 0010 (FFE2)
x = 5;
y = !x;    // = 0
x = !y;    // = 1 (i.e. !(!x) normally not equal
           // to x)
```

Program 1.5 (UNARYOP.cpp) illustrates the above examples. Try the program out and see if you can understand how each statement works before continuing.

Program 1.5
```
//: UNARYOP.cpp - illustrating some basic unary operators
//. examples of &, *, -, ~ and !
#include <conio.h>
#include <iostream.h>
#include <stdio.h>
// ....................................................
void main()
{
int   n1, n2, n, ncomp, x, y;
char  ch, *pch;

    clrscr();
    cout << " Some UNARY operators " << endl;
    cout << " ==================== " << endl << endl;

    ch = 'U';
    pch = &ch;     // p is the address of ch
    cout << "  ch  = " << ch << endl;
```

```
cout << "   *pch = " << *pch << " same as ch " << endl;

printf(" &ch = %X   the address of ch \n", &ch);
printf(" pch = %X   also the address of ch \n\n", pch);
*pch = 'a'; // change the contents of ch to 'a'
cout << " use *pch = \'a\' to change the contents of ch " << endl;
cout << "   ch = " << ch << endl << endl;

n1 = 37;
n2 = -n1;
cout << " n1 = " << n1 << " n2 (= -n1) = " << n2 << endl;

n = 29; // assuming n is a 2-byte int n = 0000 0000 0001 1101
ncomp = ~n;   // ncomp =   1111 1111 1110 0010
cout << "   n = " << n << " ncomp (~n) = " << ncomp << endl << en
cout << "   Now n and n comp in hexadecimal " << endl;
cout << hex << endl; // use hex o/p modifier to print in
                     // hexadecimal
cout << "   n = " << n << " ncomp = " << ncomp << endl;
cout << dec << endl; // return o/p to decimal
printf(" using printf() : \n\n");
printf("   n = %X   ncomp = %X \n", n, ncomp);
x = 5;
y = !x;
cout << "   x = " << x << " !x = " << y << endl;
x = !y;
cout << " !y = " << x << " not the same as the original x "
                         << endl;
}
```

1.5.1 Analysis of UNARYOP.cpp

Let's look first of all at the declarations in this program. The only new aspect is the presence of the * in the declaration of pch. Declaring pch as char *pch tells the compiler that the variable pch will be used to 'point to' the address of another char. Before we can do anything with pch we need to give it a value (i.e. initialise it), in this case we initialise it by giving pch the address of another char variable, by means of the statement pch = &ch;. We can assign a value to ch (i.e. store a character in ch) either by means of normal assignment, as in ch = 'U';, or by via the pointer variable pch, as in *pch = 'a';. What we *cannot* do is to assign a value by means of *pch = before we have given pch a location to point to. *pch, when it is first declared does not itself point to any particular location, it is not initialised, so if we try to give *pch a value we will be placing the value assigned in an unknown location in memory – which could have disastrous consequences –, e.g. the computer may hang because an important memory location has been corrupted. Note that C++ does not stop you doing this, you may get a warning but that isn't guaranteed, so the onus is on you, the programmer, to make sure that pointer variables are properly initialised.

The next point to note is the use of the bitwise complement operator (~).

The simple example given in the program illustrates what this operation does. The decimal number 29 is stored as a two-byte integer as 0000 0000 0001 1101. Taking the bitwise complement produces 1111 1111 1110 0010 which is −30. The program uses two methods of displaying an integer in hexadecimal, one using `printf()` and one using `cout`. Notice that the conversion string `%X` is used in `printf()` for this process (i.e. outputting a hexadecimal number) whereas when using `cout` the manipulator `hex` is used in the output stream. (If you are unfamiliar with `printf()` then please refer to Chapter 4 where you will find more details.) The `dec` manipulator is then required so that subsequent output will revert to the decimal representation. (Incidentally if we add 1 to this latter figure we arrive at 1111 1111 1110 0011 which is −29 – modify the program to check this.)

The final point worth noting about this program is the behaviour of `!` when applied to an integer. This operator can be used with any logical expression, indeed with any integer expression, but when used with integer expressions you need to take particular care. If the original value of the expression is non-zero and not equal to 1 then the result of `!(expression)` will be zero. If we then apply the same operator to this new value (y in the program) we end up with 1, not the original value (which in the program is 5). Normally this will not cause any difficulty since we should only be concerned with whether the expression is TRUE or FALSE (i.e. non-zero or zero), but it is as well to be aware of this fact.

Having dealt briefly with some of the most important operators we are now in a position to review the various control structures available to us.

1.6 Conditional and relational operators

As you may be aware the control of execution of program statements employs the concepts of *sequence*, *selection* and *iteration* plus the use of *modules* (subroutines, procedures, functions, units etc.– known as functions in C and C++). In the absence of selection and iteration a program will execute sequentially – i.e. statements will be executed in the order in which they appear in the source code. The only exception is that when a function call is encountered (e.g. the use of `clrscr()` or `printf()` or `scanf()`) execution will be transferred to that function – control being passed back to the following statement once the function call has been successfully executed. However a program will be of little practical use until selection or iteration structures are included.

1.6.1 Conditional expressions

In order to control the execution of statements we need to use conditional expressions – i.e. expressions which evaluate to TRUE or FALSE. However before looking at how these are constructed in C or C++ we need to know what is TRUE and what is FALSE. There is no preset Boolean data type in these languages as there is for example in Pascal; instead any integer expression can be used as a conditional expression. An expression is FALSE if it produces a zero integral value, and TRUE otherwise – i.e. any positive or negative (non-zero) integral value. The new standard does however include a `bool` type (see Table 1.3)

1.6.2 Relational operators

C and C++ use the same set of relational operators which are available in most languages. However there are a couple of unfamiliar symbols with which you will may need to familiarise yourself. Table 1.4 gives the relational operators used in C/C++.

Table 1.4 Relational operators

Operator	Meaning	Example
==	equal to	`ch == 'a'`
!=	not equal to	`n != 100`
<	less than	`i < 100`
>	greater than	`count > 50`
<=	less than or equal to	`ch <= 'z'`
>=	greater than or equal to	`ch >= 'a'`

In addition to the above we have available three logical operators, which can be used to combine conditional expressions to produce more complex expressions:

Table 1.5 Logical operators

Operator	Meaning	Example	Comment
!	not	`! (ch == 'a')`	equivalent to `ch != 'a'`
&&	and	`(ch >= 'a') && (ch <= 'z')`	select all lower case letters
||	or	`(n >= 0) || (count > 50)`	TRUE if n is greater than or equal to zero OR count is greater than 50

Note: It is very important to remember that when the above double character combinations are used (==, != etc.) there is no space between the two symbols: = = is not the same as ==, in fact the first of these will give a compilation error, so be warned!.

In C and C++ there are two basic ways of selecting which code is to be executed, the first uses `if` (and if necessary `else`), whilst the second uses the `switch` statement. We will take a brief look at both of these methods in this section.

1.7.1 if and if ... else

The basic control structure for selection is the `if ... else` statement. This has two forms:

i) `if (expression)`
    statement1
    statement2

or

ii) `if (expression)`
      statement1
  `else`
      statement2
  statement3

where `expression` is any valid integral expression (i.e. any expression, however simple or complex, which produces an integral value) and `statement1` is any valid C/C++ statement. Note that every statement is either a simple statement which ends with a ; or a compounds statement (block) – which encloses a number of statements in braces (`{` and `}`). The operation of these two if statements are as follows:

In i)   `expression` is evaluated, if it is TRUE then `statement1` is executed after which control passes to `statement2`, if `expression` is FALSE then control passes directly to `statement2`.

In ii)   if `expression` is TRUE `statement1` is executed after which control passes to `statement3`, if `expression` is FALSE then control passes to *statement2* before moving on to `statement3`.

Program 1.6 illustrates a simple use of the `if ... else` structure.

Program 1.6

```
//: IFELSE1.cpp -- Example using if ... else
#include <iostream.h>
#include <conio.h>
// ...........................................................
void main()
{
int   i;
   clrscr();
   cout << " IFELSE1\n";
   cout << " ======= " << endl << endl;
   cout << "  type in an integer and press ENTER : ";
   cin >> i;
   if ( i > 20 )
      cout << " the number is greater than 20 " << endl;
   else
   if ( i < 20 )
      cout << " the number is less than 20 " << endl;
   else
      cout << " the number is equal to 20 " << endl;
}
```

The first part of the program requests the user to enter a number and then outputs a message depending on whether the number is greater than, less than or equal to 20.

Notice the ; at the end of each cout statement. Try removing one of them from the program and see what happens.

Now modify the program so that:

a) the number entered is also output, e.g. to produce

```
The number 6 is less than 20
```

b) the user can enter, when the program is run, the number to be compared, e.g. 100 instead of 20.

1.7.2 Nested if statements

A second program (Program 1.7) illustrates the nesting of if statements.

Program 1.7

```
//: IFELSE2.cpp -- Example using nested if ... else
#include <iostream.h>
#include <conio.h>
// ...........................................................
void main()
{
int   i;
   clrscr();
   cout << " IFELSE2\n";
```

```
cout << " ======= " << endl << endl;
cout << "  type in an integer and press ENTER : ";
cin >> i;
if ( i < 20 )
   if (i > 10 )
      cout << " 10 < i < 20 " << endl;
   else
   cout << " i <= 10 " << endl;
else
   cout << " i >= 20 " << endl;
}
```

In this example the second if...else statement (testing for values of i less than 20) is enclosed within the first (i.e. it is 'nested' within the first if ... else statement). An examination of this code should tell you what conditions are being tested. The first expression tested (i<20) is used to distinguish a) between values of i less than 20, in which case the next if ... else statement is executed and b) those values greater than or equal to 20, in which case the final else statement is executed. The second expression tested (i>10) is used to distinguish between values of i greater than 10 but less than 20 and those less than or equal to 10.

Try out the above program and check that it works correctly before reading on.

It is interesting to ask what happens if the lines

```
else
   cout << " i <= 10 " << endl;
```

are removed from the program? Does it still work correctly (i.e. as originally intended)? This program illustrates an important point concerning if statements in C and C++. An else attaches itself to the nearest if, so that by removing the above two lines we change the logic of the program. The new code is:

```
if ( i < 20 )
   if ( i > 10 )
      cout << " 10 < i < 20 " << endl;
   else
      cout << " i >= 20 " << endl;
```

and, although the indentation indicates the *intention* the logic is somewhat different. The else is now attached to the if (i>10) expression not, as intended, the first one (if (i<20)), and so a value for i of 15 for example will produce the output i>=20. Also, values of i>=20 will produce no output at all! This presents a problem since there may well be circumstances when we want a construct like our modified program, and at first sight it looks as if there is no way around this problem. However the problem can be solved by means of an *empty statement*. An empty statement is simply a statement which does nothing but which is needed to preserve the correct logic. So in our current example, supposing we aren't bothered if a number is less than or equal to 10, then we can rewrite the code as follows:

```
if ( i < 20 )
    if ( i > 10 )
        cout << " 10 < i < 20 " << endl;
    else
        ; // ignore values <= 10
else
    cout << " i >= 20 " << endl;
```

The presence of the two lines:

```
else
    ; // ignore values <= 10
```

preserves the desired logic and thus solves our problem. The comment `//
ignore values <= 10` is a useful indication to the programmer, or another programmer, that this is intentional.

1.7.3 switch

The `switch` statement is the final selection method available in C and C++ and enables a statement (or statements) to be selected depending on the value of an integral expression. It can often be used in place of an `if ... else` statement. The form is:

```
switch (integral_expression) {
    case integral_value1 : statement1  break;
    case integral_value2 : statement2  break;
        ...
    default : default_statement
}
```

where

integral_expression	is any valid expression which evaluates to an integral value,
integral_value1	etc. are different integral values (also called case constants),
statement1	etc. are valid C/C++ statements which are executed when the *integral_expression* equals the corresponding *integral_value*, and

is a valid statement which is executed if no match exists between the *integral_expression* and any of the preceding *integral_values*.

Note: we are using the statement in the above in the strict sense where a statement is an expression followed by a semi-colon, which is the reason we have not placed the semi-colon after each statement – it is already included in 'statement1', etc.

The break statement is necessary here to prevent execution 'falling through', that is without break once a match has been found all succeeding statements are executed. Occasionally this is a useful facility but generally we use switch to choose between different options (e.g. in a menu) and we only want the selected options to be processed.

Although we have used only single statements in each of the options any number of statements can be included as the following example shows.

```
cin >> choice;
switch (choice) {
   case 'a' : result = a + b;
      cout << " a + b " = result;      break;
   case 's' : result = a - b;
      cout << " a - b " = result;      break;
   case 'm' : result = a * b;
      cout << " a * b " = result;      break;
   case 'd' : result = a / b;
      cout << " a / b " = result;      break;
   default  : cout << " Invalid selection \n";      break;
}
```

If the char variable choice matches any of the case constants ('a', 's', etc.) then the appropriate statements are executed followed by exit from the switch statement due to break. If choice does not match any of the case constants then default is chosen. It is not necessary to include the default option in which case none of the case options will be selected and the switch statement will be ignored.

1.7.4 The conditional operator (? :)

As we have seen the if ... else control structure is one means of selecting different statements. A similar function can be achieved by using conditional expressions (as opposed to conditional statements constructed using if ... else). Such expressions use the two characters ? and : which essentially replace the if and else keywords respectively. This conditional expression, which uses the only ternary operator in C/C++, has the form:

expression1 ? *expression2* : *expression3*

where *expression1* is an expression which evaluates to an integral value – normally a conditional expression itself (e.g. `a < 10`, `ch != 'Z'`, `total >= 100`) – if *expression1* evaluates to a non-zero integral value (i.e. TRUE) then *expression2* is evaluated; if it evaluates to a zero value then *expression3* is evaluated. Although the behaviour of the `if ... else` statement and the conditional expression (using `?` and `:`) are similar, they are used in different contexts. A conditional expression can be used in any expression whereas an `if ... else` statement cannot, e.g.

```
t = ( c < 0 ? -c / 10 : c * 10) + 8;
```

using `if ... else` we could write:

```
if (c < 0)
    t = (-c / 10) + 8;
else
    t = (c * 10) + 8;
```

or, using a temporary variable `temp`:

```
if (c < 0)
    temp = (-c / 10);
else
    temp = (c * 10);
t = temp + 8;
```

The first of these alternatives. i.e. using the conditional expression, is more efficient than either of the other two.

Another example illustrates the use of a conditional expression within an output stream:

```
cout << "The smaller of a and b is: " << (a<b?a:b) << endl;
```

which might be written using `if ... else` as:

```
cout << " The smaller of a and b is : ";

if (a < b)     cout << a << endl;
else           cout << b << endl;
```

1.8 Iteration

Iteration is a means whereby a block of code can be repeated a number of times. In C and C++ this can be achieved in three ways: using the `while`, `do`

... `while`, or `for` statements. Which one is most suitable will depend on the precise purpose of the code. We will take a quick look at each of these methods.

1.8.1 while

The `while` statement is used when the test has to be at the beginning of the loop and has the form:

```
while (expression)
    statement1
statement2
```

In a `while` loop *statement1* (which can be a single, or a compound, statement) is executed so long as *expression* evaluates to TRUE (i.e. to a nonzero value) – once *expression* becomes FALSE control passes to the statements following the while statement (i.e. *statement2* and any statements following). To illustrate a simple use of iteration we will suppose that we wish to compute the product of the first n integers (i.e. $1 \times 2 \times 3 \ldots \times n$ – the factorial of n) – this can be achieved using any of these iterative structures. Using a `while` construct we might produce the code:

Program 1.8 (extract)
```
//: Factorial
int i, n, fact;
    cout << " Factorial n (n!) Program " << endl;
    cout << " enter the value of n : ";
    cin >> n;
    i = 1;   // initialise i and fact
    fact = 1;
    while ( i <= n )
    {
       fact *= i;
       i++;
    }
```

This program fragment (Program 1.8) uses two arithmetic operators with which you may not be familiar, namely `*=` and `++`. So, let's digress for a moment to look at some more arithmetic operators. The complete list is given in Table 1.6.

In addition to the normal arithmetic operators which we mentioned earlier (+, −, * and /), we have the mod operator (%) which produces the remainder after division by the second operand and a number of double operators (++, −−, += etc.). These appear frequently in C/C++ programs and, if you are not already familiar with them, you soon will be!

Table 1.6 Arithmetic operators

Operator	Meaning	Example	Comment
=	assign	`i = 1`	
+	addition	`i + j`	
−	subtraction	`n - 1`	
*	multiplication	`a * 10`	
/	division	`total / number`	
%	remainder	`j % 10`	the remainder after `j` is divided by 10
++	increment	`++i, or ++i`	equivalent to `i=i+1`
--	decrement	`i--, or --i`	equivalent to `i=i-1`
+=	add value to	`sum += i`	equivalent to `sum=sum+i`
-=	subtract value from	`n -= 6`	equivalent to `n=n-6`
*=	multiply by and assign	`a *= 10`	equivalent to `a=a*10`
/=	divide by and assign	`b /= 5`	equivalent to `b=b/5`
%=	get remainder and assign	`n %= 10`	equivalent to `n=n%10`

Now to return to iteration. You should be able to work out how this example works, but we will explain it anyway! First of all we need a value for n, this is obtained using `cin >> n`. The variables `i` and `fact` are both initialised and then we reach the `while` loop itself. The expression `(i<=n)` is tested and if TRUE the body of the `while` statement is entered and the statements there executed. The first statement `fact *=i;` takes the current value of `fact`, multiplies it by the current value of `i` and then assigns the new value to `fact`. The next statement `i++;` is used to increment the current value of `i` (i.e. `i=i+1`). The expression `(i<=n)` is tested again and if `i` is still less than n the body of the `while` loop is again executed. This process continues until `(i<=n)` becomes FALSE (i.e. `i` becomes greater than n). At this point the `while` loop is left and processing continues sequentially.

There are two points worth noting about the `while` construct. First you must ensure that there is an expression within the body of the loop which will, at some stage, make the 'control' expression FALSE (i.e. in our example an expression which will enable the expression `i<=n` to become FALSE). If this is not the case then the `while` loop will continue executing forever, or at least until the computer is switched off, or processing is interrupted. The second point is that testing of the 'control' expression only occurs after all the statements in the body of the `while` loop have been executed. So, if for example it is important to stop executing the loop as soon as the 'control' expression becomes FALSE, no matter where in the body of the loop this occurs, then other steps must be taken to ensure that this happens.

The `while` example (Program 1.8) will work for small integral values of n, but what happens if you use large values of n? Can you explain? Is there any way round the problem? One solution is to make the variable fact a `long int` instead of an `int`.

1.8.2 do ... while

An alternative method of implementing iteration is to use the `do ... while` statement:

```
do
```

statement1

```
while (expression);
statement2
```

The `do ... while` loop works by executing `statement1`, testing the `expression` and if this is found to be TRUE executing `statement1` again. This process is repeated until `expression` becomes FALSE, at which point control passes to `statement2`. We can illustrate this method of iteration by modifying our factorial program to read:

```
do {
    fact *= i;
    i++;
} while (i <= n);
```

Before moving on to the final method of iteration in C and C++ we should look at an important difference between the `while` and `do ... while` statements. Since with the `while` statement the testing is carried out at the start of the loop there is a possibility that the expression being tested may be FALSE to begin with, which means that the body of the loop will not be executed at all. Conversely in a `do ... while` loop, since the test does not take place until the body of the loop has been executed, the body will always be executed at least once.

One final point; you will find it very easy to miss off the semicolon (;) from the end of the `do ... while` loop (i.e. by writing } `while (i <= n)` instead of } `while (i <= n);`, so watch out for this when entering programs.

Examples of the two different uses of loops mentioned above are illustrated in programs 1.9 and 1.10 – try them out and check that they work as intended.

⬚ Program 1.9
```
//: MENU.cpp -- simple menu program demonstrating
//. the use of 'break' and 'continue'.

#include <iostream.h>
```

```
#include <conio.h>
// .............................................................
void main()
{
char c; // to hold response
   clrscr();
   cout << " MENU - using while, if, break & continue "
   << endl;
   cout << " ======================================== "
   << endl << endl;
   while(1) {
      cout << "MAIN MENU:" << endl;
      cout << "1 for MENU1, 2 for MENU2, q to quit: ";
      cin >> c;
      if ( c == 'q' )  break; // out of 'while(1)'
      if ( c == '1' ) {
         cout << " MENU 1 :" << endl;
         cout << "select a or b: ";
         cin >> c;
         if ( c == 'a' ) {
            cout << "you chose 'a'" << endl;
            continue; // back to main menu
         }
         if ( c == 'b' ) {
            cout << "you chose 'b'" << endl;
            continue; // back to main menu
         }
         else {
            cout << "you should choose a or b!" << endl;
            continue; // back to main menu
         }
      }
      if ( c == '2' ) {
         cout << " MENU 2 :" << endl;
         cout << "select c or d: ";
         cin >> c;
         if ( c == 'c' ) {
            cout << "you chose 'c'" << endl;
            continue; // back to main menu
         }
         if ( c == 'd' ) {
         cout << "you chose 'd'" << endl;
         continue; // back to main menu
         }
         else {
            cout << "you should choose c or d!" << endl;
            continue; // back to main menu
         }
      }
      cout << "you must enter 1 or 2 or q!" << endl;
   }
   cout << "exiting menu ... " << endl;
}
```

☐ Program 1.10

```
//: MENU2.cpp -- simple menu program demonstrating
//. the use of do ... while

#include <iostream.h>
#include <conio.h>
// ............................................................
void main()
{
char c, cdum; // to hold response
 clrscr();
 cout << " MENU2 - using do ... while " << endl;
 cout << " ========================= " << endl << endl;
 do {
    clrscr();
    cout << endl;
    cout << "   MAIN MENU" << endl << endl;
    cout << " 1 : FIRST MENU " << endl << endl;
    cout << " 2 : SECOND MENU " << endl << endl;
    cout << " q : quit " << endl << endl << endl;
    cout << "    > ";
    cin >> c;
    if ( c == '1' ) {
       do {
          clrscr();
          cout << " FIRST MENU " << endl << endl;
          cout << " a : option a " << endl << endl;
          cout << " b : option b " << endl << endl;
          cout << " r : return to main menu " << endl << endl << e]
          cout << "    > ";
          cin >> c;
          if ( c == 'a' )
             cout << "you chose 'a'" << endl;
          else if ( c == 'b' )
             cout << "you chose 'b'" << endl;
          else
             cout << "you should choose a, b or r!" << endl;
          cout << endl << " Press enter to continue ";
          do
             cin.get(cdum);
          while (cdum != '\n');
       } while (c != 'r');
    }
    else if ( c == '2' ) {

       do {
          clrscr();
          cout << " SECOND MENU " << endl << endl;
          cout << " c : option c " << endl << endl;
          cout << " d : option d " << endl << endl;
          cout << " r : return to main menu " << endl << endl << e]
          cout << "    > ";
```

```
        cin.get(c);
        if ( c == 'c' )
           cout << "you chose 'c'" << endl;
        else if ( c == 'd' )
           cout << "you chose 'd'" << endl;
        else
           cout << "you should choose c, d or r!" << endl;
        cout << endl << " Press enter to continue ";
        do
           cin.get(cdum);
        while (cdum != '\n');
     } while (c != 'r');
   }
   else
      cout << "you must enter 1 or 2 or q!" << endl;
   cout << endl << " Press enter to continue ";
   cdum = ' ';
   do
      cin.get(cdum);
   while (cdum != '\n');
 } while (c != 'q');
 cout << "exiting menu ... " << endl;
}
```

1.8.3 continue

You will have noticed in Program 1.9 that a new statement has been introduced, namely `continue`. This statement has similarities with `break` in that it
alters the normal sequential execution of statements but is different in its precise effect. Whereas `break` is used to 'jump out of' the innermost loop or
switch statement, `continue` is used only with loops (`do`, `while` and `for` −
which we look at next) to 'jump to the end of' the innermost loop, the loop
continuation condition is then evaluated.

1.8.4 The for loop

The final method of providing iteration is by means of the `for` loop. This
takes the form:

```
for (statement1; expression2; expression3)
  statement2
statement3
```

The execution of the `for` loop is a little more complicated than either of the
other two, simply because three expressions are involved rather than one. The
process is as follows: immediately the `for` statement is encountered *state-
ment1* is evaluated, this is followed by the evaluation of *expression2*. If this
expression is TRUE then *statement2* (i.e. the body of the `for` statement) is
executed after which *expression3* is evaluated. At this stage control returns
to *expression2* and the process repeated until *expression2* evaluates to

FALSE at which point execution of the `for` statement terminates and control passes to *statement3*. A standard construct for the `for` statement is for *statement1* to be used to initialise a variable, *expression3* used to modify this variable (e.g. increment it) and *expression2* used to determine when the loop should terminate. So, to execute *statement2* six times we could use a `for` loop of the form:

```
for( i = 1; i <= 6; i++)
    ...
```

The factorial example can also be modified so that it uses a `for` statement – one way of doing this is:

```
fact = 1;
for ( i = 1; i < n; i++)
    fact *= i;
```

More complex expressions can be used for all of the three expressions in the `for` statement, but for now we will mention only one variation which is available in C++ but not in C. Take a look at the following program fragment:

```
fact = 1;
for ( int i = 1; i < n; i++)
fact *= i;
```

You will see that there is only one difference between this and the previous piece of code, namely the presence of `int` as part of *statement1*. (This is why we have used *statement1* in our definition of the syntax of the `for` statement rather than *expression1* – int i = 1; is a statement, not an expression.) C++ allows identifiers to be declared where they are first used, which in this particular example is quite convenient. Note however that the earlier declaration of `i` in the program has to be removed if we are to use this new `for` construct. Note also that the scope of `i` (i.e. where in the program `i` is available) is from its point of declaration (immediately outside of the `for` loop) to the end of the program.

1.8.5 The comma operator

A comma is used as an operator in expressions of the form:

expression1, expression2

In examples of this sort both expressions are evaluated in the order in which they occur (i.e. *expression1* before *expression2*) and then the whole comma expression is set equal to that of *expression2*. One example when the comma operator comes in useful is the following. Suppose we wish to read in positive integers and compute their sum – the list is terminated by a negative integer or zero. We can use the following piece of code:

```
// using the comma operator in a non-trivial example
sum = 0;
while (cin >> i, i > 0)
    sum += i;
```

Here the first expression in the parentheses reads in integers from the keyboard (or standard input stream), the second expression then carries out a test and the value of the resulting test is assigned to the complete expression. So, as long as i is greater than zero the sum will be updated using the latest value of i, but as soon as the value of i read in is less than or equal to zero the loop terminates.

1.9 Operator precedence and associativity

In this chapter we have discussed a number of fundamental operators but have not mentioned explicitly anything about the precedence of operators or their associativity. In this section we rectify that and at the same time introduce most of the remaining operators. Let's begin by looking at associativity. The associativity of an operator determines how an expression which uses that operator is evaluated. For example the expression n + 6 - p + 12 is equivalent to ((n + 6) - p) + 12. In other words the expression n + 6 is evaluated first, after which p is subtracted from the result which is finally added to 12. The + and - operators therefore have left to right associativity. An example of right to left associativity which we have already encountered is the assignment operator (=). Thus the in expression total = n + 5 the expression n + 5 is evaluated first and the result assigned to total. The complete list of operators and their associativity is given in Table 1.7, but before looking at that we will discuss the related idea of precedence.

The precedence of an operator determines the order in which an expression is evaluated in expressions containing a mixture of operators. Thus in the expression 3 * p - 12 / n, because both * and / have higher precedence than -, the expressions which contain * and / are evaluated before that containing the - operator. That is the expression is equivalent to (3 * p) - (12 / n). (We have used the fact here, and in our discussion of associativity, that parentheses have the highest precedence – which everyone will be familiar with from their experience of simple arithmetic and algebra!) Table 1.7 lists all the operators in descending order of precedence. Operators on the same line all have equal precedence and so if it is important that an expression using one of these operators is evaluated before an expression involving an operator of the same precedence then either parentheses should be used to force earlier evaluation or, perhaps better the expression should be broken down into smaller expressions and dummy variables used as necessary. Generally speaking if you find yourself getting confused over the order of evaluation and need to introduce too many parentheses to make evaluation clear then the expression is too complex and should be broken down. If you are already familiar with C then the majority of these operators should already be familiar to you. In any case by the time you have reached the end of this book you should understand how all the operators are used.

Appendix B gives a complete list of all C++ operators together with a brief description. This appendix includes all the operators now included in the ISO/ANSI standard and as such will list some not covered in detail in this book and possibly not available in existing implementations. However it is hoped that the list will be of use for future reference. Those included in Table 1.7 which follows are however available and will be discussed at some point in this text.

Table 1.7 Precedence and associativity of operators

Highest precedence	Associativity
() [] :: . ->	left to right
unary ! ~ + - * & ++ -- new (type) sizeof delete	right to left
.* -> *	left to right
* / %	left to right
+ -	left to right
<< >>	left to right
< > <= >=	left to right
++ !=	left to right
&	left to right
^	left to right
|	left to right
&&	left to right
||	left to right
?:	right to left
= += -= *= /= %= &= |= ^= <<= >>=	right to left
,	left to right

1.10 Summary

This brings us to the end of the first chapter. The majority of the topics covered here should have been no more than revision for those of you already familiar with C but nevertheless I hope you found them useful. Just to remind you we list below the main points from this chapter. Check that you are familiar with them all, and understand the basics, before moving on.

Topics covered:

- *Structure* of a C++ program.
- Use of the keyword `void` in the definition of `main()`.
- Comments `//`.
- C++ I/O - use of `cin >>` and `cout <<`.
- Escape sequences (see Table 1.1).
- I/O modifiers `endl`, `oct`, `hex` and `dec`.
- *keywords* (see Tables 1.2 and 1.3).
- Arithmetic operators `+ - * / %` (see Table 1.6).
- Fundamental data types – `int`, `char`, `float`.
- Type modifiers – `unsigned`, `signed`, `short` and `long`.
- Unary operators `& * ! + - ~ ! ++ --` (see Page 13).
- Other Arithmetic operators `+= -= *= /= %=` (see Table 1.6).
- The conditional operator `? :`.
- Relational operators `== <= >= !=` (Table 1.4).
- Logical operators `! && ||` (Table 1.5).
- The *comma* operator.
- Control structures: selection `if`, `if ... else` and `switch`.
- Control structures: repetition `while`, `do ... while` and `for`.
- The `break` and `continue` statements.
- Local declarations (e.g. `int i = 1` as part of a for statement).
- Operator precedence and associativity (Table 1.7); see also Appendix B.

1.11 Exercises

As a check on the material you have covered in this chapter try out the following exercises. Some exercises require you to write complete programs, whilst others ask you to complete or modify existing programs. If you get stuck then you can refer to selected answers given in Appendix C.

1.12.1 Enter Program 1.4 (DATATYPE) and use it to check the size of the C++ basic data types in your implementation.

1.12.2 Write a program to read in an integer and compute the sum and difference of the last two digits, e.g. `number entered = 376`, `sum = 13, difference = 1`.

1.12.3 Write a program which requests the user to enter two integers and which then prints out the sum, difference, product, division and modulo of the pair of integers. What do you notice about division?

1.12.4 Write programs to test the two uses of conditional expressions discussed in Section 1.7.

1.12.5 Write a program to read in a series of positive integers and display the total number entered, the number of times a number is immediately followed by a smaller number and the number of times a number is immediately followed by a larger one.

1.12.6 Modify the factorial program (Program 1.8) so that it uses the do...while construct. What happens if n = 0? or n = –3? Can you explain? How might you change the program to improve its operation, remembering that mathematically the factorial of a negative number is not defined, and that 0! = 1?

1.12.7 Make the changes suggested in the text, and any other changes which may be necessary, so that the factorial program uses the for loop.

1.12.8 Modify Program 1.10 (MENU2.cpp) program so that it uses switch.

1.12.9 Write a program to carry out simple arithmetic calculations (limit it to addition, subtraction, multiplication and division of two floats entered from the keyboard). Use a menu-driven program to enable the correct operation to be selected.

1.12.10 Write a program which reads in text from the keyboard and works out the percentage of vowels in the text. Display this percentage and the total number of characters read in.

1.12.11 Modify the above program so that the length of the longest and shortest words are computed.

1.12.12 Write a program to display in a tabular form all the ASCII character codes in decimal, octal and character form. Use the decimal range 32 to 255. What happens if you extend the range so that it starts from zero? Can you explain why?

2 Some C++ Enhancements

2.1 Introduction

In this chapter we continue on the road from C to C++. We will be reviewing some more elements of C and introducing more C++ enhancements. Some basic concepts concerning functions and program structure will be discussed. We will be looking at where and in what ways *variables* can be accessed, how functions can be used to improve program *structure* and how *arrays* of simple data types can be used. We will be introducing ways of modifying the use of cout through the use of output manipulators and will look at some examples using references.

2.2 Functions

You will already have come across functions if you have looked at C and, if you are familiar with any other programming languages you are likely to have encountered subroutines, procedures or paragraphs. In C and C++ there is only one form of structure other than a program – namely functions. In C and C++ no function can be defined inside another function – in a simple program the functions will normally be defined after the main program code; in more complex programs they may be defined in a separate header file or even pro-totyped in a header file and then included as library files during the compilation and linking process. Wherever they are physically stored they lie at the same level as the main program. This makes life easy without loss of freedom. In C++ a function can be restricted in its use to objects of a particular class, this provides an extremely important tool in the construction of abstract data types, the importance of which will be revealed in later chapters.

The essential point about functions is that they are designed to carry out a particular well defined task (e.g. formatted output, in the case of printf() in C). Another important feature of functions is that they save repeating code. So if we repeatedly need to find the value of y in the equation $y = 4x^2 + 7x - 9$ then we could write a function which takes x as a parameter and returns the value of y. Or more importantly we could write a function which would find the value of y (if one exists) for any quadratic equation of the form $y = ax^2 + bx + c$.

In C and C++ functions can return a value (int, float, char, etc.) or return no value, in which case the function must be declared using the keyword void. Our first look at functions will be at a void function. Before using a function it needs to be defined so let's take a look at how that is achieved.

2.2.1 Definition and declaration

Suppose we wish to write a function which outputs the sum, difference, product and ratio of two real numbers (floats). The function will have two parameters x and y. To make the function a little more interesting we wish it to check the divisor (y) and if it is non-zero simply output the ratio, otherwise if y is zero and x is negative output $-1e20$ (i.e. a large negative number), if y is zero and x is positive output $+1e20$ and finally, if x is zero output 0. Program 2.1 illustrates how this might be achieved.

📋 **Program 2.1**

```
//: FUNDEMO1.cpp
//. A simple illustration of functions in C++
#include <iostream.h>
#include <conio.h>
// ....................................................
void main()
{           //function declaration
    void arith(float x, float y);
    float xx, yy;

    clrscr();
    cout << " Enter two real numbers : ";
    cin >> xx >> yy;
    cout << ednl << " The results are: " << endl;
    arith(xx, yy );
    cout << endl << " End of FUNDEMO1 " << endl;
}
// ....................................................
// function definition
void arith( float x, float y)
{
    cout << " Sum        = " << x + y << endl;
    cout << " Difference = " << x - y << endl;
    cout << " Product    = " << x * y << endl;
    cout << " Ratio      = " << ( y != 0 ? x / y :
        (x > 0 ? 1e20 : ( x < 0 ? -1e20 : 0.0))) << endl;
}
```

In this example the function `arith()` is declared inside the function `main` and defined after `main()`. (We can also say that the function is prototyped inside `main`.) The difference between declaration and definition is that the definition of a function is the function itself – i.e. the statements which are used to perform the action required by the function – (and this is unique, but see later for partial exceptions) – whereas the declaration (or prototype) is simply an announcement that the function will be used (and this can occur many times – although only once in any one function).

The function `arith()` is used in the program simply by inserting it as a statement with the appropriate arguments. This is known as calling the function. The function is called, where appropriate, with the relevant arguments, and once executed successfully the program statement immediately after the function call is executed (i.e., in the above program, after the statement `cout << " \n End of FUNDEMO1 \n ";`). When the function `arith()` is called the values of the arguments are assigned to the variables x and y within the function.

2.2.2 Scope of functions

The function `arith()` in FUNDEMO1.cpp is declared within `main()` and is therefore only available within `main` – i.e. from where it is first declared to the end of the file. If we had another function `fun1()` say which also used `arith()` then we could make `arith()` available to both `main` and `fun1()` by adopting a number of strategies. The first is simply to declare both `arith()` and `fun1()` before `main()` is defined, i.e.:

☐ Extract from Program 2.1

```
...
void arith( float x, float y);  // declaration of arith
void fun1( ... ); // declaration of fun1
            // - ... would be replaced by the
            // parameter list
void main()
{           // arith and fun1 both available
            // to main
   ...
}

void fun1( ... )   // definition of fun1
{
...
}
void arith( float x, float y)   // definition of arith
{           // could use identifiers other
...           // than x & y but using the same
...           // identifiers as those used in
...           // the declaration aids
...           // readability
}
```

Since `arith()`, and for that matter `fun1()`, are declared outside `main()` they are both global functions – i.e. they have global scope and are therefore available throughout the program up until the end of the file.

There are occasions when a function declaration and its definition coincide. This was the original method used in C but, except for small functions declared within a class, it is now usually superseded by separate definition and declaration. Program 2.2 illustrates combined definition and declaration.

Program 2.2

```cpp
//: BITWISE.cpp -- bit manipulation demo, also illustrating
//. combined declaration and definition of a function

#include <conio.h>
#include <iostream.h>

// The following function takes a single byte and displays each
// bit. The (1 << i) produces a 1 in each successive bit
// position; in binary: 00000001, 00000010, etc.
// If this bit bitwise ANDed with num is nonzero, it means there
// was a 1 in that position in num.

// print_binary() defined and declared at the same time

void print_binary(const unsigned num)
{
        for(int i = 7; i >= 0; i--)
                if( num & (1 << i) )
                        cout << "1";
                else
                        cout << "0";
        cout << endl;
} // end of print_binary

// note use of unsigned - normally don't want signs when working
// with bytes, so use unsigned.
void main()
{
        unsigned a, b;

        clrscr();
        cout << " BITWISE operators"; cout << endl;
        cout << " ================="; cout << endl;

        cout << " Enter a number between 0 and 255: ";
        cin >> a;

        cout << " a in binary:     "; print_binary(a);
        cout << " Enter another number between 0 and 255: ";
        cin >> b;

        cout << " b in binary:     "; print_binary(b); NL;
        cout << " a | b =          "; print_binary(a | b);
        cout << " a & b =          "; print_binary(a & b);
        cout << " a ^ b =          "; print_binary(a ^ b);
        cout << " ~a =             "; print_binary(~a);
        cout << " ~b =             "; print_binary(~b);

        unsigned c = 0x5A;
        cout << " c in binary:     "; print_binary(c);
```

```
   a |= c;
   cout << " a |= c; a =     "; print_binary(a);
   b &= c;
   cout << " b &= c; b =     "; print_binary(b);
   b ^= a;
   cout << " b ^= a; b =     "; print_binary(b);
}
```

2.2.3 Bit manipulation

As you will have gathered by the name of the program this demonstrates how individual bits can be manipulated, and by doing so we can introduce the bit manipulation operators. Table 2.1 summarises these operators.

Table 2.1 Bit manipulation operators

Operator	Description	Operator	Description
&	Bitwise AND	|	Bitwise OR
^	Bitwise XOR (exclusive OR)	~	Bit inversion
<<	Shift left	>>	Shift right

As we saw in Chapter 1, although we can output numbers in decimal, octal and hexadecimal forms we cannot in C or C++ output a number in binary form using standard I/O functions or manipulators. So perhaps the best place to start is with the `print_binary()` function itself which is used to output a number in binary form:

```
void print_binary(const unsigned char num)
{
   for(int i = 7; i >= 0; i--)
      if( num & (1 << i) )    cout << "1";
      else                    cout << "0";
   cout << endl;
} // end of print_binary
```

In order to understand how this works consider the binary number `01100101`. The `for` loop steps through the binary digits and at each stage shifts the single bit (1) one place to the left, this is then bitwise anded with `num`. If the bit in that particular place is a 1 then '1' is output otherwise a '0' is output. Table 2.2 shows some successive steps in this `for` loop.

If you read the column under result, from top to bottom, you will see that the bits obtained correspond to the original binary number reading from left to right (i.e. from the most significant bit to the least significant bit). This illustrates both how the left shift operator and the bitwise AND operator (`&`) work. Note the reason for writing the for loop in the form `for(int i = 7; i >= 0; i--)` is now obvious – we need to output the binary digits starting with the most significant one, so we start with a 1 in the left-most position in our 8-bit number.

Table 2.2 Dry run of `print_binary()`

```
i   1 << i        num & (1 << i)          Result
7   10000000      01100101
              &   10000000                  0
6   01000000      01100101
              &   01000000                  1
5   00100000      01100101
              &   00100000                  1
```
etc.

Note the parameter declaration for this function `const unsigned char num`. We have used `char` here as we only want to deal with a single byte. (You could use `short` if that takes up a single byte, but in my implementation it is the same as an `int`, i.e. 2 bytes.) We need `unsigned` since we are not concerned with signed numbers and we wish to deal with all 8 bits. Finally we have used `const` to indicate that the parameter itself (`num`) is not modified by the function. (The use of `const` is discussed in more detail later on in this chapter.)

Now let's take a look at the rest of the program. Once two integers (between 0 and 255) have been entered we simply use `cout` statements to display the result of the various bit operations. First of all using the three binary operators and the unary operators:

```
cout << " b in binary:    "; print_binary(b);
cout << " a | b =         "; print_binary(a | b);
cout << " a & b =         "; print_binary(a & b);
cout << " a ^ b =         "; print_binary(a ^ b);
cout << " ~a =            "; print_binary(~a);
cout << " ~b =            "; print_binary(~b);
```

Test run 2.1 shows a sample run with `a` equal to 58 and `b` equal to 67.

Test run 2.1

```
BITWISE operators
==================

Enter a number between 0 and 255:
a in binary:     00111010

Enter another number between 0 and 255:
b in binary:     01000011

a | b =          01111011
a & b =          00000010
a ^ b =          01111001
~a =             11000101
~b =             10111100
```

The last part of the program uses the bitwise operators with assignment which are summarised in Table 2.3.

Table 2.3 Bit operators with assign

Operator	Description	Operator	Description
&=	Bitwise AND and assign	|=	Bitwise OR and assign
^=	Bitwise XOR and assign	<<=	Bit inversion and assign
>>=	Shift left and assign		

The code which uses the first three of these operators is:

```
unsigned char c = 0x5A;
cout << " c in binary:      "; print_binary(c);
a |= c;
cout << " a |= c; a =      "; print_binary(a);
b &= c;
cout << " b &= c; b =      "; print_binary(b);
b ^= a;
cout << " b ^= a; b =      "; print_binary(b);
```

The statement a |= c; takes the current value of a, ors it with c and then places the result back in a. The other operators work in a similar way.

Test run 2.2 shows a test run for a = 58 and b = 67.

Test run 2.2

```
c in binary:       01011010

a |= c; a =        01111010
b &= c; b =        01000010
b ^= a; b =        00111000
```

Before leaving this section we should point out that the bit manipulation operators discussed here, and the logical operators discussed in Chapter 1, have aliases defined in the new ISO/ANSI C++ standard as follows.

Table 2.4 ISO/ANSI C++ bit manipulation and logical operators

operator	alias	operator	alias	operator	alias
&&	and	&&=	and_eq	&	bitand
|	bitor	~	compl	!	not
!=	noteq	||	or	||=	or_eq
^	xor	^=	xor_eq		

This list of aliases is stated purely for completeness as it is unlikely that you will require them in your own programming and you are unlikely to encounter much code which uses them.

2.2.4 Functions of type other than void

The functions `arith` and `print_binary` are both of type `void` because they do not return any value to the function from which they are called. In general, however, functions do return a value and we can illustrate this by writing a program to find the minimum of three real numbers. The definition is:

```
float min( float x, float y, float z)
{
   if ( y < x ) x = y;
   if ( z < x ) x = z;
   return(x);
}
```

This might be called in the `main` program as follows:

```
...
cout << "\n Enter three real numbers : ";
cin >> xx >> yy >> zz;
cout << " The minimum is " << min( xx, yy, zz) << endl;
...
```

The `return` statement in `min()` returns the value of `x` – in effect this is assigned to the function name `min` (which, in this example, must be declared to be of type `float`).

2.2.5 Modifying function arguments

Suppose we wish to write a function which works out the minimum and maximum of three float numbers. We can't do this with a simple function like `min` (see above) because return only allows one variable to be returned (although there are ways around this) neither can we use simple `float` arguments. Program 2.3 gives an example.

Program 2.3

```
//: MINMAX1.cpp
//. passing parameters 'by value'
//  minmax function example 1 - doesn't work!
void minmax(float x, float y, float z, float min, float max)
{
   min = x;
   if ( y < x ) min = y;
   if ( z < x ) min = z;
   max = x;
   if ( y > x ) max = y;
   if ( z > x ) max = z;
}
```

If this function is used in a statement such as `minmax(4, 9, -6, mn, mx);` then neither of the variables `mn` or `mx` will be modified by the function.

2.2.6 The reference operator (&)

You may already be familiar with the way C solves this problem, if not we mention it briefly later, but what of the C++ solution? In C++ we can use the operator & to declare the parameters min and max as reference parameters. The function definition now becomes as in Program 2.4.

Program 2.4

```
//: MINMAX2.cpp
//. illustrating the use of reference parameters i.e. 'call by
//. reference'. minmax function example 2 - should work
//  using reference parameters - only for C++, not C
void minmax(float x, float y, float z, float &min, float &max)
{
  min = x;    // note that we can still refer to min
              // (and max) directly i.e. no need
              // to use & in the function
  if ( y < x ) min = y;
  if ( z < x ) min = z;

  max = x;
  if ( y > x ) max = y;
  if ( z > x ) max = z;
}
```

the declaration, in main, might be:

```
void minmax(float x, float y, float z, float &min, float &max);
```

and the call might be:

```
minmax(3.4, 5.6, -7.3, minimum, maximum);
```

Notice the way in which the arguments minimum and maximum are written in the function call, without the & (which is required in the function definition). Notice also that minimum and maximum must be variables – we cannot for example write maximum+1, or minimum-1 in place of maximum and minimum, neither can we pass constants e.g. the call:

```
minmax(3.4, 5.6, -7.3, 10.0, 25.0);
```

is obviously invalid.

The important point concerning reference parameters is that both the value and the address of the variable are available to the function – which is why we are able to change the values of minimum and maximum in the above example. The method of passing parameters in this way is known as 'passing by reference' in contrast to 'passing by value' which is used in C, as we now go on to illustrate.

The simplified definition, declaration and use of the `minmax()` function becomes apparent when you compare this new (C++) method with the earlier C method. In C, when the argument to a function may be modified by the function we must pass the address of the variable(s). So, the function definition becomes as in Program 2.5.

Program 2.5

```
//: MINMAX3.cpp
//. illustrating the use of pointer parameters
//. minmax function example 3 - this should work
//. using pointers - works with C as well
void minmax(float x, float y, float z, float *min, float *max)
{
    *min = x;
    if ( y < x ) *min = y;
    if ( z < x ) *min = z;

    *max = x;
    if ( y > x ) *max = y;
    if ( z > x ) *max = z;
}
```

The program fragment used to call this function might be:

```
...
float minval, maxval;
minmax(3.2, -8.6, 9.5, &minval, &maxval);
        // note use of & operator for
        // minval and maxval
...
```

This method, although still usable in C++, should generally be avoided in preference to the previous method using reference arguments.

2.3   Scope

In this section we will be taking another look at the visibility of objects in programs, in other words their scope. In Section 2.2 we discussed scope, in passing, when examining the declaration and definition of functions (see our discussion of the `arith()` and `fun1()` functions). In this section we pursue a more general discussion regarding the scope of objects in a C++ program.

The scope of an object is determined by where it is declared. Objects can be declared in three different places:

- **Globally**. Outside any functions (including `main()`).

- **As formal parameters**. To a function.
- **Locally**. In a function definition.

We will illustrate each of these types of declaration my means of a set of simple programs. We begin by looking at global declaration. Program 2.6 illustrates a global declaration of a variable.

🗂 Program 2.6

```
//: SCOPEG1.cpp
//. illustrating how scope affects the visibility of variables

#include <conio.h>
#include <iostream.h>
int i = 10;          // a global declaration and initialisation
void main()
{
   void printi(void); // prototype for printi() //- no parameters

   clrscr();
   cout << " SCOPEG1" << endl;
   printi();  // 1st call of printi() - prints 10,then 11
   printi(i)  // 2nd call of printi() - prints 11,then 12
   i--;     // decrement i
   printi()   // 3rd call of printi() - prints 10,then 11
}

void printi(void) // no parameters
{           // no parameter, or local declaration of i,
            // so i is the global variable
   cout << " in printi() " << endl;
   cout << "   i = " << i << endl;
   i++;
   cout << " i++ = " << i << endl << endl;
}
```

This program illustrates how global variables work – all functions declared after the declaration of the variable have direct access to that variable. Try the program out for yourself and verify that it works as indicated. Test run 2.3 shows a sample run.

Two important points to note arising from this example are:

- Both main() and printi() have access to the variable i, in the sense that they can use its value (e.g. to display it on the screen).
- Both functions can modify the value of i. So the i++ within printi() and the i-- in main() both affect the global i. In most cases this is very undesirable and if followed will lead to undesirable side effects. For example, if printi() was really only doing what its name suggests then it should be unable to modify i – it should only be allowed to print it!

```
SCOPEG1
=======

in printi()
  i   = 10
i++ = 11
in printi()
  i  = 11
i++ = 12
in printi()
  i = 11
i++ = 12
```

2.3.1 Local declarations

Program 2.7 has an additional declaration of i (still int) within main() – this effectively hides (or overrides the global i and makes it invisible within the body of main(). Test run 2.4 shows a sample test run.

The first value of i displayed (in my case 1092 – yours will be different) is simply the uninitialised value of the local variable i – that is local to main(), and this could have any value. Notice though that when printi() is called the global value of i is used within the function, just as in the previous example. The reason for this is that the initial global declaration of i (before main()) is global to both functions – what is important is not where the function is used that governs the i which is being processed but where the function is defined in relation to the variable. Within main() when we decrement i we are decrementing the local variable but this has no effect on the global i, as is illustrated by the third call of printi().

📋 **Program 2.7**

```cpp
//: SCOPEG2.cpp - illustrating how scope affects the visibility
//. of variables, this time showing how a local
//. declaration hides the global variable

#include <conio.h>
#include <iostream.h>

int i = 10;   // a global declaration and initialisation
// ............................................................
void main()
{
   void printi(void); // prototype for printi()
            // - no parameters

   int i;  // local declaration (to main)
        // this i not initialised so will print ???
   clrscr();
   cout << " SCOPEG2 " << endl;
   cout << " ======= " << endl << endl;
   cout << " i (in main) = " << i << endl;
```

```
    printi();  // 1st call of printi() - prints 10, then 11
    printi();  // 2nd call of printi() - prints 11, then 12
    i--;       // decrement i (not the global i!)
    cout << " i (in main) = " << i << endl;
    printi();  // 3rd call of printi() - prints 12 then 13
}

// printi() definition here - as before
```

```
SCOPEG2
=======

i (in main) = 1092
    i = 10
i++ = 11
    i = 11
i++ = 12
i (in main) = 1091
    i = 12
i++ = 13
```

2.3.2 Function parameters

The third program in this series illustrates the use of a parameter in a function call. Program 2.8 gives the complete program and Test run 2.5 shows a sample test run.

📋 **Program 2.8**

```cpp
//: SCOPEG3.cpp
//. illustrating how scope affects the visibility of
//. variables using a formal parameter in a function

#include <conio.h>
#include <iostream.h>

int i = 10;   // a global declaration and initialisation
// ................................................................
void main()
{
    void printi(int i);   // prototype for printi()
                // - one parameter

    int i;   // local declaration (to main)
        // this i not initialised so will print ???
    clrscr();
    cout << " SCOPEG3 " << endl;
    cout << " ======= " << endl << endl;
    cout << " i (in main) = " << i << endl;

    printi(i); // 1st call of printi() - prints ???, then ???+1
    printi(i); // 2nd call of printi()- prints ???, then ???+1
    i--;       // decrement i (not the global i!)
    cout << " i (in main) = " << i << endl;
    printi(i); // 3rd call of printi() - prints ???-1,then ???
```

```
        cout << " Finally printi() called with a "
             "constant as argument (7) " << endl;
        printi(7);
}
//  ...............................................
void printi(int i) // one parameter
{            // the actual value passed will now depend on the
             // details of the function call
        cout << "   i = " << i << endl;
        i++;
        cout << " i++ = " << i << endl;
}
```

🖥 **Test run 2.5**

```
SCOPEG3
=======

i (in main)  = 1150
   i = 1150
i++ = 1151
   i = 1150
i++ = 1151
i (in main)  = 1149
   i = 1149
i++ = 1150
Finally printi() called with a constant as argument (7)
   i = 7
i++ = 8
```

Notice that in this case the first three calls of printi(), with i as the argument, use the local variable i (i.e. the i declared within main()). At this stage, and with C programs, we have no means of accessing the global i within main() or within printi() – but in C++ we can ... so stay around. Before we look at the C++ extensions to scoping, take a look at the final (fourth) call to printi() in Program 2.8. You will notice that we have used a constant as an argument (the integer 7) and the printi() function has worked as expected. Notice that it appears that we can even increment a constant since printi() outputs:

```
i = 7
i++ = 8
```

when 7 is passed as the argument. However we are not in fact incrementing a constant – the increment operators and the rest of the family of double arithmetic operators cannot be applied to constants as a little thought will verify. What happens when the statement printi(7); is executed is that a (temporary) local variable is set up within printi() and given the initial value 7 (that is the variable i declared in the argument to printi()). Since this is a normal variable we are quite at liberty to change its value (i.e. in this case increment it), however the actual parameter (in this case 7) remains unchanged.

2.3.3 The scope resolution operator (::)

Now for the last program in this series. This one illustrates the added flexibility of C++ in providing greater control over access to variables. Take a look at Program 2.9.

Program 2.9

```cpp
//: SCOPEG4.cpp
//. illustrating how scope affects the visibility of variables
//. using a formal parameter in a function
//. and the scope resolution operator ::

#include <conio.h>
#include <iostream.h>

int i = 10;   // a global declaration and initialisation
// ...............................................................
void main()
{
    void printi(int i);  // prototype for printi()
                // - one parameter

    int i;         // local declaration (to main)

    clrscr(); // this i not initialised so will print ???
    cout << " SCOPEG3 " << endl;
    cout << " ======= " << endl << endl;
    cout << " i (in main) = " << i << endl;

    printi(i); // 1st call of printi()- prints ???, then ???+1
    printi(i); // 2nd call of printi()- prints ???, then ???+1
    i--;       // decrement i (not the global i!)
    cout << " i (in main) = " << i << endl;
    printi(::i); // 3rd call of printi() - prints 10 then 11
    cout << " Finally printi() called with a constant as
                argument (7) " << endl;
    printi(7);
}
// ...............................................................
void printi(int i) // one parameter
{          // the actual value passed will now depend
           // on the details of the function call
    cout << "   i = " << i << endl;
    i++;
    cout << " i++ = " << i << endl;
}
```

One line of code has been changed (from Program 2.9), that is the third call to `printi()`. That line now reads:

```cpp
printi(::i); // 3rd call of printi() - prints 10 then 11
```

We have also added another block with yet another local declaration of `i`:

```
{
    int i = 89;
    printi(i);    // a fourth call - prints 89 & 90
    printi(::i);  // a fifth call - prints 10 & 11
}
```

The `printi(i)` call in this last extract uses the local variable `i` (which has a value of 89) and behaves as we have come to expect. However the third and fifth calls behave rather differently. The argument to `printi()` in these two calls is `::i` – it consists of the variable `i` preceded by the special operator `::` (i.e. two colons – no space) which is known as the scope resolution operator. This special operator allows the programmer to gain access to a variable which is hidden by a local declaration. So we can use it in this program to gain access to the global variable `i`. Notice that it doesn't matter how deeply nested blocks are, when we use *::global_name* the name referred to will always be the global one (obviously it must exist!). This operator will become very familiar once we get into the topic of classes, but it does no harm to give you an early introduction to it.

Now that we have finally covered the basic rules of scope and you have learnt about local and global variables we can move on to an examination of the storage class modifiers.

2.4 Storage class

As we have already seen when variables are declared storage is made available in the computer's memory. As well as specifying the type of variable we can also specify how the computer will store the variable and what other parts of the program will have access to it. These issues are covered by the term *Storage Class*. In C++ (as in C) there are four storage class modifiers `extern`, *static*, *register* and *auto* which can be used to specify the way in which the computer stores variables (including functions). They are used in the declaration of variables in the following way:

storage_class_specifier type variable_name;

where:

storage_class_specifier is one of `extern`, `static`, register or auto;
type is any valid C++ data type (built-in or user-defined);
variable_name is any valid C++ *variable_name*.

2.4.1 *extern*

The `extern` keyword is mostly used for large programs or projects where the various functions, variable declarations, classes and so on are split up amongst a number of separate files. In C++ you are only allowed to declare global variables once. If a variable in one file is required by another file then we need a method of informing the compiler that such a variable does indeed exists in another file. This is where the `extern` storage class modifier comes in. Consider a program which is made up to two files: Program 2.10 and Program 2.11.

Program 2.10

```
//: EXTERN1.cpp
//. illustrating the use of extern and separate compilation
//. use with extern2.cpp

#include <conio.h>
#include <iostream.h>
extern int i;          // an extern declaration
extern void printi(int i); // ... and for a function
// ...................................................
void main()
{
   int i = 34;   // local declaration (to main)
                 // i is initialised to 34
   clrscr();
   cout << " EXTERN1 " << endl;
   cout << " ======= " << endl << endl;
   cout << " i (in main) = " << i << endl;

   printi(i);    // 1st call of printi(), prints 34 & 35
   printi(::i); // 2nd call of printi(), prints 10 & 11
}
```

Program 2.11 contains the global variable `i` and the function `printi()`.

Program 2.11

```
//: EXTERN2.cpp
//. a second file with a global variable i and a function
//. printi()

#include <iostream.h>

int i = 10;       // a global declaration and initialisation
// ..............................................
void printi(int i)
{
   cout << "   i = " << i << endl;
   i++;
   cout << " i++ = " << i << endl;
}
```

Notice the use of `extern` in Program 2.10; this is used to tell the compiler that the variable `i` and the function `printi()` are to be found in another file. Provided that these two files are linked correctly (by using a project file in Borland C++ for example) then the output should be as Test run 2.6.

One advantage of the use of separate files is that modifications can be made in one file without worrying about the detail in other files. Another advantage is that separate files can be built up which hold functions, variables etc. needed for a particular task. These might be quite general tasks, such as I/O, or more specialised tasks perhaps needed only for one particular program. When we get on to discussing classes we will see yet another reason why placing code in separate files is useful.

⌨ **Test run 2.6**

```
EXTERN1
=======

i (in main) = 34
    i = 34
  i++ = 35
    i = 10
  i++ = 11
```

2.4.2 static

The keyword `static` is another storage class modifier which can be applied to variables in a file. In addition it can be used within functions. When a variable is declared as `static`, even though the variable is not visible outside the file or function in which it is declared, it will retain its value between calls. We can apply `static` to both local and global variables and the effect varies depending on which type of variable is being referred to.

When `static` is applied to local variables they retain their values between uses – they can be used in blocks in C++, as the next example shows, as well as within functions and files as we shall see in a moment. Program 2.12 gives a simple usage of a `static` variable in a block. Test run 2.7 shows a sample run.

📋 **Program 2.12**

```
//: STATIC1.cpp
//. how the static storage class type modifier works

#include <conio.h>
#include <iostream.h>
// ..................................................
void main()
{
    int i;

    clrscr();
```

```
cout << " local declaration & initialisation " << endl;
cout << " int j = 10 " << endl;
for(i = 1; i <= 4; i++)
{
    int j = 10;
    cout << " i = " << i <<
                " j = " << j << endl;
    j++; //j incremented but then reinitialised by int j = 10;
}
cout << " now using static " << endl;
cout << " static int j = 10 " << endl;
for(i = 1; i <= 4; i++)
{
    static int j = 10;
    cout << " i = " << i <<
                " j = " << j << endl;
    j++; // j incremented and new value retained by use of
         // static in the declaration and initialisation of j
}
}
```

⌨ Test run 2.7

```
local declaration & initialisation
int j = 10
i = 1 j = 10
i = 2 j = 10
i = 3 j = 10
i = 4 j = 10
now using static
static int j = 10
i = 1 j = 10
i = 2 j = 11
i = 3 j = 12
i = 4 j = 13
```

This, not very useful, program simply uses a `for` loop to declare and initialise another integer `j`, print out the index variable (`i`) , the variable `j`, and then increments `j`. As the first few lines of output show `j` is initialised to 10 each time the body of the for loop is executed – the incrementing of `j` has no effect (except within the loop – each time it is increased to 11, but that only lasts until the end of the block).

The second set of output, beginning `now using static`, shows that the first time the body of the for loop is executed `j` is initialised to 10, but thereafter the last value assigned to `j` is retained and used in subsequent processing.

Incidentally this program illustrates the way C++ allows variable declaration at points other than at the beginning of a function, or globally. We have declared `j` twice in two separate blocks; the first time simply as a 'normal' `auto int` variable, and the second as a `static int` variable. We could not do this in C – although we could do it in a function. You might be tempted to think that we could use this facility to declare `i` within each `for` loop, e.g.:

```
for( int i = 0; i <= 4; i++)
```

and then repeat the same line for the second for loop. However this is not allowed because both for loops are in the same block and so i would be declared twice – which is illegal, even in C++. The block structure of this program is:

```
        // start of block1
...
void main()
{       // start of block 2, inside block 1
   ...
   for( i = 0; i <= 4; i++)
   {    // start of block 3, inside block 2
      ...
   }    // end of block 3
   ...
   for( i = 0; i <= 4; i++)
   {    // start of another block 3, inside
        // block 2
      ...
   }    // end of 2nd block 3
}       // end of block 2
        // end of block 1, program and file
```

This outline program structure should reveal why we cannot declare i in the first statement of each for loop – both are part of the same block: block 2. It is legal to declare j within the body of each for loop (both blocks 3) because they are separate blocks. We can, if we are sufficiently perverse, add two more levels of block simply by surrounding each existing block 3 with { }. Each for statement is now in its own self-contained block and so we can now declare i in the first statement of each for loop. The program fragment below illustrates this:

```
{          // new block started
   for(int i = 1; i <= 4; i++)
   {
      int j = 10;
      cout << " i = " << i <<
              " j = " << j << endl;
      j++; // j incremented but then
           // reinitialised by int j = 10;
   }
}          // end of this new block

cout << " now using static " << endl;
cout << " static int j = 10 " << endl;
{          // another new block
   for(int i = 1; i <= 4; i++)
           // this now ok
   {
```

```
          static int j = 10;
          cout << " i = " << i <<
                  " j = " << j << endl;
          j++; // j incremented and new value retained by use of
               //static in declaration and initialisation of j
     }
}              // end of the 2nd new block
```

Such a contrived block structure rarely has any practical application, but it does serve to illustrate the scope of variables and the way in which blocks work. Try out these two programs and experiment with the placement of declarations to make sure you understand how the scope rules and block structure are handled in C++.

2.4.3 Functions with static variables

Now let's look at the use of static variables within functions. There is very little that need be added to the foregoing discussion, a simple example should be sufficient. Consider Program 2.13.

Program 2.13
```
//: STATICF.cpp
//. example using static variables in functions

#include <iostream.h>
// ........................................................
void count_call()
{
   static int i = 1;
   cout << " This function has been called ";
   cout << i++ << " time. " << endl;
}

void main()
{
   count_call(); // 1st call of f()
   count_call(); // 2nd call of f() etc.
   count_call();
}
```

Type in the above program and try it out. What do you find?

Now remove the word static in the function definition. What happens now? You will not be surprised at the output – you should have found that in the first example the output is given in Test run 2.8. Test run 2.9 shows the output when the keyword static is removed.

Test run 2.8
```
This function has been called 1 time.
This function has been called 2 time.
This function has been called 3 time.
```

```
This function has been called 1 time.
This function has been called 1 time.
This function has been called 1 time.
```

Making `i` a static variable within the function definition means first of all that it will be initialised the first time the function is called (i.e. used). Subsequently `i` is incremented and the new value output. This is exactly the behaviour that we would have expected following our discussion above.

2.4.4 static global variables

It only remains to take a look at how the keyword `static` affects global variables, so let's do just that. Whereas static local variables retain their values within functions and between function calls even though they are invisible outside the function, the scope of static global variables is confined to the file in which they are declared. Therefore a static global variable can only be modified by statements (including functions) *within the file*. One use of static global variables as opposed to static local ones is when two or more functions require access to a variable. For example suppose we wish to compute successive terms of the series $x_{n+1} = x_n + a$, $x_0 = b$ for various values of a and b. So if $a = 2$ and $b = 4$ we will get the successive terms 4, 6, 8, 10, 12 etc. and for $a = -3$ and $b = 7$ we will get 7, 4, -1, -4, -7, etc. We could write a program using two functions, one to initialise the series and another to return the next element in the series. The file containing the necessary functions is given in Program 2.14 and Program 2.15 gives the main program.

📋 **Program 2.14**

```
//: SERIES.cpp
//. separate file holding the functions required
//. in the generation of the series x(n+1) = x(n) + a, x(0) = b

static int a, term;
// ...................................................................

void init_series(int aa, int b)
{
   term = b;  // 1st term in the series
   a = aa;
}

int get_next_term(void)
{
   term = term + a;
   return(term - a); // needed so we can get the 1st term
}
```

Program 2.15

```
//: STATICG.cpp
//. static global variables
//. this uses the functions in SERIES.cpp

#include <iostream.h>
#include <conio.h>

extern void  init_series(int a, int b);
extern int   get_next_term(void);

void main()
{
   int a, b;

   clrscr();
   cout << " enter a value for a (int) > ";
   cin >> a;
   cout << " enter a value for b (int) > ";
   cin >> b;

   init_series(a, b);
   for ( int i = 1; i < 10; i++ )
      cout << " term " << i << " = " << get_next_term() << endl;
}
```

Before reading on try out the program and check that it works correctly (use the values for a and b given above). Remember you will have to ensure that the files are compiled and linked correctly.

Test run 2.10 shows a test run for a=2 and b=4. This gives the results that would be expected.

Test run 2.10

```
term 1 = 4
term 2 = 6
term 3 = 8
term 4 = 10
term 5 = 12
term 6 = 14
term 7 = 16
term 8 = 18
term 9 = 20
```

Now that we have some output we can take a look at how the program works. Let's look first at the file holding the functions (i.e. Program 2.14). The first statement:

```
static int a, term;
```

is required to ensure that a and term retain their values within this file. The function init_series simply initialises the variable a with the first argument of the function and initialises `term` with the second argument. The function `get_next_term` takes the current value of `term` and adds `a`, it then returns this new value minus `a`! This rather odd piece of coding means that we are able to get the first term of the series by calling `get_next_term` instead of making `init_series` return the first term which we would otherwise have to do.

The main program (Program 2.15) should require little additional comment, the only thing we need to be careful of is to declare the two functions as `extern` so that the compiler recognises the fact that they are to be found in a separate file. Notice though that neither `term` nor `a` need to be made `extern` – which means that the program has no direct access to them. In order to demonstrate this add a line to the main program to output the value of `term`, e.g. `cout << term;` and rebuild the files. If you try this out you will find that `term` is an unknown variable within Program 2.15 but nevertheless so long as we do not try to access `term` directly (via the `cout` statement, for example) the program will work.

2.4.5 register

Register variables are worth mentioning in passing, but you will only occasionally find any need to use them. This storage specify is used to tell the compiler that access to the variables should be as fast as possible. This is a rather less specific instruction than was the case for register variables in early implementations of C, which stated that register variables should be stored, if possible, in the register of the CPU, thus guaranteeing the fastest possible access (hence the name register). Such variables could then only be of type `char` or `int`. However in C++ the application of the register specifier has been widened to include any data type – hence the more general meaning of register variables. In practice however only `int` or `char` variables are likely to be used. The advantage of using a register variable becomes obvious when the variable is being accessed frequently, for example in a loop.

There are two other restrictions concerning register variables which you should be aware of:

i) they can only be local variables or formal parameters in a function, and
ii) since the compiler may store register variables in the CPU registers you cannot access the address of such variables.

Finally you can declare as many register variables as you wish (so long as you keep to i) above) and the compiler will sort out which variables really become register variables.

2.4.6 auto

This final storage class modifier describes variables which are only temporarily allocated memory. Any variables that are not static or global will be of type auto, e.g. local variables in functions. Memory locations for local variables are automatically assigned on entry to the function and removed on exit – hence they are referred to as *automatic variables* – the keyword auto can be used to emphasise this but it is rarely required since they will of this type anyway!

2.5   Arrays

An array is a collection of items of the same data type. The type can range from the basic C/C++ types (e.g. int, char and float) through collections of various types (via the use of structures) to collections of objects belonging to a particular class, to name only a few possibilities. Each of the elements in an array is referenced by the same name but using a different index (or indexes in the case of arrays of more than one dimension). Successive elements of an array are stored in adjacent locations in memory. The first element in the array corresponds to the lowest address and the last element corresponds to the highest address.

We can declare an int array using:

```
int marks[20];
```

which enables the following variables to be used

```
marks[0], marks[1] ... marks[19]
```

Notice that the elements range from marks[0] to marks[19], not from 1 to 20 as, for example, in Pascal. The constant dimension (20 in this case) specifies the number of elements in the array – the first element is always 0 and the last element 1 less than the number of elements specified.

Any int variable, as well as any expression which evaluates to an int, can be used to index the array (i.e. to refer to an array element). However the programmer must be careful to control the range of this index (e.g. in the above case the index must be greater than or equal to 0 and less than or equal to 19) – if an index outside the array bounds is used then errors will obviously occur.

Arrays can be declared to be of any type (e.g. char, float, double, as well as more complex types), however the index (or subscript) must always be of type int (or unsigned).

Good programming practice dictates that a symbolic constant is used, for example when array sizes are specified. In both C and C++ this can be achieved by using a #define statement. So for example, suppose we wish to declare an array name consisting of 40 characters we could write:

```
#define NAME_SIZE        40
char     name[NAME_SIZE];
```

This method is to be preferred over the previous one (where an integer was used – 20) since firstly it is obvious whenever we are referring to the size of the array name, because we use the symbolic constant NAME_SIZE – for example: `for (i = 0; i < NAME_SIZE; i++) name[i] = ' ';` which places spaces into all elements of the array name. Any other occurrences of 40 will refer to some other constant, but should not refer to the size of the array name. Secondly it is a simple matter to change the size of the array – replace the 40 in the #define pre-processor instruction with a different value – this might be needed for example during testing and debugging to save typing in 40 characters each time, or we might decide that 40 is too small and a larger size for the array is required. Note that the #define instruction is not a C/C++ statement and therefore does not normally end with a semi-colon – if you do then the symbolic constant will also include the semi-colon.

In C++ there is yet another way of defining constants:

```
const int NAME_SIZE = 40;
```

the array can then be declared as before:

```
char name[NAME_SIZE];
```

(The const statement is also available in ANSI C but you cannot declare arrays using a const in ANSI C, whereas you can in C++.)

Program 2.16 is a simple program that uses an array and a const int to specify the length of the array. Type it in and try it out. Before running it work out what it does!

Program 2.16
```
//: ARRAY1.cpp
//. Simple program illustrating the use of an array
//. and the keyword const
#include <iostream.h>
#include <conio.h>
// ......................................................
void main()
{
const int  WORD_LENGTH = 10;
int        i;
   char    word[WORD_LENGTH];
   clrscr();
   cout << " ARRAY1 - using cin " << endl;
   cout << " ================== " << endl;
   cout << " Enter " << WORD_LENGTH << " characters:" << endl;
   for ( i = 0; i < WORD_LENGTH; i++)
   cin >> word[i];
```

```
    cout << " The string was: " << endl;
    for ( i = 0; i < WORD_LENGTH; i++)
        cout >> word[WORD_LENGTH - i - 1];
}
```

This program works well enough so long as at least WORD_LENGTH number of characters are entered and none of them are white spaces. (A white space is any of space, tab or new-line.) All white spaces are ignored, so if the input was:

today is Thursday

then the output would be:

uhTsiyadot

i.e. the first 10 non-white space characters in reverse order. This is a feature of cin, any white spaces that occur in the input stream, even when reading a single character, are ignored. We can overcome this by either reverting to C syntax (i.e. using scanf and the char conversion specifier %c, or one of the C get functions e.g. getchar(), getche() or getch()) or by use of one of the get member functions of cin. We will be looking at these later on in the book once we have introduced classes.

Of course it may be the case that we do not always wish to enter exactly WORD_LENGTH characters. If this is the case then, as usual, there are a number of alternatives. Before reading on what other alternatives can you think of?

One alternative is to use a while statement instead of a for statement to read in the characters to the array – we would then stop reading as soon as a white space has been entered. The relevant statements now look something like this:

```
    int nchars;
    cout << " Enter no more than " << WORD_LENGTH
         << " characters : \n ";

    i = 0;
    word[i] = cin.get();
    while ( word[i] != ' ' && word[i] != '\t' && word[i] !=
        '\r' && word[i] != '\n' && i < WORD_LENGTH-1)
    {
        i++;
        word[i] = cin.get();
    }
    nchars = i;
    cout << " the string was: " << endl;
    for ( i = 0; i < nchars; i++)
        cout << word[nchars - i - 1];
}
```

Notice a couple of things about this. First we need to know how many characters have been read in – we do this by introducing another `int` variable `nchars` which is assigned to `i` on exit from the `while` loop. This is then used in the `for` loop to check that only the same number of characters are output as were input.

Second we have used `cin.get()` which is a member function of `istream` and is used with the `cin` object to allow a single character to be read – more about this later.

Third notice the nature of the expression at the beginning of the `while` statement. This is rather cumbersome and a better alternative uses one of the standard functions in `ctype.h` (`isspace()`) which tests for a character being any white space (i.e. any of `space`, `tab`, `return`, `new-line`, `form-feed` or `vertical tab`), which is actually more comprehensive than our expression given above. With the use of this function, the new `while` statement therefore begins like this:

```
while ( !isspace(word[i]) && (i < WORD_LENGTH-1))
{
    ....
```

Another alternative to the above methods, although not particularly good style, is to use the keyword `break` which we looked at briefly in Chapter 1. You will remember that this can be used in a `loop` or `switch` statement to prematurely end the execution of the code in that block. Once `break` is encountered control passes to the next statement following the end of the block. So our first modified program might now contain the lines:

```
for ( i = 0; i < WORD_LENGTH; i++)
{
    word[i] = cin.get();
    if (word[i] == '\n') break;
}
```

Once the ENTER key is pressed the `for` loop is terminated irrespective of the value of `i`.

Yet another way of using `break` in our program is the following:

```
for( ; ; )
{
    word[i] = cin.get();
    if ((word[i++] == '\n') || (i>WORD_LENGTH))
        break;
}
```

Without the use of `break` the body of the `for` loop would continue to be executed until the computer is switched off or some other similar drastic measure is taken.

2.5.1 Initialising arrays

The most important point to remember about the initialising of any object is that before doing so memory must be allocated. In the case of simple data types this is straightforward – the declaration allocates space, as in `unsigned short int i; char ch;` or `double speed_of_light;` – it is when we declare pointers that problems can occur, but we will be looking at such issues in Chapter 3. For the moment we are concerned with arrays. So long as an array is declared and the number of elements is known there will be no problems about initialisation.

First of all remember that, in general, array elements will have no predetermined value. Thus if we declare an array

```
const int size = 10;
int a[size];
```

and then print out the values, using:

```
for (int i = 0; i < size; i++)
   cout << a[i] << " ";
```

then we cannot tell what values we are likely to get. For this reason, if for no other, we need to be able to initialise array elements.

The initialising of array elements can be carried out through simple assignment. Suppose we have the array as declared above then we can initialise certain elements, as in:

```
a[0] = 2;   a[1] = 5;   a[3] = 12;
```

or we can initialise all elements to a given value (e.g. 0):

```
for (int i = 0; i < size; i++)
   a[i] = 0;  // set each element to 0
```

or to different values:

```
for (int i = 0; i < size; i++)
   a[i] = i * i; // set each element to the
                 // square of its index
```

However, we also have another method available. The statement

```
int a[size] = { 2, 5, 0, 12 };
```

(assuming size is still 10) will have the same effect as the first method above except that in addition all remaining elements will be set to 0. It will be obvious in this last example, that we also need to set the, previously uninitialised, element 2 to some value (in this case 0), but if the remaining elements are to be set to zero then there is no need to explicitly specify their values in the list.

Finally we have two exceptions to our first comment that we cannot pre-determine the uninitialised values of array elements. These concern global and static variables (this will also work for types other than arrays). Both global and static arrays have all their elements set to zero on declaration. So an array declared outside `main()` or one declared inside `main()` as a static array will have all elements set to zero.

Program 2.17 illustrates all of the above points.

Program 2.17

```
//: ARRAYINI.cpp - initialising arrays
//. showing three methods of initialising 1-dimensional arrays
#include <conio.h>
#include <iostream.h>
const int  sizeb = 5;
int        b[sizeb];
// ........................................................
void main()
{
   const int sizea = 10;
   int a[sizea];

   clrscr();
   cout << " ARRAYINI " << endl;
   cout << " ======== " << endl << endl;
   cout << " a[] = ";
   for( int i = 0; i < sizea; i++)
      cout << a[i] << " ";
   cout << endl;

   cout << " b[] = ";
   for( i = 0; i < sizeb; i++)
      cout << b[i] << " ";
   cout << endl;

   cout << endl << " initialising elements 0, 1 & 4 " << endl;
   a[0] = 2; a[1] = 5; a[3] = 12;
   cout << " a[] = ";
   for( i = 0; i < sizea; i++)
      cout << a[i] << " ";
   cout << endl;

   cout << endl << " setting all elements to 0 " << endl;

   for( i = 0; i < sizea; i++)
      a[i] = 0;
   cout << " a[] = ";
   for( i = 0; i < sizea; i++)
      cout << a[i] << " ";
   cout << endl;

   cout << endl << " setting all elements to square of index "
        << endl;
```

```
    for( i = 0; i < sizea; i++)
       a[i] = i * i;
    cout << " a[] = ";
    for( i = 0; i < sizea; i++)
       cout << a[i] << " ";
    cout << endl;

    cout << endl << " new array c (8 elements) " << endl;
    const int sizec = 8;
    int c[sizec] = {3, 8, 5, 0, 4};
    cout << " c[] = ";
    for( i = 0; i < sizec; i++)
       cout << c[i] << " ";
    cout << endl;

    cout << endl << " finally a static array d (6 elements) "
       << endl;
    const int sized = 6;
    static int d[sized];
    cout << " d[] = ";
    for( i = 0; i < sized; i++)
       cout << d[i] << " ";
    cout << endl;
}
```

2.5.2 Arrays as function parameters

In this section we will take a brief look at using arrays with functions. We will be concerned only with one-dimensional arrays, of the type we have already been discussing. A simple array can be declared as an argument in a function as:

```
void function(int a[]);
```

However such a declaration can be dangerous unless some indication of the size of the array is given. This can be achieved by passing the size of the array as a separate variable:

```
void function( int a[], int size_of_a);
```

where size_of_a is the number of elements in a. This might then be called by means of the statement:

```
function(b, sizeb);
```

where we have previously made the declarations

```
const int  sizeb = 15;
int        b[sizeb];
```

This method has the advantage that arrays of variable size can be passed to the function. Can you think of any other method of informing the function of the size of the array?

One alternative is to use the first element of the array (e.g. b[0]) to hold the size of the array. You must then remember that the array no longer behaves like a 'normal' C/C++ array in that the first element will be a[1] and not a[0]. Thus all indexing expressions will need to be modified to take account of this.

One important point needs to be made about arrays as function arguments. Whilst the parameter sizeb cannot be changed by the function the contents of b can be changed. This is because when declaring an array as an argument we are indicating the address of the first element of the array. It is therefore advisable if we are writing a function which uses the array elements but does not change them to declare the array as a const, we might also reinforce the fact that the size_of_a argument cannot be changed by making this a const argument as well. Thus our function declaration becomes:

```
function( const int a[], const int size_of_a);
```

Of course if our function is supposed to modify the contents of the array then we would use the declaration:

```
function( int a[], const int size_of_a);
```

The exercise at the end of this chapter will give you the opportunity to experiment with arrays as arguments to functions.

2.6   Structures

One important element of program design is matching the data structures used in a program to the problem being solved. The ability to do this is mainly confined in C to the use of structures, similar to records in Pascal, which provide a limited means of data abstraction. Structures in C++ are an extension of the stuctures available in C and may be thought of as an early attempt at creating abstract data types. In this section we will look at how they operate in C++ – if you already use structures in C then it would be instructive to compare the differences between the two implementations. (Remember though that if necessary a structure in C++ can be used exactly as in C, although generally speaking the C++ alternative is simpler and 'cleaner' and should be used in preference to the C alternative whenever possible.)

As a means of introducing structures we will take a look at a simple problem, namely how to implement a date structure to hold the three elements of a date (day, month and year). The simplest way of doing this is by using three int variables day, month and year. However we would really like to treat these as a single collection (a single type) called `date`. We can do this by using a `struct` to define the representation of a `date` and a set of functions for manipulating variables of this type:

```
struct date {
    int day, month, year;
};

date today;
void set_date(date &dte, int d, int m, int y);
void next_date(date &dte);
void print_date(date &dte);
```

This is a reasonable first attempt, however we know that `day` will be in the range 1 to 31 and `month` in the range 1 to 12, so it would be worthwhile making both `day` and `month` chars. Program 2.18 (`DATES1.cpp`) illustrates the use of this structure for the date data type. (An alternative to defining `day` and `month` as `char` types is to define them as `unsigned short` data types and since year cannot be negative (assuming the year is AD) then this could be defined as `unsigned` (int – by default). This alternative implementation is left as an exercise for the reader.)

📋 **Program 2.18**
```
//: DATES1.cpp
//. dates using struct

#include <iostream.h>
#include <conio.h>
// ..........................................................
struct date {
    char day, month;
    int year;
};
// ..........................................................
void main()
{
    date today;
    void set_date(date &dte, char d, char m, int y);
    void next_date(date &dte);
    void print_date(date &dte);

    clrscr();

    cout << " dates1.cpp - using struct" << endl;
    cout << " ==========================" << endl << endl;

    set_date(today, 2, 3, 1994);
    cout << " today is : ";
    print_date(today);
    cout << endl;
    next_date(today);
    cout << "\n ... and tomorrow will be : " << endl;
```

```
        cout << "              ";
        print_date(today);
        cout << endl;

        cout << " \nPress <ENTER> to Quit ";
        cin.get();
}
// ...........................................................
void set_date(date dte, char d, char m, int y) {
        dte.day = d;
        dte.month = m;
        dte.year = y;
}

void next_date(date &dte){
// simplistic version !
// improve so that it works correctly
// i.e. no 32 / 3 / 1994 etc. include leap years if you wish!
        dte.day++;
}

void print_date(date dte) {
        cout << (int) dte.day << " / " << (int) dte.month <<
                    " / " << dte.year;
}
```

Notice in this program how we have used reference variables as parameters to the two functions `set_date()` and `next_date()`. This, as we have already mentioned, makes such functions simpler to use as well as providing a 'cleaner' interface for the user. In contrast, in C, it would be necessary to pass the address of a date to any function which might need to modify its value. So, for example, the `next_date()` function would be implemented in C in the following way:

```
/* C form of next_date() */
void next_date(date *dte){
        dte->day++;
}
```

and this would be called, in the main program, like this:

```
next_date(&today);
```

In this function we have used the -> operator. This operator, known as the structure pointer operator, allows us to access individual members of the structure. This is a shorthand notation which replaces the slightly more cumbersome equivalent which uses the usual dereferencing operator *. Thus

```
dte->day
```

is equivalent to:

```
(*dte).day
```

both operate on a pointer to an object (the `struct date` in this example) and allow access to members of that object.

Notice also, in the `print_date()` function, that we need to cast the `day` and `month` variables to an `int` before having `cout` display them. If we didn't do that we would output the characters represented by the relevant ASCII code.

Now to return to the C++ program. If you try it out you should find that it works satisfactorily, however, as there are no explicit connections between the functions and the date type, anyone can write any new function to manipulate the structure `date` - that is everyone has access to the various elements (members) of this structure. This can be partially overcome by including the functions as *member functions* within the declaration of `date`:

```
struct date {
    char day, month;
    int year;
// the following functions are member functions of date
    void set(char d, char m, int y);
    void next();
    void print();
};
```

These member functions can be used only for a specific variable of the appropriate type (i.e. of type `date`). Notice that the functions are also simpler than in the previous example – their names can be shortened to `set`, `next` and `print` and we no longer need to pass (even) a reference to `date` as an argument to the first two functions. This form of `struct` provides an extension to the `struct` definition as used in C – in C member functions are not allowed. So with this form of `struct` we are moving closer to the implementation of abstract data types where the functions are 'tied to' the types which they are used to manipulate.

📋 **Program 2.19**
```
//: DATES2.cpp -- dates using struct
//. with member functions

#include <iostream.h>
#include <conio.h>
// ...............................................
struct date {
    char day, month;
    int year;
    void set(char d, char m, int y);
    void next();
    void print();
};
```

```
//  ..........................................................
void main()
{
    date today;

    clrscr();
    cout << " dates2.cpp - using struct with member functions";
    cout << endl;
    cout << " ================================================";
    cout << endl << endl;
    today.set(2, 3, 1994);
    cout << " today is : ";
    today.print();
    cout << endl;
    today.next();
    cout << "\n ... and tomorrow will be : " << endl;
    cout << "                  ";
    today.print();
    cout << endl;
    cout << " \nPress <ENTER> to Quit ";
    cin.get();
}
//  ..........................................................
void date::set(char d, char m, int y) {
    day = d;
    month = m;
    year = y;
}

void date::next(){
    day++;
}

void date::print() {
    cout << day << " / " << month << " / " << year;
}
```

Notice in Program 2.19 (DATES2.cpp) how we use the scope resolution operator (: :) when defining the member functions of the struct date, e.g.

```
void date::set(char d, char m, int y) {
    day = d;
    month = m;
    year = y;
}
```

You were introduced to this operator earlier in this Chapter 2 when it was
used to gain access to a global variable otherwise hidden by a local variable of
the same name. What we have here is a much more common use of this operator, albeit to perform a similar task. Since the definition of the set()
function, for example, occurs outside the block which defines the date structure a definition of the form void set(char d, char m, int y) {...} will
not be recognised by the compiler as belonging to the date structure. This
problem is overcome by prefixing the names of member functions defined

outside of the structure definition with the structure name and the scope resolution operator (i.e. in this case by date::).

2.7 Enumeration types

Enumerations or enumeration types provide an important method of clarifying
code. They enable the programmer to declare a set of named integer constants
through the use of the keyword enum. Any variables declared of such a type
will only have the values specified in the enum statement as valid values.

We can use the concept of enumerators in a number of ways. Perhaps the
simplest is to use enum to declare simple constants. e.g.

```
enum {ZERO, ONE, TWO };
```

will declare three integer constants with the values 0, 1 and 2 respectively.
This statement then is equivalent to the three const statements:

```
const int ZERO = 0;
const int ONE = 1;
const int TWO = 2;
```

This shows that the list of enumerator constants are given the integral values
0, 1, 2 etc. However we can force initialisation as follows:

```
enum { I = 1, V = 5, X = 2 * V, L = 50, C = 100,
         D = 5 * C,  M = D + D};
```

which sets up the Roman numerals using explicit initialisation. Once an item
in the list is initialised, in the absence of further explicit initialisation, the
value given to an item will be one more than the value of the previous item.
Thus

```
enum { I = 1, V = 5, X = 2 * V, L = 50, C, D, M};
        // wrong values for C, D & M
```

will give C the value 51, D 52 and M 53.

Enumerated types can be manipulated in the usual way except that direct
input and output cannot be used. Since a named element in the enumerated set
is simply a tag or alias for an integral value any attempt to input, say M (for
1000) to a variable of type roman_num will fail. Also, trying to output a ro-
man_num n using cout << n will produce the number in decimal form, not
roman. For these reasons enumerated types are often used in places where direct i/o is not required.

You may be wondering why we need to use enum in this way when we have two other methods of setting up constants – one using the const keyword and the other via a #define preprocessor statement. One reason is that it is better to restrict the use of preprocessor statements to a minimum – they do have their uses but using #define statements is going against the philosophy of data abstraction since it removes the definition from the abstract data type.

If we include a name between the keyword enum and the opening brace then we create an integral type which can then be used to declare variables of this type which can only be assigned the values given (by the names) in the enumerator list. Thus:

```
enum roman_num {I = 1, V = 5, X = 2 * V, L = 50,
          C = 100, D = 5 * C,  M = D + D};
```

together with

```
roman_num n, m;
```

will provide us with two variables n and m which can be assigned the Roman numbers given in the enumerator list. In C++ the assignment can only be via the name, not through assignment to the value as it can in C. So

```
n = D;
```

and   m = V;

are both valid in C and C++, whereas

```
n = 500;
```

and   m = 5;

are only valid in C, not in C++.

The final variation on enum is to include a list, or a single identifier, after the closing brace, thus enabling the definition of the new integral type and the declaration of a variable (or variables) of that type to be made all in one go. So

```
enum { I = 1, V = 5, X = 2 * V, L = 50, C = 100,
          D = 5 * C,  M = D + D} n, m;
```

will declare n and m as before. However now we cannot declare any other variables of this type as we could before.

2.8 Summary

The majority of the topics covered here should have been revision for those of you already familiar with C but nevertheless I hope you found them useful. Just to remind you we list below the main points from this chapter. Check that you are familiar with them all, and understand the basics, before moving on. The Exercises should help you to consolidate what you have learnt.

Topics covered:

- *Functions* – definition and declaration.
- void functions.
- The scope of functions.
- Bit manipulation operators (Table 2.1).
- Bit operators with assignment (Table 2.3).
- Functions returning a value.
- Modifying function arguments.
- Functions and the reference operator (&).
- The scope of variables.
- The scope resolution operator (::).
- Storage class – extern, static, register and auto.
- Functions with static variables.
- Arrays.
- Using const.
- Initialising arrays.
- Arrays as function arguments.
- Structures.
- Enumeration types.

2.9 Exercises

As a check on what you have covered in this chapter try out the following exercises. Most of the examples just ask you to write functions, but you should also include each function in a suitable program and test in thoroughly. Use the const keyword wherever necessary to improve the readability of functions.

2.9.1 Enter the Program 2.1 (FUNDEMO1.cpp) and try it out. The observant amongst you will notice the use of the ? and : operators in the calculation of the ratio x/y, i.e.:

```
(y != 0 ? x/y : (x>0 ? 1e20 : ( x<0 ? -1e20 : 0.0)))
```

2.9.2 Modify the program so that it uses `if ... else` statements instead of the conditional operator.

2.9.3 Copy Table 2.2 and complete it, to make sure that you understand how the `print_binary()` function works.

2.9.4 Write a function which takes as parameters the width (w) and height (h) of a rectangle and displays the rectangle using suitable symbols (e.g. asterisks, or _ and ı characters, or the graphics characters in the extended ASCII character set – this is slightly more complicated).

2.9.5 Write a function which takes an integer n and computes and returns a digit (1 to 9) which is the sum of the decimal digits which make up the number. So for example, 237 would return 3 (2 + 3 + 7 = 12, 1 + 2 = 3).

2.9.6

a) Modify the Program 2.5 so that the function `void minmax(float x, float y, float z, float *min, float *max)` is used and test it. What happens?

b) Save this program with a `.c` extension and make any other necessary modifications to convert it into a C program e.g. use `stdio.h`, `printf()` and `scanf()` instead of `iostream.h`, `cout` and `cin`. Test this program. Does it still work?

You should have found that both of the above programs worked. That is they work in both C and C++.

2.9.7 A function is required to sort three `float` numbers into either ascending or descending order depending on whether the `char` parameter order is set to 'A' (ascending) or 'D' (descending). Write such a function and test it.

2.9.8 Modify the `print_binary()` function discussed in the text so that either `int` or `long int`s can be used.

2.9.9 These functions all require an understanding of the bit operators so check the relevant section before tackling them.

a) Write functions called unsigned int shift_left(unsigned int n, int d) and unsigned int shift_right(unsigned int n, int d) which take an int parameter n and returns the number shifted left (or right) d places.

b) How might you modify one of these functions so that it could shift the digits either way? Write and test such a function.

c) Write a function which rotates (left or right) a positive integer. With this function digits moved from the left should reappear on the right and vice versa.

2.9.10 Write a program to test the above code. Remember to make the screen user-friendly. For example use clrscr() to start with a fresh screen, tell the user what the program requires for input and output the result.

2.9.11 An undetermined, at compile time, set of real numbers are to be entered from the keyboard and some simple statistics computed. Write functions (to be stored in a separate file from the main program) which compute these statistics (average, minimum, maximum, standard deviation). Note that the standard deviation(s) of a set of numbers is given by:

$$SD = \sqrt{\sum_{i=1}^{i=n} \frac{(x_i - x_{av})^2}{n}}$$

2.9.12 Rewrite the Program 2.17 (ARRAYINI.cpp) so that it uses a function (print_array()) to display the contents of a variable-length array.

2.9.13 Write a function which will take a variable-length float array and initialise all elements to the same value (this should be one of the function arguments). In addition you should use a function to display all elements in the array.

3 | Pointers and their uses

3.1 Introduction

In this chapter we take a look at pointers and some of their most important uses. Although you may be able to avoid many of the more esoteric uses of pointers with C++ you cannot avoid them altogether. Pointers can be very useful tools provided they are used with care and it is important that you are aware of the range of tools available, just as when using a hammer you choose the correct one for the job – hopefully you will not use a sledge hammer to knock a nail into a wall – otherwise you will have a much larger hole than you intended.

You have already come across the occasional use of pointers and they will crop up again at various places throughout this book so this is an appropriate point to take a rather more in-depth look at them. We will be looking at pointer expressions and arithmetic as well as referring again to references as they are used in C++. A discussion of pointers leads naturally onto the topics of arrays and strings. Finally we look at how dynamic memory management is achieved in C++ through the use of new and delete and hence how to implement dynamic arrays.

3.2 Pointers

If you are familiar with C then you will have already come across the idea of pointers. In this section we are going to review pointers and look at some of their uses in C++. We begin by recalling that a variable has an address in memory – and each memory cell can be selected by using its address. A pointer is just a special type of variable which holds an address, usually of another variable, and which thereby allows us to manipulate addresses. Figure 3.1 illustrates a pointer stored in memory location 10000, containing 10006 and thus pointing to the location 10006.

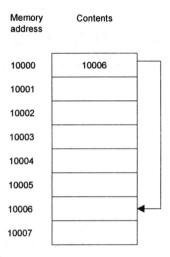

Figure 3.1 Block diagram of a simple computer system

Pointers can also be used to address functions (i.e. a pointer to a function), in which case they would be used when passing functions as arguments to other functions. However when used with functions it is not permissible to perform arithmetic operations on them. We will be looking at pointers and references once classes have been introduced (Chapter 5).

A pointer variable is declared using the unary operator * and it can be used with any of the fundamental data types of C/C++ as well as with user-defined data types. So for example we might have:

```
char* pchar;
int * pint;
float *pfloat;
```

which declare three variables respectively as a pointer to a char, a pointer to an int and a pointer to a float. Notice the (intentional) difference between these declarations. In the first we have used char* pchar; (no space between the type and *), in the second int * pint; (spaces either side of *) and in the third float *pfloat (a space before the * but none after it). There is no difference between these declarations – all of them declare pointers (to specific data types), but see below for which is preferable. Program 3.1 illustrates the use of these three pointer variables and Test run 3.1 shows a sample run.

📋 **Program 3.1**
```
//: POINTER1.cpp
//. illustration of pointer variables,the * and & operators.
#include <conio.h>
#include <iostream.h>
#include <stdio.h>
// ...........................................................
```

```
void main()
{
    char* pchar; // note all these are uninitialised pointers
    int * pint; // they must be initialised before use
    float *pfloat;

    char c = 'z';
    int i = 10;
    float f = 3.5;

    pchar = &c;   // pchar now holds the address of c
    pint = &i;    // the address of i
    pfloat = &f;  // the address of f

    clrscr();
    cout << " POINTER1 " << endl;
    cout << " ======== " << endl << endl;
    cout << " c = " << c << " \t address = " << &c << endl;
    printf(" \t\t address of c = %p \n", &c);
    cout << " i = " << i << "\t address = " << &i << endl;
    cout << " f = " << f << "\t address = " << &f << endl;

    cout << "now the contents of the pointers & their addresses "
                << endl;
    cout << " pchar = " << pchar << "\t address = " << &pchar
                << endl;
    cout << "  pint = " << pint << "\t address = " << &pint
                << endl;
    cout << " pfloat = " << pfloat << "\t address = "
                << &pfloat << endl;
}
```

```
POINTER1
========
c = z    address = zèÿìÿïÿ
i = 10   address = 0x3be8ffec
f = 3.5    address = 0x3be8ffe8
now the contents of the pointers & their addresses
pchar = zèÿìÿïÿ    address = 0x3be8fff4
  pint = 0x3be8ffec    address = 0x3be8fff2
pfloat = 0x3be8ffe8   address = 0x3be8fff0
        address of c = FFEF
```

Note two things about the above output; first we used the %p conversion specifier in the call to printf – this gave the address of c in the default format for
my computer (i.e. FEFF), secondly if you compare the source code for the
program and the output above you may be surprised at the position in the output of the printf() line. According to the code address of c = FFEF
should have followed the first cout output, i.e. after c = z address =
zèÿìÿïÿ but it comes at the end. Why? The reason is that the output you see
here was obtained by running the compiled program pointer1.exe and redirecting its output to a text file. This output is exactly as it appears in the text

file! The output on the screen is as we would expect, it is simply when redirecting the output to another file that problems occur. You might wish to try this out for yourself and compare your output with what you would expect and the above.

The addresses will almost certainly be different but they should be addresses, i.e. output in hexadecimal format. All, that is, except for the address output by cout for the char variable c. cout outputs the contents of c, not its address, in order to display the address to which pchar points we can use printf, – the second line output is done using printf (see the program for more details). Using the above information we can draw a memory map for these variables in Figure 3.2.

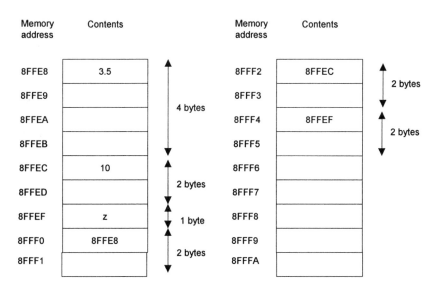

Figure 3.2 Schematic 'memory map'

If you examine Figure 3.2 carefully you should notice two things. First the three variables c, i and f each take up a different amount of memory; c 1 byte, i 2 bytes and f 4 bytes. However the pointers to these three variables each occupy the same number of bytes, namely two. Now take a look at the output when you run the same program (Program 3.1) and draw up a similar map. What are the differences between your 'memory map' and Figure 3.2? Make a note of them for future reference.

We mentioned earlier that although the three declarations char* pchar, int * pint and float *pfloat all produced pointer variables they weren't all equally desirable. The one to be preferred is the last one, used for the float pointer, i.e. in general the form for declaring a pointer variable should be:

```
data_type *variable_name;
```

The reason for this is connected with the syntax of C++. The operator ⋆ is not distributive over a list of variables – in other words if we make the following declaration:

```
int* pi, pj, pk; // a pointer to an int and two ints!
```

and think that we are declaring three `int` pointers then we will be mistaken! In fact what is declared is one `int` pointer variable (`pi`) and two `int` *variables* (`pj` and `pk`). So in order to avoid this possible confusion it is better to place the * immediately before the variable to which it refers. Thus:

```
int *pi, pj, pk;   // pi a pointer to an int,
                   // pj and pk int variables
```

and

```
int *pi, *pj, *pk; // three pointers to int
```

A similar argument applies to the `&` operator, the reference operator. We can declare reference variables in C++, meaning that the variables will be aliases for other variables, by prefixing the desired variables by `&` when declaring them. Thus:

```
float &px, py, pz;   // px a reference to a float,
                     // py and pz float variables
```

and

```
float &px, &py, &pz; // three reference variables to float
```

3.3   Pointer expressions

In this section we will take a quick look at some examples using pointer expressions. Generally speaking the rules for pointer expressions are the same as those for any other C/C++ expressions. We can assign pointers, we can perform arithmetic (but only those operations which make sense) and we can compare pointers.

Program 3.2 illustrates pointer assignment and Test run 3.2 shows a sample run. This illustrates that we can use assignment in the normal way. Notice that before `pint2` is set equal to `pint1`, which itself is set equal to the address of `i`, there is no telling what value will be stored in `pint2`. We must therefore be careful to assign `pint2` an address before manipulating it (e.g. before changing the contents of the address pointed to by `pint2`). So in the next example, Program 3.3, we see how `pint1` can be used to change the contents of `i`, but on no account should we attempt to use `pint2` to change `i` until it has itself been given the appropriate address. Test run 3.3 shows a sample run.

▢ Program 3.2

```
//: PASSIGN.cpp
//. illustrating assignment of pointers
#include <conio.h>
#include <iostream.h>
// .........................................................
void main()
{
    int *pint1, *pint2, i;

    i = 10;
    pint1 = &i;      // the address of i

    clrscr();
    cout << " PASSIGN " << endl;
    cout << " ======= " << endl << endl;
    cout << " address of i = " << &i << endl;
    cout << " after pint1 = &i " << endl;
    cout << "    pint1 = " << pint1 << endl;
    cout << "    pint2 = " << pint2 << endl;
                 // no value given to pint2

    pint2 = pint1; // give pint2 the address of i
    cout << " after pint2 = pint1 " << endl;
    cout << "    pint2 = " << pint2 << endl;
}
```

▦ Test run 3.2

```
PASSIGN
=======

address of i = 0x3769fff4
after pint1 = &i
    pint1 = 0x3769fff4
    pint2 = 0x376904a2
after pint2 = pint1
    pint2 = 0x3769fff4
```

▢ Program 3.3

```
//: PASSIGN2.cpp
//. assignment of pointers and changing values using the
//. dereferencing operator *
#include <conio.h>
#include <iostream.h>
// .........................................................
void main()
{
    int *pint1, *pint2, i;

    i = 10;
    pint1 = &i;      // the address of i
```

```
    clrscr();
    cout << " PASSIGN2 " << endl;
    cout << " ======== " << endl << endl;
    cout << " at start  i = " << i << endl;
    cout << " address of i = " << &i << endl;
    cout << " after pint1 = &i " << endl;
    cout << "     pint1 = " << pint1 << endl;
    cout << "     pint2 = " << pint2 << endl;
            // no value given to pint2

    *pint1 = 25; // change the contents of the location pointed
            // to by pint1 to 25 (i.e. set i to 25)

    cout << " after *pint = 25 " << endl;
    cout << "        i = " << i << endl;

    pint2 = pint1;  // give pint2 the address of i

    cout << " after pint2 = pint1 " << endl;
    cout << "     pint2 = " << pint2 << endl;
    cout << " now we can use *pint2 = 33 to set i to 33 " << endl;

    *pint2 = 33; // change i to 33

    cout << "        i = " << i << endl;

    cout << " Press any key to Quit ";

    getch();
}
```

🖳 Test run 3.3

```
PASSIGN2
========
at start  i = 10
address of i = 0x3774fff4
after pint1 = &i
   pint1 = 0x3774fff4
   pint2 = 0x37740516
after *pint = 25
    i = 25
after pint2 = pint1
   pint2 = 0x3774fff4
now we can use *pint2 = 33 to set i to 33
    i = 33
```

Try Program 3.3 for yourself and check your output. Again the addresses will be different but otherwise the program should give the same result. Notice that the address initially held by pint2 differs between the two programs – again illustrating the point that we have no idea what an uninitialised (or unassigned) pointer will contain. Notice also that we have used *pint1 and *pint2 to gain access to the variable to which pint1 and pint2 are pointing.

3.4 Pointer initialisation

Variables often need to be initialised – i.e. given values at declaration. Two points are worth noting about initialisation:

i) Variables can only be initialised when memory locations have been assigned to them. This is very important and should not be forgotten. The consequences of not adhering to this can be disastrous. Program 3.4 illustrates the danger of assigning a value to an uninitialised pointer. In this program ip is not given an address, however it may well have, depending on the compiler, a value which will be some unknown, and almost certainly an unwanted address. Any attempt to modify the value stored at the address pointed to by ip will result in the accidental change to an unknown section of memory – this could corrupt the compiler, the operating system or ...

ii) Some compilers automatically assign the value 0 to all static or global variables. This concerns the possibility of automatic assignment of variables to 0, and is a little more controversial – since not all compilers will initialise variables to 0 it is better to assume that none does. This means that it is up to you, the programmer, to initialise explicitly all variables before use.

Program 3.4

```
//: POINT1.cpp
//. illustrating the need for initialisation of
//. pointer variables before use
#include <conio.h>
#include <iostream.h>
// ...........................................................
void main()
{
    int *ip, i;

    i = 6;
    clrscr();
    cout << "address of  i (&i)      "
        << &i << " value " << i << endl;
    cout << "address of ip (&ip)     "
        << &ip << " value " << ip << endl;
    cout << "address of *ip (&*ip = ip) "
        << &*ip << " value " << *ip << endl;
}
```

Test run 3.4

```
address of  i (&i)        0x2c97fff2 value 6
address of ip (&ip)       0x2c97fff4 value 0x2c971723
address of *ip (&*ip = ip) 0x2c971723 value -19517
```

3.5 Pointer arithmetic

3.5.1 How point arithmetic works

Now let's take a look at pointer arithmetic. We can use the basic increment and decrement operators (++ and --) and their extensions (+= and +-) on pointer variables, but not as we said above, the multiplication or division operators. But what might pint1++ give us? If pint1 contains the address 0x3774fff4 then you might expect the value after pint1++ to be 0x3774fff5, in fact it will be 0x3774fff6. That is the address is incremented by 2 bytes, the size of an int. Similarly if pfloat1 points to a float then pfloat1++ will increment the stored address by four bytes. Program 3.5 illustrates this. Try it out.

⬛ Program 3.5

```
//: PARITH1.cpp
//. incrementing and decrementing pointers
#include <iostream.h>
#include <conio.h>
// ...........................................................
void main()
{
    int *pint, i = 100;
    float *pfloat, f = -8.6;
    double *pdble, d = 3.231456;

    pint = &i;
    pfloat = &f;
    pdble = &d;

    clrscr();
    cout << " PARITH1 " << endl;
    cout << " ======= " << endl << endl;
    cout << "  pint = " << pint;
    pint++;
    cout << "  pint++ = " << pint << endl;
    cout << " pfloat = " << pfloat;
    pfloat++;
    cout << " pfloat++ = " << pfloat << endl;
    cout << " pdble = " << pdble;
    pdble++;
    cout << " pdble++ = " << pdble << endl;
    cout << " Now to put them back to their original values "
                         << endl;
    pint--;
    cout << "  pint-- = " << pint << endl;
    pfloat--;
    cout << " pfloat-- = " << pfloat << endl;
    pdble--;
    cout << " pdble-- = " << pdble << endl;
    cout << " Press any key to Quit ";
    getch();
}
```

After examining the output from this program you should begin to see how pointer arithmetic works. Specifically, addresses are incremented and decremented according to the size of the data type originally given to the pointer. So, assuming an `int` takes up 2 bytes, a `float` 4 and a `double` 8, then adding 1 to a pointer to an `int` will in fact increase the address by 2 bytes; adding 1 to a pointer to a `float` will increase the address by 4 bytes; and adding 1 to a `double` pointer will add 8 bytes to the address.

What other arithmetic operations can be carried out on pointers? As well as adding and subtracting one we can add or subtract any integer. So we might add 10 to an `int` pointer variable to point to the 10th `int` beyond the current int. However there is no guarantee that this memory location will actually contain an `int`! Care must therefore be taken when such operations are carried out. Normally operations using pointer arithmetic such as those we have been discussing will most likely be carried out on arrays, where we can guarantee that we will still be looking at the correct type (so long as we are careful not to increment or decrement beyond the array bounds). We will be looking at these applications shortly.

There is one further arithmetic operation which can be carried out on pointer variables and that is finding the difference between two pointers. Thus if `pint1` and `pint2` are pointers to `int`s and `pint1` has the value `0x3774fff4`, `pint2` the value `0x3774ffe0` then `pint1-pint2` will give 8 which represents the number of integers between these two addresses. (Not 16 which is the number of *bytes* between these two addresses.) Program 3.6 illustrates the subtraction of addresses. Have a look at it and try it out.

Program 3.6

```
//: PDIFF1.cpp
//. illustrating how addresses can be subtracted
#include <iostream.h>
#include <conio.h>
// ..........................................................
void main()
{
   int *pint1, *pint2, i, idiff;

   pint1 = &i;
   pint2 = pint1 + 20;
   idiff = pint2 - pint1;
   clrscr();
   cout << " PDIFF1 " << endl;
   cout << " ====== " << endl << endl;
   cout << " pint2 = " << pint2 << endl;
   cout << " pint1 = " << pint1 << endl;
   cout << " diff = " << idiff << endl;
   cout << "     = " << idiff * sizeof(i) << " bytes " << endl;

   cout << " Press any key to Quit ";
   getch();
}
```

This program not only computes the number of integers between the two addresses given by `pint2` and `pint1` but also the actual number of bytes. This is achieved by using the `sizeof()` function which returns the number of bytes occupied by its argument, in this example the argument is `i` which is an `int`, which in my implementation takes up 2 bytes.

3.5.2 Comparing pointers

Since we can carry out a limited amount of arithmetic using pointers it should not surprise you that we can also compare pointers. For example we might implement a stack using pointers and have one pointer pointing to the top of the stack (`top`), another pointing to the bottom of the stack (`bottom`) and yet another pointing to the last item added (`last`). We might then need to check if a) the stack is empty or b) the stack is full. We could achieve a) by testing whether `last` is equal to `bottom` and b) by testing whether `last` is equal to `top`. A simple implementation is given in Program 3.7.

☐ **Program 3.7**

```
//: PCOMP1.cpp
//. implementing a stack as an example of pointer comparisons

#include <conio.h>
#include <iostream.h>
// .........................................................
void main()
{
   const int SIZE = 10;
   int stack[SIZE];
   int  *const top = &stack[SIZE-1],      // fixed pointer
        *const bottom = &stack[0];        // fixed pointer
   int *last = bottom;

   clrscr();
   cout << " PCOMP1 " << endl;
   cout << " ====== " << endl << endl;

   cout << " bottom = " << bottom << " top = "
     << top;
   cout << " last = " << last << endl;

   for( int i = 0; i < SIZE; i++)
   {
     cout << " i = " << i;
     if( last == bottom )
        cout << " stack EMPTY " << endl;
     else
     if( last == top )
        cout << " stack FULL " << endl;
     else
        cout << " last = " << last << endl;
     last++;
   }
}
```

In this program the pointer `last` is compared with the pointers `bottom` and `top` to test whether the stack is empty or full respectively.

If you look carefully at this program you will see that we have found another use for `const` – the two pointers `bottom` and `top` are initialised to the first and last address of the stack elements (i.e. `stack[0]` and `stack[SIZE-1]`), this is done with the statement:

```
int *const top = &stack[SIZE-1],
    *const bottom = &stack[0];
```

Since neither `top` nor `bottom` will change it makes sense to initialise them as constants. However notice the form of this statement. The `*const` qualifier is used for each identifier and not just once as you might at first expect. (However if you think back to our previous discussion concerning the position of `*` in pointer definitions perhaps you shouldn't be surprised.)

This use of `const` with pointers is not the only one. We can also write:

```
const int *pint;
```

which declares a pointer to an `int`, but this time, instead of the address being a constant the contents of whatever is pointed to by `pint` is treated as a constant and cannot be modified by de-referencing the pointer. Consider the following program fragment.

```
const int *pint;    // pointer to an int
int total = 100;
int *pint2;         // another int pointer

pint = &total;
(*pint)++;          // attempt to increase total
                    // by pointer dereferencing

cout << " total = " << total << endl;
total++;            // incrementing total directly using
                    // the increment operator

cout << " total = " << total << endl;
pint2 = &total;     // initialise pint2
*pint2 = 100;       // reset total using pointer
                    // dereferencing
cout << " total = " << total << endl;
```

When this is included in a complete program any attempt to compile the program will result in a compilation error. The statement `(*pint)++;` produces the error message:

```
cannot modify a const object
```

which illustrates exactly what the statement `const int *pint;` is attempting to do, it is setting up a pointer to an object which, as far as `pint` is concerned, is a constant. We know that the object itself (i.e. `total`) is not a constant since `total++;` and `*pint2 = 200;` both successfully modify it. Once the offending statement is removed or commented out we obtain Test run 3.5.

🖳 **Test run 3.5**
```
PCONST1
=======

*pint = 100 total = 100
 (1) after total++
 total = 101
 (2) after pint2 = &total
 ... and *pint2 = 200
 total = 200
```

Notice the difference in the way `pint` and `pint2` are declared:

```
const int *pint;
int *pint2;
```

Now, even though both `pint` and `pint2` are set equal to the address of `total` we cannot use `*pint` to modify `total` but we can use `*pint2` to do so, as a close examination of the output from the program shows.

Before leaving our discussion of `const` in relation to pointers we need to look at one further combination. So far we have seen the use of definitions like `int *const top = &stack[SIZE-1]` and `const int *pint`, which provide us with, respectively, a pointer whose value cannot be changed (i.e. it always points to the same address) and a pointer which points to an object whose value cannot be changed through de-referencing. How do we combine both methods and what will it give us? A little thought will suggest that a statement such as:

```
const int *const pint = &i;
```

will do the job of combining the two uses of `const`, where `i` is an `int` identifier. The first reference to `const` ensures that we cannot modify the de-referenced value of `pint`, whereas the second one ensures that we cannot alter the actual value of `pint`, which is the address to which it is pointing (i.e. the address of `i`). Such definitions are useful when you need to use pointers to access information but you wish to restrict the powers the user has to modify the information.

Since we are talking about pointers it is worth looking briefly at the statement `(*pint)++;` with which we attempted to increment `total` indirectly using `pint`. The brackets are essential here, without them we would be incrementing the address which `pint` points to and then getting the contents. It is not possible to check this use of `pint` since it is declared as a `const int` pointer, however we can illustrate the same idea using a normal pointer. Consider the following program fragment:

```
int *pint;    // pointer to an int
int i = 25, j = 11, k;

pint = &j;    // initialise pint

...
(*pint)++;    // increment j indirectly

*pint++;      // pint incremented (* superfluous)
              // pint now points to next 2 bytes
              // (actually next sizeof(int) bytes)
```

The first statement `(*pint)++` does what we want, as in the previous program, and increments the contents of the address pointed to by `pint`. However the second statement involving `pint` (i.e. `*pint++`) increments the pointer so that it now points to the next 'int chunk of memory' – whether the next 'int chunk of memory' is in fact an `int` and we what value it has, we cannot be certain. The output which I obtained when these statements are included in a complete program shows that `pint++` makes `pint` point to `i` (not `k` as you might expect).

A more sensible use of pointers in this context involves the use of arrays. We can access an individual element of an array by using the notation `a[10] = 5;` which sets element 10 of `a` to 5, but we can also use pointers to achieve the same result. Let `ptra` be a pointer to an `int` and let it be initialised with the address of `a[0]`, i.e.

```
int a[10], *ptra;
ptra = a;               // equivalent to &a[0]
```

Now to access the 10th element of `a` and set it equal to 5 we can write

```
*(ptr+10) = 5;
```

We therefore have two methods in C/C++ of accessing array elements – one using array notation, the other using pointer notation. The pointer notation is important as pointer arithmetic can be faster than array indexing and since often speed is important in programming the use of pointers, instead of array indexing, is often common in C/C++ programs. For example, we could use:

```
for (int i = 0; i < SIZE; i++)
    cout << *(ptr+i) << " ";
```

instead of:

```
for (int i = 0; i < SIZE; i++)
   cout << a[i] << " ";
```

to output the elements of the array a.

<hr>

3.6   Void pointers

So far we have been dealing almost exclusively with `int` pointers. Needless to say pointers can be of any data type, including user defined types and we shall be looking at some of those applications later on. There is one other pointer type that you should be aware of and that is the void pointer. You might wonder what use a void pointer is since it would appear that a variable of this type points to nothing – deep into outer space maybe! In fact in C++ declaring a void pointer means that the pointer can point to any data type and void pointers come in useful when we need to use a pointer but do not know beforehand what type of object it will be pointing (e.g. whether the object is a `char` or a `float`). As an example, suppose that we wish to allow the user of our program to enter a date in a number of different formats, let's say ones of the form 21 Mar 1996, 21 3 1996 and March 21 1996. We could think of other formats, but these will do for now. This problem requires a little thought and involves more than simply the use of void pointers, but hopefully you will find it an instructive example. The first thing to notice is that we can't tell before the data is entered what format will be chosen and so our input routine needs to take account of the three possibilities we have suggested. Take a look at the Program 3.8.

Program 3.8
```
//: VOIDP1.cpp
//. void pointers - a simple example!

#include <conio.h>
#include <iostream.h>
#include <ctype.h>
£include <string.h>
// ...........................................................
char input[3][20];

void get_date(char input[][20]);
void parse_date(char input[][20], int &day, int &dmonth,
             char *month, int &year, int &type);
void print_date(int d, void *m, int y, int type);
// ...........................................................
void main()
```

```
{
   int day, dmonth, year, type;
   char month[10], ch;

   void *pmonth;      // declaring a void pointer

   clrscr();
   cout << " VOIDP1 " << endl;
   cout << " ====== " << endl << endl;

   cout << " Please enter a date in one of the formats: "
                       << endl;
   cout << " 23 5 1996, 23 May 1996 or May 23 1996 " << endl;
   cout << " > ";

   get_date(input);

   parse_date(input, day, dmonth, month, year, type);

   if (type == 1)      // select the appropriate type
      pmonth = &dmonth;
   else
      pmonth = month;

   print_date(day, pmonth, year, type);

   cout << " Press any key to Quit ";
   getch();
}

// ..........................................................

void get_date(char input[][20])
{
   int i;
   char *p, ch;

   for(i = 0; i < 3; i++ )
   {
      p = &input[i][0]; // set p to point to array of char
      do {
         cin.get(ch);

         if ((ch == ' ') || (ch == '\n') || (ch == '\t'))
            ch = '\0';
         *p++ = ch;
      } while( ch != '\0');
   }
}

// ..........................................................

void parse_date(char input[][20], int &day, int &dmonth,
            char *month, int &year, int &type)
{
   int i;
   char *p;
```

```
type = 1;              // 1 = all numeric (25 6 1996)
                       // 2 = mixed (25 Jun 1996 or Jun 25 1996)
for(i = 0; i < 3 ; i++)
{
   p = &input[i][0];
                       // set p to first character (input[0][0])

   if (isalpha(*p)){ // check for alphabetic character
      strcpy(month, p);
      type = 2;          // mixed type
   } else if (isdigit(*p)){
      int num = 0;       // convert string to int *** A ***
      while(isdigit(*p)) {
         num = 10*num + (int) (*p - '0');
         p++;
      }                  // *** B ***

      if (i == 0)
         day = num;
      else if ((i == 1) && (type == 2))
         day = num;
      else if ((i == 1) && (type == 1))
         dmonth = num;
      else
         year = num;
   }
}
}

// ...............................................................
void print_date(int d, void *m, int y, int type)
{
   cout << " Date was : " << d << " ";
   switch(type) {
      case(1) :    // 23 5 1996
         cout << *((int *) m);
                    // cast m to pointer-to-int and o/p contents
         break;
      case(2) :    // 23 May 1996 or May 23 1996
         cout << ((char *) m);
                    // cast m to pointer-to-char and o/p contents
         break;
   }
   cout << " " << y << endl;
}
```

In this program we have declared a character array month[10] which is used
to hold a month entered as a string and an int dmonth used when the month is
entered as a number. We have also declared a void pointer (*pmonth) which
will be used to point to the appropriate month variable (month or dmonth).
Don't worry about the two functions get_date() and parse_date() for the
moment – all we need to know is that the second of these two functions returns the day and year as ints, month and dmonth (only one of which will be
given a value) and type which tells us which of the two versions of month has
been input. The next statement:

```
if (type == 1)
   pmonth = &dmonth;
else
   pmonth = month;
```

converts the void pointer pmonth to the correct type and assigns it to the address of the appropriate month variable. Notice the difference between the two statements, one requires the address to be explicitly specified (by using &), whereas the other (because month is the address of the char array month) does not need the &. Next, the call to print_date simply requires pmonth to be passed as a parameter – this is because the argument for pmonth is declared as a pointer (void *m) in the print_data() parameter list. Finally, within print_data() we use a switch statement and the appropriate casts to output the appropriate month:

```
void print_date(int d, void *m, int y, int type)
{
   cout << " Date was : " << d << " ";
   switch(type) {
      case(1) :   // 23 5 1996
         cout << *((int *) m);
         break;
      case(2) :   // 23 May 1996 or May 23 1996
         cout << (char *) m;
         break;
   }
   cout << " " << y << endl;
}
```

Again, the important points to notice about this function are the ways the pointer m is cast to enable the correct version of the month to be output. Recall that m is a pointer (strictly speaking a void pointer) so it needs to be cast into the appropriate type (by either (int *) or (char *)) and then, for the int version we need the contents of the address pointed to by the (now) int pointer – so we need to de-reference it using another *, however for the array of char version we simply need to output m (as a char *) so that the whole month (with as many characters as were input) is displayed.

One final point to notice in this example is the way in which the void pointer (pmonth) is assigned the address of dmonth or month. In neither case do we need a cast when converting from any type to a void pointer, however a cast is essential when going from a void pointer to a pointer of any other type.

Section 3.7 will help you to understand the subtleties of outputting arrays of char (or strings), but before that we will take a brief look at the use references as return values and compare the use of pointers and references.

3.7 References as return values

3.7.1 Using the reference operator

In Chapter 2 we looked briefly at the use of reference parameters. We are now in a position to see how we might use the reference operator when returning a value from a function. Take a look at Program 3.9 (FUNREF.cpp).

Program 3.9
```
// FUNREF.cpp - using reference as return value
#include <iostream.h>

int &larger(int &x, int &y); // declaration

void main()
{
   int n = 7, m = 60;

   cout << "n = " << n << " m = " << m << endl;
   cout << " The larger of these is " << larger(n, m) << endl;
   larger(n, m) = 0; // function call as the left - hand side
   cout << " after setting the larger to zero ..." << endl;
   cout << " we have " << endl;
   cout << " n = " << n << " m = " << m << endl;
}

int &larger( int &x, int &y)
{
   return( x > y ? x : y);
}
```

The first call of `larger()`, embedded in the second `cout` statement, is a straightforward one – it simply returns the larger of the two arguments. However the second call returns the address of the argument (not simply its value) and so this can be used as a variable (identifier) on the left of an assignment statement. Such calls are not allowed in C or in most other languages – it is allowed in C++ because of the concept of references.

A final point to note about the use of a function which returns a reference. Since, in the second call of the `larger()` function we are modifying the value stored in one of the arguments addresses we should not pass a constant as an argument to the function – since you can't change the value of a constant! So using the `larger()` function in a call such as `larger(6, 7) = 0;` although it will compile and run, is meaningless. Similarly if we declare m as a constant int (`const int m = 60;`) and then call `larger(n, m) = 0;`, m will still equal 60. Such calls are obviously to be avoided.

3.7.2 Recap on pointers and references

Now that you have seen, in this chapter and the previous one, some simple examples of the use of pointers and references with functions we are in a position to look a little more deeply into the differences between these two important methods of manipulating data.

First of all a general point as an introduction. One important design philosophy in software engineering is that functions should be easy to use. The purpose of a function should be clear to any user and the way the function is called – the parameter type and the return type of the function – should not require a detailed understanding of how the function is implemented (or coded).

Now recall how, in C, we declare parameters and pass arguments to a function when we wish the arguments themselves to be modified by the function (look back at the `minmax` function in Chapter 2 if you need a simple reminder). Parameters that are to be modified by the function must be declared using the pointer operator (e.g. `void max(int n1, int n2, int *maxint)`). The user of such a function needs to be aware of the fact that the third parameter is a pointer to an `int` and so the corresponding argument in any function call of `max` must represent the address of an `int` variable. The user has therefore to consider the way the writer of the function has implemented the solution. It would be preferable if the user could ignore such implementation considerations. References, which as we have seen have been introduced to C++, provide a means of clarifying function uses and thus allow the user of class libraries, or even just functions, to concentrate on what the class or function does instead of spending time deciding whether an address or a value should be passed to a function. (If you have come to C++ through C you will be aware of the ease with which you can miss off the address operator (&) in calls to `scanf` – e.g. writing `scanf( "%d", num);` instead of `scanf( "%d", &num);`). By using reference variables such details are taken care of by the class or function programmer and the user need not be concerned with them.

Again, when using pointers as parameters we need to *de-reference* the identifier when manipulating this variable within the function. If you never see the inside of the function, then perhaps that doesn't matter too much. But what if the function returns an address? For example we might use a function `char *ch(char *c)` to return a pointer to the character c. We could display this character, using `cout` as follows:

```
cout << " c = " << *ch(*c) << endl;
```

We could even give the character c a value using this function:

```
*ch(*c) = 'z';
```

However, in both of these cases the use of the pointer only complicates the code. It would be much better if we could use just `ch(c)` to manipulate the appropriate element – once again we can do this by making use of references.

Program 3.10

```cpp
//: CPOINTR.cpp
//. a function returning the address of a variable using
//. pointers

#include <conio.h>
#include <iostream.h>
// .............................................................
char *ch(char *c)
{
   *c = 'a';  // set c to 'a'
   return c;  // return the address of c
}
// .............................................................
void main() {

   clrscr();
   cout << " CPOINTR " << endl;
   cout << " ======= " << endl << endl;

   char c;

   c = 'n';
   cout << " c = " << c << endl;
   cout << endl;
   cout << " Now to check that the function works " << endl;
   cout << " c = " << *ch(&c) << endl; // displays 'a'
   cout << " c = " << c << endl;       // also displays 'a'
   cout << endl;

   cout << " Can also use ch to set c to a value other than
       'a' " << endl;
   *ch(&c) = 'z'; // a roundabout way to do c = 'z' !!

   cout << " c = " << c << endl;       // displays 'z'
   cout << endl;

   cout << " Press any key to Quit ";
   getch();
}
```

Take a look at Program 3.10 – this, very contrived example, illustrates what we have been discussing in relation to the use of pointers. Try the program out and check that you understand how it works. Now look at Program 3.11.

Program 3.11

```cpp
//: CREF.cpp
//. using references to return the address of a variable

#include <conio.h>
#include <iostream.h>
// .............................................................
char &ch(char &c)    // using references to ch and c
{
   c = 'a';
```

```
    return c;      // because of the &ch in function header
}              // this returns the address of c
// ...........................................................
void main() {

    clrscr();
    cout << " CREF " << endl;
    cout << " ==== " << endl << endl;

    char c;

    c = 'n';
    cout << " c = " << c << endl;
    cout << endl;
    cout << " Now to check that the function works " << endl;
    cout << " c = " << ch(c) << endl;
    cout << " c = " << c << endl;
    cout << endl;
    cout << " Can also use ch to set c to a value other than
        'a' " << endl;
    ch(c) = 'z';
    cout << " c = " << c << endl;
    cout << endl;

    cout << " Press any key to Quit ";
    getch();
}
```

This is a version of the previous program, but this time using references throughout. The code is more straightforward and should be easy to follow. Try this program out and again make sure you understand how it works. The points we have been discussing above are summarised in Table 3.1 and Table 3.2. We will be looking at more of the intricacies in the use of pointers and references once we have introduced classes in Chapter 5.

Table 3.1 Function parameters

	Variable declaration	Argument	Getting its value
pointer	type *x	&x	*x (de-reference)
reference	type &x	x	X

Table 3.2 Return values

	Function declaration	Function called and used
pointer	type *func_name(...)	*func_name(...)
reference	type &func_name(...)	func_name(...)

As we have already hinted, strings are basically arrays of characters and pointers are often used when dealing with strings. Recall that an address can appear in a number of forms:

- As the value of a pointer.
- In an expression starting with `&` (e.g. `&a[5]` – the address of `a[5]`).
- As the name of an array (e.g. `arr` if `arr` is declared as `int arr[20]` say).

One further way in which an address can occur is when a string constant is used, as in "Hello World". So given a pointer to a character `p` we can assign this to a string constant. For example:

```
char *p;
p = "Hello World";
```

This can be thought of as equivalent to setting up an array of 12 characters with element 0 = `'H'`, 1 = `'e'` ..., 10 = `'d'` and 11 = `'\0'`. Remember that the last character in a string must be set to `'\0'` in order for the string to be terminated correctly. Note that with the above assignment this character will be added automatically, but if we set up an array of `char` and assign each character individually to the relevant array element then we would also need to assign `'\0'` to the last element if we wanted to treat the array as a string and use string functions on it. If you think back to the very first program in this book then it should come as no surprise to you that in C++ we can output the string `"Hello World"`, and move to a new line, using `cout` in the following way: `cout << p << endl;`

The act of assigning `p` to `"Hello World"` places the address of the first character in the string in the pointer `p`. It is important to note that unlike `i = 8` which sets (an `int`) `i` to 8, `p = "Hello World"` does not copy the string to `p` (however we can use operator overloading to achieve this in C++ – details will be given later).

We can carry out pointer arithmetic even on string constants. A few examples will illustrate this and help you to understand the nature of strings and their relationship to pointers. Consider first what `*"Hello World"` might yield. Bearing in mind that `p = "Hello World"` retrieves the address of the first character in the string constant, and that applying the `*` operator to an address yields the contents of the address, then `*"Hello World"` will give us `'H'`, i.e. the first character in the string. To obtain other characters from the string we can use pointer arithmetic, e.g.:

```
*("Hello World" + 1)  gives  'e'
*("Hello World" + 5)  gives  ' '
```

```
*("Hello World" + 10) gives   'd'
```

You will find an exercise on this at the end of the chapter.

3.9   Arrays of pointers

An array of pointers is declared as follows:

```
float *p_to_float[5];
```

Thus each element of the array holds the address of a float object. How might we use such a construct? Consider the task of sorting a series of floats into ascending order. We can store these numbers in an array in the order in which they are entered. They can then be sorted, *in situ*, if we wish. However we may wish to retain the original order as well as the sorted set. We could do this by copying them into another array in the correct order or we could use an array of pointers to hold the addresses of the numbers in ascending order (i.e. ascending order of numbers, not addresses!). As an illustration of the use of arrays of pointers we will adopt this second method (Program 3.12).

📋 **Program 3.12**
```
//: APOINT1.cpp
//. using an array of pointers

#include <conio.h>
#include <iostream.h>
// ........................................................
void swap(double **d1, double **d2);
// ........................................................
void main()
{
    const SIZE = 5;
    double a[SIZE], // array of double
        *p[SIZE]; // array of 5 double pointers
    int i;

    clrscr();
    cout << " APOINT1 " << endl;
    cout << " ======= " << endl << endl;

    cout << SIZE << " real numbers " << endl;

    a[0] = 13.4; a[1] = 3.8;
    a[2] = 2.6; a[3] = 0.5; a[4] = 12.8;

    cout << " i    p[i]    *p[i] " << endl;
    for(i = 0; i < SIZE; i++)
```

```
    {
        p[i] = &a[i]; // store addresses of
                // elements of a in array of
                // pointers (p)
        cout << " " << i << " " << p[i] <<
                " " << *p[i] << endl;
    }

    cout << " now sort the array of pointers " << endl;

    for(int j = 0; j < SIZE-1; j++)
    {
        for(i = j+1; i < SIZE; i++)
            // check values pointed to by p[j] and p[i]
            if (*(p[j]) > *(p[i]))
                // swap the addresses stored in p[j] and p[i]
                swap(&p[j], &p[i]);
    }

    cout << " *p[] : ";
    for(i = 0; i < SIZE; i++)
        cout << *p[i] << " ";
    cout << endl;

    cout << endl << "End of APOINT1" << endl;
}
// ..............................................................
// this function is used to swap addresses held in d1 and d2
void swap(double **d1, double **d2)
{
    double *temp; // local variable - temp: pointer
            // to a double

    temp = *d1;
    *d1 = *d2;
    *d2 = temp;
}
```

There are a number of important points worth noting in this example. First,
the declaration:

```
double *p[SIZE];
```

declares an array of SIZE double pointers (or an array containing SIZE pointers to a double) and not a pointer to an array of doubles. Secondly notice that
the addresses of the elements p[j] and p[i] have to be passed to the function
swap. Obviously if we missed off the address operator (&) no swapping would
occur. Thirdly notice how the arguments to swap are declared (void   swap
(double **d1, double **d1)). Remember that we are passing addresses of
doubles (pointers to doubles) and so we can't simple refer to them using double *d1 for example. Such a declaration would infer that we will be passing a
double, not the address of a double. Finally, notice how the swap function is
coded. We declare a temporary variable (double *temp) to hold the address

of a double. All the operations on the arguments (d1 and d2) then refer to them as pointers (*d1 and *d2) since they hold addresses and we are swapping the addresses pointed to by these arguments.

3.9.1 Declaration and initialisation of arrays

Incidentally there is an alternative way of initialising the array a to a set of values other than by direct assignment of each element. This can be done when a is declared, as follows:

```
double a[] = {13.4, 3.8, 2.6, 0.5, 12.8};
```

This method, sometimes known as aggregate initialisation, can at times be very useful and can be applied to multi-dimensional arrays as well as to other structures, as you will see later on.

3.9.2 Another use of arrays of pointers

If you have come to C++ with a good grounding in C then you will already be familiar with the idea of program parameters and you may have been reminded of their use in the previous discussion. A program which requires command-line arguments (e.g. copy file1.cpp file2.cpp which would copy the contents of file1.cpp to file2.cpp) would use an array of pointers in the declaration of main. The standard declaration, when command-line arguments are required is:

```
void main(int argc, char *argv[])
{
    // program
}
```

this declares an int (argc) and an array of pointers to arrays of chars (argv). An alternative declaration is:

```
void main(int argc, char **argv)
{
    // program
}
```

Now, what do argc and argv hold? argc and argv are initialised when a C++ program (or a C program for that matter) starts up. The first argument (argc) contains the number of arguments (including itself and the program name). This means that a command line with no arguments would have an argc of 1 (the program name). The second argument (argv) is an array of argc pointers to the command-line strings. Program 3.13 illustrates the use of an array of pointers to chars in passing command-line arguments to the program.

Program 3.13

```
//: PPARAM.cpp
//. illustrating the use of command-line arguments
//. uses an array of pointers

#include <conio.h>
#include <iostream.h>

// .........................................................
void main(int argc, char *argv[]) {
      // argc no. of command-line arguments
      // including the program name
      // argv[] array of pointers to char

   clrscr();
   cout << " PPARAM " << endl;
   cout << " ====== " << endl << endl;

   cout << " argc = " << argc << " no. of arguments " << endl;

   cout << endl << " These are the elements in the command-
                       line: " << endl;
   for( int i = 0; i < argc; i++)
      cout << " argv[" << i << "] = " << argv[i] << endl;

   cout << endl;
   cout << " Press any key to Quit ";

   getch();
}
```

Type in the program and run it without any additional arguments (i.e. just the program name) then try it with various strings as arguments (e.g. PPARAM TESTING COMMAND_LINE ARGUMENTS).

3.10 New and delete

The new and delete keywords are used in C++ to allocate and release memory. The new operator returns a pointer to the memory which has been allocated. If there is not enough memory available then a null pointer is returned. The general form of new is:

```
pointer_variable = new type;
```

where type can be any of the fundamental data types in C/C++ or combinations, e.g. an array of int, structures, classes, arrays of classes, etc. So to allocate memory for a float, and then release it, we could use Program 3.14.

Program 3.14

```
//: ALLOC.cpp
//. allocating memory for a float
#include <iostream.h>
#include <stdlib.h>
// .....................................................
void main()
{
  float *fp;    // declare a pointer to a float

  fp = new float; // allocate memory for a float
  if (!fp)
  {
    cout << " Unable to allocate memory for float " << endl;
    exit(1);
  }

  *fp = 326.8; // give the float a value
  cout << " Address of float (fp) = " << fp << endl;
  cout << " contents of float (*fp) = " << *fp << endl;

  delete fp;
}
```

Notice that we first of all declare a pointer to a `float` (`*fp`) and then we allocate memory for the `float` by use of the statement:

```
fp = new float;
```

After use we release the memory allocated with the statement

```
delete fp;
```

(Notice, in passing, the use of the `exit(1);` statement to terminate the program if an error occurs in an attempt to allocate memory. In order to use this function we need to include the header file `stdlib.h`)

Initialisation can also be carried out when memory is allocated. So we could combine the two statements:

```
        fp = new float;
and     *fp = 326.8;
```

to produce:

```
fp = new float (326.8);
```

Any (simple) data type can be initialised and allocated space in the above manner. Just include in brackets the value you wish the newly declared variable to have.

Of course, the above could be achieved at lot easier using a `float` variable without the explicit need to use `new` and `delete`, however we shall see shortly examples when `new` and `delete` are more useful.

Consider the task of allocating an array of `int`'s. We can do this using `new` by including the number of elements in square brackets after the allocation of memory. E.g.

```
int *ip;
ip = new int [20];
```

which allocates an array of 20 `ints`.

To release the allocated memory we again use `delete`, but this time it is advisable to include empty square brackets after `delete` to indicate to the compiler that an array is being deleted. (Some earlier compilers required the number of elements being deleted to be enclosed in the square brackets and some more modern compilers may not need the square brackets at all. However it is good programming practice to include the (empty) square brackets to make it clear that memory allocated to an array is being released. Check your own compiler to see what `delete` requires.)

```
delete [] ip;
```

The allocation and release of memory using arrays is illustrated in Program 3.15, which you should now try out.

Program 3.15

```
//: NEW2.cpp
//. memory allocation: using new and delete to declare an array
#include <iostream.h>
#include <stdlib.h>
#include <conio.h>
// ........................................................
void main()
{
    int *ip, i;  // declare a pointer to an int and an int
            // allocate memory for an array of 20 ints
    ip = new int [20];

    clrscr();
    cout << " NEW2 " << endl;
    cout << " ==== " << endl << endl;

    if (!ip)
    {
       cout << " Unable to allocate memory for int array \n";
       exit(1);
    }

    for ( i = 0; i < 20; i++)
       ip[i] = i * i;  // give the array some values
```

```
    for ( i = 0; i < 20; i++)
      cout << ip[i] << " ";

    delete [] ip;    // release memory
    cout << endl;
    cout << " Press any key to Quit ";
    getch();
}
```

Note: Although you can initialise simple types (`int`, `float`, etc.) at the same time as you allocate storage space using `new`, you cannot do that with arrays. Therefore initialisation must take place after space has been allocated to an array.

3.11 Dynamic arrays

One important use of new is to allow dynamic arrays to be created. Supposing we do not know, until run-time, how many elements we require in our array. We can overcome the problem by declaring a pointer (of the correct type – e.g. to an int), read in the size of the array and then use the new operator to allocate memory for this array. Look at Program 3.16 – this illustrates how a dynamic array can be constructed.

Program 3.16
```
//: NEW3.cpp
//. illustration of new and delete to declare a dynamic array
#include <iostream.h>
#include <stdlib.h>
#include <conio.h>

void main()
{
    int *ip, i;    // declare a pointer to an int

    int size;

    clrscr();
    cout << " NEW3 " << endl;
    cout << " ==== " << endl << endl;

    cout << " Enter no. of elements required: ";
    cin >> size;
                    // allocate memory for an array of size ints
    ip = new int [size];
    if (!ip){
        cout << " Unable to allocate memory for int array \n";
```

```
        exit(1);
    }
    for ( i = 0; i < size; i++)
        ip[i] = i * i;  // give the array some values

    for ( i = 0; i < size; i++)
        cout << ip[i] << " ";

    cout << endl;
    cout << " address of ip[0] = " << &ip[0] << endl;
    cout << " and of ip[size] = " << &ip[size-1] << endl;

    delete [] ip;      // release memory

    cout << " Press any key to Quit ";
    getch();
}
```

The essential elements of this program are:

```
int *ip, i;
int size;
```
which declares the `int` pointer `ip` and the `int` array `size`,

```
ip = new int [size];
```

to allocate the correct amount of memory, and

```
delete [] ip;
```

to release the memory.

Now suppose we wish to create a two-dimensional array. There are a number of important issues to understand when creating two-dimensional arrays. The first is that only the first array dimension can be unknown at compile time. So:

```
int a[3][6];         // a 3 × 6 element array
int m[4][5][10];     // a 4 × 5 × 10 element array
int n[][6];          // an array of unknown first dimension
                     // but with 6 as the second dimension
int p [][3][5];      // an array of unknown first dimension
                     // but with second & third dimensions
                     // of 3 and 5
```

are all valid, whereas the following

```
int a[3][];
int m[4][][6];
int n[][];
```

are all invalid.

The second issue is how do we declare the pointer which we will need to use in order to allocate memory for a two-dimensional array? Remember that a pointer to an `int` is declared as `int *p;` and that we are wishing to declare a pointer to an array of (say) 5 elements. We might think that the declaration for our pointer would be:

```
int *ip[5];      // incorrect
```

But, as the comment states this is not correct. The reason lies in the precedence of the `*` and `[]` operators – the `[]` operator has a higher precedence than the `*` and so this declaration constructs an array of five pointers to `int`s, and not what we want which is a pointer to an array of five `int`s. We must therefore use parentheses to over-ride the order of precedence. Thus the declaration becomes:

```
int (*ip)[5];    // correct
```

Finally, once we know the size of the first dimension, we can allocate storage for the two-dimensional array:

```
ip = new int [size][5];
```

Program 3.17 illustrates this example.

Program 3.17

```
//: NEW4.cpp
//. illustration of new and delete to declare an array with 2 or
//. more dimensions

#include <iostream.h>
#include <stdlib.h>
#include <conio.h>
// ..............................................................
void main()
{
    int (*ip)[5];
        // declare a pointer to an int array of 5 elements
    int i, j;

    int size;

    clrscr();
    cout << " NEW4 - 2d array " << endl;
    cout << " ==== ========== " << endl << endl;

    cout << " Enter no. of elements required: ";
    cin >> size;

    ip = new int [size][5]; // allocate memory for an array
                  // of size x 5 ints
```

```
    if (!ip) {
        cout << " Unable to allocate memory for int array \n";
        exit(1);
    }


    for ( i = 0; i < size; i++)
        for ( j = 0; j < 5; j++)
            ip[i][j] = i * j;// give the array some values

    for ( i = 0; i < size; i++)
    {
        for ( j = 0; j < 5; j++)
            cout << ip[i][j] << " ";
        cout << endl;
    }

    cout << endl;

    cout << " address of ip[size-1][4] = " << &ip[size-1][4] << end
    cout << "      and of ip[0][0] = " << &ip[0][0] << endl;
    cout << " check no. of elements " << endl;
    int n = &ip[size-1][4] - &ip[0][0] + 1;
    cout << " No. of elements = " << n << endl;

    delete [] ip;   // release memory

    cout << " Press any key to Quit ";
    getch();
}
```

Arrays with more dimensions can be set up in a similar way, as long as we keep to the restrictions outlined above concerning which dimension must be known at compile time. Thus

```
float (*ip)[5][8];
fp = new float [size][5][8];
```

will allow a three dimensional array of type float to be constructed.

3.11.1 Memory checking

A simple use of new and delete is to check available memory. We can repeatedly attempt to allocate blocks of memory until there is no more available. When this stage has been reached we know how much memory can be allocated. Program 3.18 provides a simple way of doing this. Take a look at it now and try it out.

📋 **Program 3.18**
```
//: AVMEM.cpp
//. testing to see how much memory is available

#include <conio.h>
#include <iostream.h>
```

```
// .............................................................
void main() {
   char *pmem;    // pointer to a byte

   clrscr();
   cout << " AVMEM " << endl;
   cout << " ===== " << endl << endl;

   // pmem = new char[10000];    // allocate a block of 10K
   // delete pmem;               // release this block

   for (int i = 1; ; i++) {      // do forever!
      pmem = new char[10000];    // try allocating 10KB
      if (pmem == 0) break;
      cout << " Another 10KB allocated: Total = " << 10*i
           << "KB" << endl;
   }

   cout << " Press any key to Quit ";
   getch();
}
```

This program uses blocks of 10KB and so continues to allocate blocks of this size until no more is available. Since new returns a null (i.e. 0) if it is unable to allocate memory we can use this fact to stop allocating memory when there is none left to allocate! The statement:

```
if (pmem == 0) break;
```

does just that. Test run 3.6 shows a sample run.

Test run 3.6
```
AVMEM
=====

Another 10KB allocated: Total = 10KB
Another 10KB allocated: Total = 20KB
Another 10KB allocated: Total = 30KB
Another 10KB allocated: Total = 40KB
Another 10KB allocated: Total = 50KB
Another 10KB allocated: Total = 60KB
Press any key to Quit
```

In the program you will see the following two lines of code:

```
// pmem = new char[10000]; // allocate a block of 10K
// delete pmem;            // release this block
```

Try the following:

1. Remove the comment from the beginning of the pmem = ... line, recompile your program and run it. What output do you get?

Obviously since a block of 10KB has been allocated before entering the loop only a further 50KB can be allocated.

2.   Now remove the comment from the following line. What output do you get this time?

This illustrates that delete does actually release memory, since now the amount allocated by the loop is back to the original value (in my case 60KB).

3.11.2 Using set_new_handler

An alternative to testing for pmem to return a NULL value to determine when no more memory is available we can use a built-in function set_new_handler(). This function (in new.h) allows the programmer to control what happens when memory is exhausted. This is done by using an internal function pointer (_new_handler). This normally returns NULL when new runs out of memory, but by using the set_new_handler() function we can replace the NULL with the address of a function to call when memory is exhausted. Take a look at the Program 3.19 (AVMEM2.cpp).

Program 3.19

```
//: AVMEM2.cpp
//. testing to see how much memory is available
//. introducing the _new_handler function pointer
//. and set_new_handler
#include <conio.h>
#include <iostream.h>
#include <stdlib.h>
#include <new.h>

static void no_more();
// ...............................................................
void main() {
   set_new_handler(no_more);
   char *pmem;   // pointer to a byte

   clrscr();
   cout << " AVMEM2 " << endl;
   cout << " ====== " << endl << endl;

// pmem = new char[10000]; // allocate a block of 10K
// delete pmem;       // release this block

   for (int i = 1; ; i++) {// do forever!
      pmem = new char[10000]; // try allocating 10KB
      cout << " Another 10KB allocated: Total = " << 10*i
           << "KB" << endl;
   }
```

```
}
static void no_more() {
   cerr << endl << " No more memory available" << endl;
   exit(1);
}
```

In this we have a function:

```
static void no_more() ...
```

which contains a simple message. Within `main()` we use the `set_new_` handler() function to specify which function to call when memory is exhausted:

```
set_new_handler(no_more);
```

Test run 3.7 shows an example run.

🖥 **Test run 3.7**

```
AVMEM2
======
Another 10KB allocated: Total = 10KB
Another 10KB allocated: Total = 20KB
Another 10KB allocated: Total = 30KB
Another 10KB allocated: Total = 40KB
Another 10KB allocated: Total = 50KB
Another 10KB allocated: Total = 60KB

No more memory available
```

Warning: Before trying this program with your compiler check how `set_new_` `handler` works.

3.12 Pointer notation – a summary

In this chapter we have spoken a good deal about pointers. We have used them with the reference operator and when accessing array elements (both one-dimensional and two-dimensional). In this section we bring together all the uses you have encountered so far. Make sure that you understand the various uses before leaving this chapter. Some pointer examples are given next:

`char *pmonth;`	pointer to a char, pmonth will hold an address
`int *i, j, k;`	i pointer to int but j and k ints (not pointers)
`int &x;`	reference to an int

`func( int &x)`	function definition or prototype
`func( x);`	function call – don't need to pass an address
	x can still be modified by `func`
`int *const bottom =` `    &stack[0];`	constant pointer to element 0 of `int` array `a[]`
`int *last = bottom;`	pointer `last`, initialised to `bottom`
`last++;`	move pointer (`last`) to next `int`
`const int *pint;`	`pint` will point to an `int` value which cannot be modified
`int total = 100;`	give `total` a value
`pint = &total;`	`pint` now pointing to `total`
`(*pint)++;`	ILLEGAL – can't modify a constant (i.e. `total`)
`int *pint2;`	another pointer to an `int`
`*pint2 = 200;`	set `total` to 200
`(*pint2)++;`	increase `total` by 1 to 201
`const int *const` `    pint = &i;`	pointer to a constant address, the contents of which is a `constant int`
`int a[10];`	array of 10 ints
`int *ptra;`	pointer to an `int`
`ptra = a;`	set `ptra` to the address of a
	(equivalent to `ptra = &a[0];`)
`*(ptra+10) = 5;`	set `a[10]` to 5
`void *pvoid;`	create a void pointer (generic pointer)
`pvoid = &i;`	`pvoid` now points to an `int` (assuming `int i;`)
	– no cast required
`pchar = (char *) pvoid;`	cast needed when converting from `void` pointer
`void func(int a[]);`	passing a complete array into `func`[1]
`void func(int a[][4]);`	passing a two-dimensional array into a function[1]
`void func(int *a);`	equivalent to the above (`int a[]`)
`void func(*int[4]);`	equivalent to `int a[][4]`
`a[i]`	equivalent to `*(a+i)`
`a[i][j]`	equivalent to `*(a[i]+j)`
	also equivalent to `*(*(a+i)+j)`
`&a[i]`	equivalent to `a+i`
`&a[i][j]`	equivalent to `a[i]+j`
	also equivalent to `*(a+i)+j`
`*p_to_int[6];`	an array of pointer to ints
`(*p_to_array_of_ints)[6];`	a pointer to an array of (6) ints

---

[1] *Notice in these cases that the first array length is omitted – otherwise we would be passing only one element of the array.*

3.13 Summary

In this chapter we have continued the examination of functions in C++ and introduced further C++ syntax and semantics. The topics covered are listed below. As always check that you have grasped the ideas behind them before moving on. Try out the Exercises – these should help to consolidate what you have learnt.

Topics covered:

- Pointers, see also Table 3.2.
- Pointer expressions.
- Initialisation of variables.
- Pointer arithmetic.
- Comparing pointers.
- Using void pointers.
- References as return values.
- Using pointers or references (Table 3.1).
- Strings.
- Arrays of pointers.
- Command-line arguments.
- new and delete.
- `set_new_handler()` function.
- Dynamic arrays.

3.14 Exercises

3.14.1

    a) Write a function which returns the character at position n in the string s (`chr( int n, char *s)`).

    b) What happens if the position chosen is greater than the number of characters in the string? Modify the program by writing and incorporating a function `strlen` which returns the number of characters in the string.

3.14.2   Write a program which uses pointers to `int` and `float` and then experiment with different additions to and subtractions from the two pointers. E.g. if `pint` is a pointer to an `int`, then output the addresses of `pint` + 4, 8, 9 and `pint` − 3, 7 and 10. Do similar pointer arithmetic for the `float` pointer.

3.14.3   Modify the program `PDIFF1.cpp` (Program 3.6) to use `float` pointers instead of `int`. Check that the output you get is what you expected.

3.14.4   Write a program which reads in a line of text and outputs the text in reverse order. You should write two versions. One version should use array notation, the second version should use pointer notation only.

3.14.5   Write another version of the above program which uses command-line parameters but only allows one word to be reversed. That is :

```
reverse ABCDEFG
```

produces the output

```
GFEDCBA
```

but `reverse Hello World`

will give a suitable error message.

3.14.6

a) In program `VOIDP1.cpp` which we looked at earlier (Program 3.8) write a function to replace the code between lines *** A *** and *** B *** inclusive. This function should return an integer indicating the day, month or the year.

b) How might the months (in character form) be checked for their validity? Write a function to do this. It should return 1 if the month is valid, 0 otherwise, and the month should be set equal to the appropriate month in the list. Thus if month equals 'Jun' the function should return 1 and set month equal to 'JUNE'.

4 Input and Output

4.1 Introduction

In this short chapter we take a look at how C++ handles *input* and *output*. It concentrates on:

- Normal methods used for I/O via streams.
- Overloaded shift operators.
- How formatted and unformatted I/O are implemented so that you have available a variety of methods at a reasonably early stage.
- A brief overview of basic C I/O.

We will inevitably be referring to some structures and concepts which are not introduced in detail until later chapters, however you should still be able to understand how I/O works and use many of the methods introduced in this chapter. Once you have worked through the book, this chapter should provide a useful reference for any I/O facilities which you may require.

4.2 Stream I/O in C++

All input and output in C++ is based on the idea of a stream. A stream is a logical device which is associated, at some stage, with a physical device in order that input and output can be performed. The exact form of this device is irrelevant as far as the user of the streams is concerned. So it is immaterial whether output is to the screen, a disk file or a printer.

The header file iostream.h includes all the prototypes for C++ I/O. This includes the basic methods of C++ stream I/O which we have already used, namely cin >> and cout <<, which respectively read data from the input stream (designated by cin) and write data to the output stream (cout). These operators are often known respectively as insertion and extraction operators: the << inserts data onto the output stream and >> extracts data from the input stream. In addition there are a number of I/O functions and I/O manipulators which provide the formatted I/O available through the use of printf() and scanf() in C.

115

At the highest level, that is the level most likely to be used by you the programmer, are three classes – istream, ostream and iostream. The class iostream is derived from both istream and ostream, which is itself derived from the ios class. The ios class use objects of type streambuf. The most important iostream classes are summarised in Table 4.1 and the pre-defined C++ stream objects are listed in Table 4.2.

Table 4.1 The basic C++ I/O classes

Class	Purpose
streambuf	To manage memory buffers
ios	To deal with stream errors and state variables
istream	To handle formatted and unformatted character input
ostream	To handle formatted and unformatted character output
iostream	To handle input and output to the same stream

cin is an object of class istream whilst cout, cerr and clog are objects of class ostream. (In some implementations there is another level of inheritance below the istream and ostream class; istream_withassign and ostream_withassign – where these are implemented the cin, cout, cerr and clog will be objects of the latter classes.) When a C++ program starts these four predefined streams are opened.

Table 4.2 Pre-defined stream objects

Object	Description	C equivalent
cin	Used for standard input, normally the keyboard	stdin
cout	Used for standard output, normally the screen	stdout
cerr	Used for error messages	stderr
clog	A buffered version of cerr – mostly used for none when large amounts of error messages are expected	

4.3 Formatted output in C++

Formatting of data can be achieved either through direct access of the ios class members, or through the use of member functions of ios which themselves access these data members, or through the use of special manipulators which are included as part of the I/O expression. Each of these will be examined in turn.

The ios class contains an enumeration type occupying two bytes (in fact stored as a long int) which hold a collection of 15 flags essential to the control of I/O formatting, they are declared as follows:

```
public:
enum {
  skipws = 0x0001,      // skip whitespace on input
  left   = 0x0002,      // left justify output
  right  = 0x0004,      // right justify output
  internal = 0x0008,    // pad for numeric o/p - after the sign or
                        // base indicator
  dec = 0x0010,         // convert o/p to decimal
  oct = 0x0020,         // convert o/p to octal
  hex = 0x0040,         // convert o/p to hexadecimal
  showbase  = 0x0080,   // show the number base
  showpoint = 0x0100,   // show the decimal point
  uppercase = 0x0200,   // use upper case letters in hexadecimal o/p
  showpos   = 0x0400,   // show '+' with positive numbers
  scientific = 0x0800,  // use scientific notation for o/p
  fixed  = 0x1000,      // use fixed number of decimal places in o/p
  unitbuf = 0x2000,     // flush the streams after insertion
  stdio = 0x4000,       // flush stdout and stderr after insertion
};
```

Notice that these flags are declared in the public section of ios and so they are available for access by the programmer provided that the class is identified and the scope resolution operator used, i.e. ios::showpoint provides access to showpoint. However we still cannot get direct access – we still need to use either a manipulator i.e. setiosflags(), prototyped in iomanip.h, or a member function of ios – setf() – in order to do this:

Program 4.1
```
//: IOSFLEX.cpp
//. illustrating simple o/p formatting
#include <iostream.h>
#include <iomanip.h>            // needed for setiosflags()

void main(){
    int i = 234;

    cout << " i = " << i << endl;
    // ios::showbase = 1;         // can't access showbase like this
    // setiosflags(showbase);     // ... nor like this
    // cout.showbase = 1;         // ... nor like this!
    cout.setf(ios::showbase);  // but like this
    cout.setf(ios::oct);       // convert to octal
    cout << " i = " << i << endl;
    cout << setiosflags(ios::hex);   // ... or like this
    cout << " i = " << i << endl;
    cout << " IOS FLAGS: ";
    cout << cout.flags();            // o/p current settings
}
```

This simple program illustrates that the default output of an integer is in base 10 (decimal); that we can use the hex manipulator (see Section 4.4) to force output in hex; and that in order to change a flag we either call the member function setf() for the object cout or include the setiosflags() manipulator in a `cout` statement. Test run 4.1 shows a sample run.

Notice that once a flag is set it remains in force (for that stream) until reset. So the member function `flags()` which returns the complete set of flags as a long int is, in this case displayed in hexadecimal form. The flags which are therefore set are:

```
1  0x0001   skipws
c  0x0040   hex
   0x0080   showbase
2  0c2000   unitbuf
```

Notice also illegal attempts at accessing the various flags. These are illegal for different reasons and it is instructive to remove the comment characters (`//`) from the beginning of these lines and try to compile the program. If you do this you should obtain the following errors:

```
ios::showbase = 1;         // Lvalue required
setiosflags(showbase);     // Undefined symbol "showbase"
cout.showbase = 1;         // Lvalue required
```

The first and last of these errors are due to the fact that `showbase` is a name (an alias) for a number (the constant `0x0080`) and therefore cannot appear on the left side of an assignment operator. The second error indicates the need to identify the class to which `showbase` belongs before it can be accessed. One further point is worth noting about the above example. The two statements which set the `showbase` and `oct` flags whilst perfectly valid would more frequently be combined in one statement like this:

```
cout.setf(ios::showbase | ios::oct);
```

which uses the bitwise or operator to combine the two flags so that they can be used as a single argument to `setf()`. A similar method can be used with any of the manipulator functions and any combination of valid flags. Finally, as the Table 4.3 implies, the `setiosflags()` function can also take as an argument a long int. Thus, reverting to the previous example, we could set the `showbase` and `oct` flags by assigning the appropriate value to a long int and then using it (or using the value directly) as the argument to `setiosflags()` (or indeed to `setf()`):

```
long f = 0x00C0;
cout << setiosflags(f);  // or cout.setf(0x00C0);
```

Table 4.3 Output manipulators

Manipulator	Used to	Flag
dec	set the decimal base format flag	dec
endl	insert new line and flush the stream	
ends	insert end-of-string null, to terminate a string	
flush	flush (clear) an ostream	
hex	set the hexadecimal base format flag	hex
oct	set the octal base format flag	oct
resetiosflags(long f)	clear the format bits specified by f	any
setbase(int n)	set the base format to n – 0, 8, 10 or 16 (0 means set to the default)	dec, oct or hex
setfill(int c)	set the fill character to c	internal
setiosflags(long f)	set the format bits specified by f	any
setprecision(int n)	set the floating-point precision to n	fixed
setw(int n)	set field width to n	
ws	extract whitespace characters	

The resetiosflags() function is used to clear the format bits specified in the argument. Thus, for example, in the previous program, if further output was desired then we could reset the bits which had been set by use of the following statement:

```
cout << setiosflags(ios::showbase | ios::oct);
```

Following the execution of this statement at the end of the above program the only flags set which would be skipws and stdio – i.e. the default settings.

If you think back to Program 2.17 in which we output the contents of some un-initialised as well as some initialised arrays, you may recall that the output looked rather untidy. A partial output when I ran the program looked like this:

🖳   **Test run 4.2**
```
ARRAYINI
========
a[] = 6335 1700 12419 0 1088 -14 8634 1088 1 1356
b[] = 0 0 0 0 0

initialising elements 0, 1 & 4
a[] = 2 5 12419 12 1088 -14 8634 1088 1 1356

setting all elements to 0
a[] = 0 0 0 0 0 0 0 0 0 0
...
```

The output from the above program may look a little untidy, especially for the uninitialised arrays. The layout can be improved by using another I/O manipulator setw() which sets the output width. Thus to space the output to a field width of 7 characters we could use setw(7) *in each cout statement* where required. Thus:

```
for(int i = 0; i < asize; i++)
    cout << setw(6) << a[i] << " ";
```

will output each element of a on a line in a field width of 7 (since the maximum number of digits taken up by (signed) ints in my implementation is 6 (i.e. -32768) we have an additional space to ensure that numbers don't run together).

Note that setw() behaves rather differently from the other manipulators we met in Chapter 1 (oct, hex and dec). With those manipulators once one was used its effect remained until reset by another manipulator. With setw(), however, its effect only lasts for the next data item output in the cout statement, so we need to use it in all the cout statements for which it is required. We also need to include the special header file iomanip.h.

Only those manipulators which have parameters require the inclusion of the header file iomanip.h – as we saw in Chapter 1 dec, oct, hex and endl are all available in iostream.h. As another example of some of these manipulators, Program 4.2 (FLOATOUT.cpp) illustrates an attempt to print a table of floating-point numbers in a reasonably well-formatted manner. Test run 4.3 shows a sample run.

📋 **Program 4.2**

```
//: FLOATOUT.cpp
//. outputting a table of floats

#include <conio.h>
#include <iostream.h>
#include <iomanip.h>
// ...........................................................
void main()
{
    clrscr();
    cout << " FLOATOUT " << endl;
    cout << " ======== " << endl << endl;

    cout << " Table of 1/(x * x) " << endl;
    for( float x = 1; x < 20; x++) {
        cout << setw(5) << setprecision(2) << x;
        cout << setw(10) << setprecision(6) << 1.0 /(x * x);
        cout << endl;
    }
}
```

```
FLOATOUT
========

Table of 1/(x * x)
     1           1
     2        0.25
     3   0.111111
     4      0.0625
     5        0.04
etc.
```

This was not what we intended. First the values of x have no decimal point and, more worrying, the values of $1/x^2$ are all over the place! The reason for this is that we need to set the showpoint flag in order to ensure that the decimal point is shown. So to get the desired output we need to add the following statement before we start outputting the table:

```
cout << setiosflags(ios::showpoint);
```

An alternative method is to use setf(), i.e.

```
cout.setf(ios::showpoint);
```

which also sets the showpoint flag.

Test run 4.4 shows how the above modifications the output.

```
FLOATOUT
========
Table of 1/(x * x)
1.00   1.000000
2.00   0.250000
3.00   0.111111
4.00   0.062500
5.00   0.040000
etc.
```

Finally, in the last part of this section we should mention the member functions and data members of ios. We have already encountered setf() as an alternative to setiosflags(), another useful function is unsetf() which can be used in the same way as setf() but instead of resetiosflags(). There are in fact 20 member functions of ios plus two constructor functions, however it is beyond the scope of this book to look in detail at these functions. If you need more control over input and output then you should consult the documentation associated with your particular implementation for further details.

4.4 Formatted input in C++

Much of the previous discussion applies to C++ stream input and so this section should be easy to follow provided that you have understood the previous one. Just as the output streams use the overloaded left-shift operator (<<) so the input streams use the overloaded right-shift operator (>>). Thus for input the operand to the left of >> must be an object of type istream and the right operand can be any type for which an overloaded >> operator exists.

One of the first problems which is often encountered when attempting to use cin concerns the way in which white spaces are handled. As a rule white spaces are skipped on input. So if we want to read in a group of characters, and retain any white spaces, then the following extract won't work as intended:

```
// read in characters including white spaces
// won't work!
char c[80];
int i = 0;
do{
    cin >> c[i++];
while (c[i-1] != '\n');
...
```

Any characters in the input stream which are white spaces will be skipped, and so even if the user presses Enter it will never be inserted into the array c. We can overcome this problem in a variety of ways. The first involves clearing the skipws flag before attempting any input. Thus:

Program 4.3

```
//: NOSKIPWS.cpp
//. One method of reading white space characters
#include <iostream.h>
#include <iomanip.h>

void main(){
    char c[80];    // to hold a line of text
    int i = 0, n;

    cin >> resetiosflags(ios::skipws);
    do{
        cin >> c[i++];
    }while(c[i-1] != '\n');
    n = i;
    for( i = 0; i < n; i++)
        cout << c[i];
}
```

This program illustrates two very important points both of which form parts of the first cin statement. First the fact that this is a cin statement at all! Remember that the ioflags are set for a specific stream so if we want to affect formatting during input then (and we are using cin) it is cin which needs to be told what flags are to be modified. Secondly, in this instance, we wish to turn the skipws flag off and so we must use resetiosflags() (or cin.unsetf()) not setiosflags(). It is very easy to fall into either of these traps with the result that the program will never terminate and drastic methods may be needed to stop the program.

A second method which will enable white spaces to be read is to use one of the member functions of cin, which we met earlier, namely get(). So the input section of this program now reads:

```
do{
    cin.get(c[i++]);
}while(c[i-1] != '\n');
n = i;
```

In this case there is no need to specifically reset the skipws flag – get() by default reads every character it encounters on the input stream. As just mentioned get() is one of the member functions of istream and this is a convenient place at which to introduce the other functions – a summary is given in Table 4.4.

Although all the member functions are given here for completeness we will only take a brief look at the get() and getline() functions. These provide further useful ways in which to read data from an input stream and it is worth spending a short time looking at them.

Table 4.4 Istream member functions

Function	Action
gcount	Returns the number of characters just extracted
get	Extracts the next character from the i/p stream or EOF
getline	Extracts characters until a delimeter is encountered or a specified maximum number of characters have been extracted
ignore	Skips characters in the input stream
peek	Returns the next character but does not extract it
putback	Inserts a character back into the input stream
read	Extracts a set number of characters into an array
seekg	Moves to an absolute position in the stream
tellg	Returns the current stream position

The get() function has a number of forms:

```
1. int get();
2. istream& get(signed char* buf, int len, char delimiter ='\n');
3. istream& get(unsigned char* buf, int len, char delimeter='\n');
4. istream& get(signed char& c);
```

```
5. istream& get(unsigned char& c);
6. istream& get(streambuf&, char delimeter = '\n');
```

Function 1, which we have already used, is the least powerful and can be used to extract the next character from the input stream. If the end of file is reached then this character is also extracted. Functions 2 and 3 behave in the same way but either for `signed` or `unsigned` chars. These continue to extract characters either until the delimeter is encountered or until len-1 bytes have been read or until EOF is encountered. The delimeter is not added to the extracted characters but a terminating null is. An error will only occur if no characters are extracted. Versions 4 and 5 extract a single character into the reference variable specified. Finally, Version 6 enables characters to be extracted into the specified `streambuf` until the `delimeter` is encountered. Note that for Versions 2, 3 and 6 the default `delimeter` is the new line character, so a call of:

```
cin.get(buf, 80);
```

will read in a line of characters i.e. read characters until ENTER is pressed, whereas:

```
cin.get(buf, 40, "*");
```

will read in characters (to a maximum of 39) until the * is encountered. Obviously for either of these statements to work correctly we must declare two character arrays with at least 80 and 40 elements respectively (e.g. `char buf[80]`).

This brings us on to the `getline()` function which has two forms, one for signed characters and one for unsigned characters:

```
1. istream& getline(signed char*, int, char = '\n');
2. istream& getline(unsigned char*, int, char = '\n');
```

These functions work in exactly the same way as their corresponding `get()` functions (i.e. 2 and 3 above) except that the delimiter is extracted and discarded, it is not added to the other characters read. Program 4.4 illustrates the use of some of these input functions.

☐ Program 4.4
```
//: GET.cpp
//. illustrating get() and getline()

#include <iostream.h>

void main(){
    char buf[80];
```

```
        int i = 0;

        cout << " GET " << endl;
        cout << " === " << endl << endl;
        cin.get(buf, 10, '*');
        cout << endl << "From get: " << endl;
        cout << buf << endl;

        cin.getline(buf, 10, '*');
        cout << endl << "From getline: " << endl;
        cout << buf << endl;
    }
```

The first `cin` statement uses `get()` to read into `buf` a maximum of 9 characters, or until an `*` is entered, whilst the second `cin` statement uses `getline()`. First note that for either of these statements to work some text has to be entered and sent to the input stream by pressing ENTER. Some examples of text entered for program get to read are:

1. `"an *"`   less than 10 characters with terminating `*`
2. `"123456789*"`   10 characters – tenth being `*`
3. `"longer input and *"`   more than 10 characters and `*`
4. `"longer input"`   more than 10 characters – no `*`

It is instructive to experiment with these various input data – the results are summarised in Table 4.5.

Table 4.5 Possible output from Get.cpp

Ref.	Input to `get()`	Output	Input to `getline()`	Output
1.	an *	an	none required	\n
2.	123456789*	123456789	none required	\n
3.	longer input and an *	longer in	none required	put and a
4.	longer input	longer in	an *	an
5.	longer input	longer in	more input	more inpu

The first important point about these results is that in all three cases when an asterisk has been entered, because it is not extracted by `get()` but just "looked at" and therefore still left to be read, any subsequent call of `getline()` or `get()` which uses the `*` as a delimiter will see the same `*` and terminate. Thus in Cases 1 and 2 the output as a result of the `getline()` call is just a new line and in Case 3 the next 9 characters are extracted. The second point to note is illustrated by Cases 3 and 5. Since no `*` is encountered, `get()` reads the first 9 characters entered, and then more data is required for `getline()` to read. Finally, in Case 4 a subsequent call to `get()`, or `getline()` will require new input either because the delimiter has been extracted by `getline()` and discarded (Case 4), or more than 9 characters have been read (Case 5).

The above analysis should help to make it clear that you need to be very careful when using these input functions. As with standard I/O it is easy to write code which can fail in certain cases. It is therefore very important to thoroughly test any input routines before incorporating them into a larger program. (This is of course true of any routines, but given the nature of some of the problems encountered with input and the many different possibilities for erroneous input by the user thorough testing is especially important here.)

4.5   File I/O with C++

It only remains, in this chapter on input and output, to deal briefly with file I/O. Much of our previous discussion in this Chapter applies to file I/O so we only mention in this section any important differences and additions.

First, in order to use file I/O you will need to include the header file `fstream.h` in your program. This header file contains definitions for several classes which have counterparts in the I/O classes which we have just been looking at. In particular it contains the classes `ifstream`, `ofstream` and `fstream` which correspond to (and are, in part, derived respectively from) `istream`, `ostream` and `iostream`. Since `istream` and `ostream` are derived from `ios` the file classes have access to the `ios` functions and operations which we looked at earlier.

Once the header file is included in your program, the next important set of operations which must be carried out is to declare an `fstream` object and use this to specify and open a file. This can be carried in a number of ways. The first is by means a declaration and call of the `open()` function. For example:

```
ofstream outfile; // declare ofstream object
outfile.open("c:\\cpp\\testdata", ios::out, 0);
```

will open the file `c:\cpp\testdata` for normal output, whereas:

```
ofstream outfile; // declare ofstream object
outfile.open("c:\\cpp\\testdata", ios::app, 0);
```

will open the same file for appending to, and:

```
ifstream myinput; // declare ifstream object
myinput.open("c:\\cpp\\testdata", ios::in, 0);
```

will open the file for input. This method gives the most control over how a file is to be opened and for what purpose. The syntax of the open method is:

```
void open(char *filename, int mode, int access);
```

where *filename, as we have seen, is the filename, including the path where necessary, of the file to be opened, mode is one or more of the constants given in Table 4.6 and access is an integer specifying the type of access (see Table 4.7).

Table 4.6 File mode types

Mode	Description
ios::app	Open file for appending to end of existing file
ios::ate	Finds end-of-file, but unlike ios::app operations can occur anywhere in the file
ios::in	Open file for input – usually redundant
ios::nocreate	Only successful if the file already exists
ios::noreplace	Only successful if the file does not already exist
ios::out	Open file for output – usually redundant
ios::trunc	Opens already existing files, destroys all data and sets the file length to zero

The above modes can be combined using the bitwise or operator (|), for example to open a file for reading from and writing to – ios::in | ios::out. As indicated in the Table 4.6, ios::in and ios::out will not normally be used (excepted in the example just mentioned) since using ifstream or ofstream of necessity implies input or output respectively.

The access code will only be used in special circumstances – e.g. when writing operating systems. The codes given in Table 4.7 correspond to the DOS attribute codes – for other operating systems you will need to check your operating system manual for the values and their meaning.

Table 4.7 Access values for DOS

Access	Description
0	Normal access
1	Read only access
2	Hidden file
4	System file
8	Set archive bit

An alternative, simpler, and more common method of opening files includes all the above operations in one declaration. Thus the first example could be written more concisely as:

```
ofstream outfile("c:\\cpp\\testdata");
```

and the third example as:

```
istream myinput("c:\\cpp\\testdata");
```

4.5.1 Text input and output

Once a file has been opened the next stage is to either read data from it or
write data to it. As far as basic text I/O is concerned these operations are the
same as for console (screen) I/O except that instead of using cin and cout we
use the stream which has already been linked to a file by one of the methods
just mentioned. Thus the following program fragment will read and display a
character, a string and an integer read from a file linked to myinput.

```
char c, string[30];
int n;
myinput >> c;
myinput >> string >> n;
cout << " c = " << c << endl;
cout << " string = " << string << endl;
cout << " n = " << n << endl;
```

As with normal input using >> white spaces will be skipped on input. Thus a
string such as "The House at Pooh Corner" stored in a file, will if read using

```
myinput >> string;
```

will only read into string "The" and leave the remaining characters to be read
by any subsequent input statement. In order to overcome such problems, as
well as for other reasons, it is often necessary to use binary input and output
to which we now turn our attention.

4.5.2 Binary input and output

A binary file is opened in the same manner as described above – the differences arise in how the data is transferred to and from the file. Two methods
are available – reading and writing single bytes or reading and writing blocks
of (binary) data.

Single byte transfer uses the two functions put() and get(), which have
the following basic syntax:

```
ostream &put(char ch);
istream &get(char &ch);
```

As we saw earlier (Section 4.4) the get() function has many forms – only the
simplest will be used in this section. On the other hand the put() function has
only the one form illustrated here.

Since get() reads single bytes from a file it can be used to read any file –
the exact nature of the data is irrelevant as far as binary reading (strictly byte
reading) is concerned. So Program 4.5 can be used to read and display the
contents of any file. The file to be read is specified on the command line e.g.

filelist address.dat will display the data stored in address.dat byte by byte, whereas filelist filelist.cpp will display the source file of filelist byte by byte and filelist filelist.exe will display the exe file byte by byte.

Program 4.5

```cpp
//: FILELIST.cpp
//. simple binary read - list a file byte by byte
#include <iostream.h>
#include <conio.h>
#include <stdlib.h>
#include <fstream.h>
void main(int argc, char *argv[]){
    char c;
    clrscr();
    cout << " FILELIST " << endl;
    cout << " ======== " << endl << endl;
    if (argc != 2){
        cout << " Incorrect usage: " << endl;
        cout << " Filelist filename" << endl;
        cout << " ... where filename is name of file to be listed "
                    << endl;
        exit(1);
    }
    ifstream ipfile(argv[1]);
    if (!ipfile){
        cout << " Unable to open file: " << argv[1] << endl;
        exit(1);
    }
    cout << " Contents of file: " << argv[1] << endl << endl;
    while(ipfile){
        ipfile.get(c);
        cout << c;
    }
    ipfile.close();
    getch();
}
```

When an end-of-file is reached the stream associated with the file becomes zero, which is why we can use the while statement in the form given (while(ipfile)). In fact, since ipfile.get(c) returns a reference to the stream ipfile, this will also be zero when the EOF is reached. We can therefore write an even more compact form of the while statement for reading the file:

```cpp
while( ipfile.get(c))
    cout << c;
```

The second method which can be used for binary input and output uses the functions read() and write(). These have the syntax:

```cpp
istream &read(unsigned char *buf, int n);
ostream &write(unsigned char *buf, int n);
```

in each case n bytes are transferred either from the file to a buffer pointed to by `buf` or from a buffer to the file. (Alternative versions of `read()` and `write()` are also available, in some implementations, which allow for signed chars to be transferred.)

4.6   Standard I/O

The standard I/O inherited from C uses both formatted and unformatted methods. Formatted I/O is most familiar in the guise of `printf()` for output and `scanf()` for input. Unformatted I/O uses functions like `getc()` and `putc()`, for single characters and `gets()` and `puts()` for a whole line of characters and blocks of data can be transferred using the `read()` and `write()` functions.

4.6.1 Formatted Output

As just mentioned, and as anyone familiar with C will know, the main function used for formatted output is `printf()`. However this is only a special case of a family of formatted output functions, a fact that is immediately obvious as they all contain the word `printf` in their function name (e.g. `sprinf()`, `fprintf()`). The `printf()` function has prototype:

```
int printf(const char *control_string, ...);
```

which shows that `printf()` is an `int` function and therefore will return an `int` value. In fact the value returned is the number of characters written, or a negative value if an error has occurred. The *control_string* (or *format_string*), which is enclosed in double quotes("), contains both text to be output and format specifiers which determine how the arguments are to be displayed. The ... (ellipsis) indicates that a variable number of arguments may follow the control string. This, by the way, can be used in any function definition where the number of arguments may vary. A detailed discussion of such functions – variadic functions – is however beyond the scope of this book.

The simplest example in which a `printf()` function might be used is one with only one argument – a double quoted string of characters, possibly including escape sequences (e.g. \n, \t, etc.). So `printf("Hello World\n");` is a valid if rather needless use of `printf()` – better would be `puts("Hello World");` or `cout << "Hello World" << endl;`.

When using more than one argument in a `printf()` function call care must be taken to ensure that the format specifiers match the argument types being output. Some examples of `printf()` statements used to output data are:

```
int i = 5, n;
float  x = 7.2;
char c = 'A';
```

```
char *str = "No. of characters written = ";
printf("i = %d", i);        // output i (5)
printf("character = %c", c);  // output character ('A')
n = printf("x = %4.1f\n", x);  // output        x = 7.2
printf("%s %d\n", str, n);   // output characters written (8)
```

The only comment which need be made concerning the above is to note that the `printf()` function returns the number of characters written – which is used in the last two examples.

4.6.2 Formatted input

Formatted input is accomplished using `scanf()`, as you will probably already be aware. This has a similar prototype to `printf`:

```
int scanf( char *control_string, argument1, ...);
```

The control string can take a variety of forms, but must include at least one format specifier similar to those used for `printf()`. As with `printf()`, `scanf()` returns an `int` value which, in this case, is the number of items of data successfully read. In the case of an error during input then `scanf()` returns EOF.

The arguments which contain the variables into which data is to be read are pointers and so the address of the variables must be passed to the `scanf()` function. Which, in the case of simple data types, usually means prefixing them with the address operator `&` (thus `scanf("%d", &n)` reads a decimal integer into the (`int`) variable n). In the case of strings where the variable name already refers to the address of the array of characters, there is no need for the address operator. Finally, if a pointer variable is passed to a function, and this is used in a `scanf()` statement, then again there is no need for the address operator. Thus if `pi` is a pointer to an `int`, as in this function:

```
void fun(int *pi)
```

then within the function this following statement would enable a value to be input from the keyboard

```
scanf("%d", pi);
```

Some simple examples of the use of `scanf()` are given next:

Declarations:

```
int n1, n2;  float f1, f2;   char c1, c2, c3; char s[6];
```

Statement	Valid Input	Invalid Input
1. `scanf("%d", &n1);`	24	29.0
2. `scanf("%d%f%d", &n1, &f1, &n2);`	12 1.6 9	23 2 12.1
	12 2 -7	c 2.4 5
3. `scanf("%c%c%c", &c1, &c2, &c3);`	abc	
	a b	
	1.5	
4. `scanf("%s", s);`	Hello	Goodbye

4.6.3 Unformatted Output

Unformatted output (and its converse unformatted input) is less complicated than the formatted output which we have already looked at, in that it deals almost entirely with the output of characters. The functions available are given in Table 4.8.

The `putchar()` function outputs a single character argument to the standard output device (`stdout`) which is normally the monitor. Output appears at the current cursor position on the screen. It is declared as returning an `int`, the value of which is the character written, if successful, or `EOF` if an error occurs.

The `puts()` function allows output of a string of characters to the screen. The character array argument is output to the screen at the current cursor position followed by a new-line character. You will often find `puts()` used when simple string output is required, instead of the more powerful `printf()`. The `printf()` function carries much unnecessary baggage with it when used for simple string output, i.e. when no numeric values are involved, whereas `puts()` takes up less room and uses less storage space. So in C programs or in C++ programs when the full power of C++ is not required it is often better to use `puts()` for string output.

Table 4.8 Unformated output

Function	Purpose	Header File
`putchar(char)`	output character to `stdout`	`stdio.h`
`putc(char, FILE)`	output character to a stream	`stdio.h`
`putch(char)`	output character to active text window	`conio.h`
`puts(char *)`	output string to `stdout` and append `'\n'`	`stdio.h`

4.6.4 Unformatted Input

Like its output counterpart this deals mainly with the reading of characters and is very useful for low-level input, i.e. when no format conversions are required immediately on input. Table 4.9 summarises the available functions.

Table 4.9 Unformatted input

Function	Purpose	Header File
getchar()	Input character from stdin	stdio.h
getc(FILE)	Input character from a stream	stdio.h
getche()	Input character from keyboard	conio.h
getch()	As for getche() but character not displayed	conio.h
gets(char *)	Input string from stdin	stdio.h

The function getchar() allows single character input from the standard input device – normally the keyboard. Any character is a valid character, thus any white space can be read (e.g. space, tab and new-line) as well as control keys (e.g. ESC, arrow-keys) and function keys. One of the difficulties with getchar() is that it is normally implemented using buffered input, so that the key strokes are not processed until the Enter key is pressed. As an alternative therefore two further function are available in most C environments – getch() and getche(). Although these are not part of the ANSI C standard they are to be found in the vast majority of implementations of C and C++. These provide very useful means of obtaining characters from the keyboard if for no other reason that the keystroke is processed as soon as the key is pressed – there is no necessity to press Enter to send the input to be processed. As indicated in the table the only difference between getch() and getche() is that the latter echoes the character to the screen. This facility is often not necessary, or even undesirable, and so getch() is frequently used for this purpose. Incidentally there is one further function which can be very useful when dealing with input from the keyboard. In some cases we don't want the program to wait around doing nothing and waiting for input – e.g. in a simple game program (using the keyboard, not the mouse). In such cases the function kbhit(), which is also prototyped in conio.h, comes in very useful. This returns a non-zero integer whenever a key has been pressed (not including Alt, Ctrl, Shift or CapsLock on their own). The key pressed can then be read by getch() or getche().

The function gets() reads in a line of text from the keyboard. The function is a char * function and so the value returned is the same as the contents of the string argument except, in the case of an error (or end-of-file), it returns NULL ('\0'). gets() also replaces the character '\n' used to terminate input, by '\0' thus ensuring that the string is terminated correctly.

4.7 Summary

This chapter has dealt with input and output in C++. There is only one exercise for this chapter but you should ensure that you try out the example programs given and use what you have learnt in any future programs you write or modify.

Topics covered:

- Stream I/O in C++ – `cout`, `cin`, `cerr` and `clog`.
- The I/O stream classes – `ios`, `istream`, `ostream` and `iostream`.
- The `ios` format state flags for formatted stream output.
- Stream output manipulators.
- `Istream` member functions (Table 4.6).
- File I/O in C++ – Text and binary I/O.
- Review of standard (C) I/O.

4.8 Exercise

4.8.1 Write a function which takes as a parameter an array of characters and displays them as part of the Contents page of a document. E.g the output from successive calls might be:

```
1......................Introduction
2...........Conditional Expressions
3.......................Functions
```

The maximum number of characters in the line (to include the number) should also be an argument to the function (so in the above example 36 characters would be specified). (Use `setfill(ch)` and `setw(w)`.)

5 Introducing Classes

5.1 Introduction

In this chapter we provide the basic ideas and the tools required to implement classes in C++. As you will be aware by now classes are fundamental to the philosophy of C++ and are a building block for object-oriented programming. You already encounter classes in-directly earlier in this book and this chapter will help you to understand how and why they are used. The implementation of abstract data types through encapsulation via the use of data members (attributes) and member functions (methods) is introduced. Managing access to class attributes and methods is discussed and the use of the keywords `public` and `private` demonstrated. We examine the use of constructors and destructors, and look briefly at constructor overloading (a more complete discussion of operator overloading follows in Chapter 6). Finally we look at the accessibility of class names (class scope) and the use of static attributes and methods. We begin our discussion by asking the question '*Why do we have classes?*'.

5.2 Why classes?

Classes provide a means of extending the basic data types available in C and C++. To understand the concept of classes we need first of all to understand how simple data types operate. Consider the built-in type double. This provides a representation of the mathematical concept of real numbers (albeit with restrictions –, e.g. not all the set of real numbers can be represented). In addition to the representation of the idea of a real number the double type also includes a set of operations that can be used with particular instances of type `double` (e.g. +, −, *, /) and a library of functions that can be used with `double` data types (e.g. `pow()`, `sqrt()` and `sin()`).

With the introduction of classes the user is able to create a representation of a concept (or idea) which has no obvious or direct counterpart among the built-in types. For example, in a drawing program the type *shape* might be defined. Such a type would allow for:

i) The definition of particular shapes (e.g. `square`, `triangle`, `circle`,...) and
ii) operations which could be performed on shapes (e.g. `move`, `rotate`, enlarge,...). Another example might be found in a word processing package where the type *paragraph* might be defined with the operations `indent`, `set_line_spacing`, `change_font`, etc.

Programs which closely match the ideas of the particular application under consideration, or problem being solved, are (usually) easier to understand and easier to modify than programs that do not. Two other advantages of well-chosen user defined types are i) programs are more concise and ii) illegal use of objects can be detected by the compiler instead of being delayed until rigorous testing has been carried out.

When defining a new type the aim should be to separate the implementation details (e.g. the way in which data is used to store an object of the declared type) from the aspects of the type which are essential to a correct use of it (e.g. the list of functions that can access the data). So, to return to the shape example, we do not need to worry about the exact way in which a shape is defined (in fact when setting up the generic type *shape* we may not know how to define all the shapes that might be used) – all we need to be concerned with, at this level, is what operations can be carried out on objects of type *shape*. (Of course we will have to be concerned with the details of how to define a square, a triangle, or a circle, etc. at some stage, but this concern can be separated from the functional or operational aspect.)

5.3 Class declaration

Now that we have looked briefly at why classes might be useful we continue, in this section, by taking a closer look at class declarations and some simple uses of class types and classes in C++.

5.3.1 Class declarations

The basic syntax for class declarations is:

```
class_key class_name <:base_list> {<member_list>};
```

where:

`class_key`	is one of the keywords *class*, *struct*, or *union*.
`class_name`	is a unique identifier (within its scope) which in certain instances (see later) can be omitted.
`base_list`	is an (optional) list (i.e. one or more) of class(es) from which `class_name` will derive (or inherit) attributes and methods.

`member_list` is a declaration of class members (i.e. attributes and methods) of `class_name`. These class members may have default and optional overriding access specifiers that may affect which functions can access which members (again these details will be explained later).

For the moment you can ignore the `<:base_list>` part of the class definition given above. The use of this will be introduced in a later chapter when we come to talk about inheritance. However the `class_key`, `class_name` and `<member_list>` will become very familiar to you by the time you have completed this chapter.

In C++ new types can be constructed using structures and unions as well as classes. Structures, unions and classes each provide variations on the implementation of abstract data types. You will be familiar with standard data types such as `int`, `float` and `char` and know that when a variable is declared, or a constant set up, as well as specifying the type of data that can be stored the operations which can be carried out on that object (variable or constant) are also specified. Abstract data types can be thought of as simply an extension of normal data types in that they also specify the type of data that can be stored (via the class attributes) and the operations which can be carried out on objects of that type (via the methods). Such types are called abstract because they abstract from, or take out from, the real world objects the essential elements. So we might model a bank account using an abstract data type and in doing so specify such elements as the type of account, amount in the account and overdraft limit and the operations which can be carried out on a bank account such as withdraw, deposit, list the balance and so on.

In order to specify which type of class is being constructed we use a `class_key` (`struct`, `union` or `class`). Such a class declaration creates a unique class type (user-defined type – called `class_name` in the above definition). Once this has been created the programmer (you!) can declare further objects (or instances) of this type as well as objects derived from this type (e.g. pointers to, references to, arrays of `class_name`, etc.).

For example we can construct classes, structures and unions of various kinds, as follows:

```
    // a class definition
class    class_c { ... };

    // now some declarations (instances)
class_c c,       // an object c
    &cr = c,     // reference to object of type class_c
    *cptr,       // pointer to object of type class_c
    carray[10];  // and array of class_c
    // a struct definition
struct  struct_s { ... };
```

```
        // ... and some declarations
struct_s s, &sr = s, *sptr, sarray[10];

        // in C this would be:
        // struct struct_s s, *sptr, sarray[10];
        // note can't have references in C
        // a union definition
union   union_u { ... };
        // a union provides a means
        // whereby data can share storage

        // .. and some union declarations
union_u u, &u = u, *uptr, uarray[10];

        // again in C this would be:
        // union union_u u, *uptr, uarray[10];
        // and again no reference variable in C
```

The examples just given help to illustrate how structures in C++ are a 'midway house' on the road to classes – they can contain member functions in addition to data members, but these functions are public functions as so available to any block in which such a structure is declared. Although object-oriented programming purists would argue that there is no need for such intermediate forms of classes, two points are worth making:

- There may be occasions when the full power of classes is not required to solve a problem and structures with public member functions may well suffice (and in some cases we may not even need structures!).
- The history of C++. This is because the language grew out of C and so, by including structures as a lower form of class, the provision was made for 'a smooth and gradual transition from traditional C-style programming, through data abstraction, to object oriented programming.' [1].

It is important to note the difference between struct and union declarations in C and C++ – the keywords struct and union are essential in C but they are only necessary in C++ when class names, e.g. struct_s and union_u, are hidden (see later).

5.4 Example - the date class

Now that the essential elements of classes have been introduced we can return to the problem discussed in Chapter 2 – that of creating a date abstract data type. You may recall that we were attempting to create an abstract data type for date so that only certain operations could be carried out on date objects. Our last attempt (Section 2.6), that of using member functions of the date defined as a struct fails to provide total encapsulation as it is still possible to access elements in the `date` structure, as we now go on to illustrate.

Suppose another user of date needs to find yesterday's date, as well as tomorrow's, you might think that all the user needs to do is to write a function `prev()` like this:

```
void date::prev() {
        day--;
}
```

However, since the function `prev()` is not a member function of `date`, the compiler objects and the attempt to get at the previous day fails. Obviously one way of gaining access to the `date` members is to prototype `prev()` in the structure `date`, thus making it a member function along with the `set()`, `next()` and `print()` functions. However that presupposes that everyone has access to the structure definition, which normally they would not. But all is not lost, our programmer can still get around this problem by passing a reference to a variable of type `date` and then modifying the `day` part, as here:

```
// passing a reference to the date struct
void prev(date &dte) {
        dte.day--;
}
```

This might then be used like this:

```
today.set(2, 3, 1994);
prev(today);
cout << endl << " . yesterday was : ";
today.print();
```

So, the public still have access!

The final solution, which provides complete encapsulation, is to use a `class`, instead of a `struct`, to define `date`. This gives us:

```
// date as a class
class date {
   char day, month;
   int year;

public:
   void set(char d, char m, int y) ;
   void next();
   void print();
};
```

with the functions defined later in the program (or for larger programs in a separate file) as follows:

```
void date::set(char d, char m, int y) {
   day = d;
```

```
        month = m;
        year = y;
}

void date::next() {
    day++;
}

void date::print() {
    cout << (int) day << " \ "
        << (int) month << " \ " << year;
}
```

Now, the only functions that can operate on objects of type `date` are those included in the original class definition (i.e. `set()`, `next()` and `print()`). If we try to declare another function, e.g. `prev()`, even by using `date::prev()` we cannot succeed, or by passing a reference to date and using a function such as `void prev(date *dte){ dte->day--; }` – neither of these attempts succeeds. Only by including the prototype for `prev()` in the class declaration for `date` can we finally use the `prev()` function. So we have at last reached a watertight abstract data type – only those functions (methods) specified in the class definition for date can use its data members (attributes – i.e. day, month and year).

5.5   Public and private

5.5.1   The important difference

In the `date` class which we have just been discussing we used a new keyword from the C++ list, i.e. public. This is used within a class definition to indicate that data members and/or member functions which follow are available in any block in which objects of this type are declared. If we omit the word public from our class definition then these member functions (in this case `set()`, `next()` and `print()`) will only be available within the class definition – which means the class has no means of communicating with the outside world!

This point also illustrates a crucial difference between structures and classes: in a `struct` definition all functions and data members are public – in a class definition all functions and data members are *by default* private.

The private nature of elements in a class definition can be emphasised by including the keyword `private` in the definition. So, for example, this definition of `date` is equivalent to the previous one:

```
// date as a class - making explicit use of private
    class date {
    private:
```

```
      char day, month;
      int year;
   public:
      void set(char d, char m, int y) ;
      void next();
      void print();
   };
```

Incidentally there is no reason why the order should be as above, we could just as easily write:

```
// date as a class
   class date {
   public:
      void set(char d, char m, int y) ;
      void next();
      void print();
   private:
      char day, month;
      int year;
   };
```

You may find classes defined using all of the three formats just described. Some authors and programmers include the private keyword to emphasise that what follows are private data members or member functions, however we will continue with the first method which doesn't require the explicit use of private and groups all the public class members together at the end of the class definition.

Finally there is one other keyword that you should be aware of which restricts the availability of data members and functions – that is protected. We will discuss the use of this later.

5.5.2 Data abstraction and abstract data types

At this point, after introducing some basic ideas concerning classes, it is worth returning to a brief discussion of abstract data types and data abstraction which we began earlier. In the date class that we finally arrived at we have employed the concept of data abstraction to create an abstract data type. Such types combine the data structure and the operations on that data structure into one entity, an abstract data type. One consequence is that a means is provided of restricting access to a data structure to an explicitly declared list of functions – either member functions such as set(), next() and print() or friend functions which we shall introduce shortly. Creating user-defined types in this way has a number of advantages:

- A self-contained module is created which contains the data structure and the operations which can be carried out on that data structure.
- The way in which the new type is implemented is hidden from the user of the type.

- Any errors, e.g. causing an illegal date, must be caused by code in a member function – so debugging begins by localising the problem – even before the program is run!
- Potential users of such a type need only examine the definitions of the member functions in order to learn how to use them.

The idea of abstract data types is not unique to C++ and applications can be found in most high-level procedural languages. As such they are not confined to object-oriented programming (OOP), however they are a necessary precursor of the approach adopted in OOP.

5.6 Unions

As mentioned above unions are another member of the family of classes, similar to structures but where different objects can be stored at different times and therefore allowing storage to be shared. The amount of storage allocated will be that of the largest object. So suppose we want to store a date as dd mm yyyy or as dd month yyyy, where each d, m and y represents a decimal digit and month represents the month as text (e.g. January, April, October). We construct a union which looks like:

```
union{        // anonymous union
   char mm;
   char month[9];
};
```

and then use it in our date class:

```
class date {
   char day;
   union{      // anonymous union
      char mm;          char month[9];
   };
   int year;
public:
   void set( char d, char m, int y) ;
   void next();
   void print();
};
```

In this example the union is an anonymous union because there is no name attached to it and no variables declared using it – the only code that has access to its two members is code in the same block, i.e. in the class date. A more general form of union declaration was given in Section 5.3 and takes the form:

```
union <union_type> { member_list; } <name_list>;
```

and, in general terms, behaves like a `struct` data type.

Even though we have created a union, on its own, this isn't sufficient to allow us to use `month`. We need functions to allow us to select the correct version of the union. All the functions we have written for this class need modification: in `set()` we need to know whether we have the numeric or text form for the month, as we do also for `print()`. The `next()` function is even more problematic since it is not obvious how we increment `month` when it is in the text form. We will address each of these difficulties in turn.

First then for the function `set()`. We can use the idea of function overloading here (see Chapter 6) and have two versions of `set()`: one as in the original and the other with an array of `char` for the `month` argument. The correct version of `set()` will then be selected automatically depending on the type of the "month" parameter. So we have:

```
void date::set(char d, int m, int y) {
    day = d;
    mm = m;
    year = y;
    m_type = 0;   // flag set to 0 to indicate
                  // numeric version used
}

void date::set(char d, char pm[], int y) {
    day = d;
    strcpy(month, pm);
    year = y;
    m_type = 1;   // flag set to 1 to indicate text
                  // version used
}
```

Notice the difference in the argument `list` for these two `set()` functions. The first uses an `int` for the `month` variable, the second an array of char (`pm[]`). (Recall that it is essential that either the type or number of parameters differs in overloaded functions.) Notice also that we have used a string function `strcpy()` to allow us to copy characters from the array `pm` to `month` (`strcpy()` is in `string.h` which must be included along with the normal header files).

On its own though function overloading of `set()` is not enough, we will need to tell the other functions, e.g. `print()` which version of month is currently being used so that the correct `cout` statement can be used. We can achieve this by setting a flag (`m_type`) − set to 0 if we are using the numeric version and 1 if the text version is being used. `m_type` must now be declared as a private member of date. So the definition of date becomes:

```
class date {
    char day;
    union {     // anonymous union
        char mm;
        char month[9];
```

```
    };
    int year;
    int m_type;   // flag indicating month type
              // (numeric or text)
public:
    void set(char d, int m, int y);
    void set(char d, char pm[], int y);
    void print();// next() not included for this
              // 1st version
};
```

Finally the modification to `print()`. This simply involves checking `m_type` and printing the correct version of the date.

```
void date::print() {
    if (m_type == 0)
        cout << (int) day << " / " << (int) mm
             << " / " << year;
    else if (m_type == 1)
        cout << (int) day << " " << month << " "
             << year;
    cout << endl;
}
```

Now that we have defined our new date class this might be used as illustrated in Program 5.1.

Program 5.1

```
//: DATEC1U.cpp -- dates using a date class
//. with member functions and month as a union

#include <iostream.h>
#include <conio.h>
#include <string.h>
// ...............................................
class date {
    char day;
    union {          // anonymous union
        char mm;
        char month[9];
    };
    int year;
    int m_type;

public:
    void set(char d, int m, int y);
    void set(char d, char pm[], int y);
    void print();
};
// date member functions defined here
    ...
// ...............................................
void main()
{
    date day;
```

```
    clrscr();

    cout << " DATEC1U - using class & a union\n";
    cout << " ==============================\n\n";

    //day.set(2, 3, 1994);
    cout << " today is : ";
    day.print();

    cout << "\n Now for the text version ... " << endl;
    day.set(2, "March", 1994);
    cout << " today is : ";
    day.print();
    cout << " \nPress <ENTER> to Quit ";
    cin.get();
}
```

Provided that we insert all the required member function definitions the above program should work correctly with the data given. However if we comment out the first call to set() i.e. day.set(2, 3, 1994); then we may get surprising results. If you have your computer handy then enter Program 5.1 and try it out, then comment out the statement as suggested. What result do you get? Section 5.7 we will go on to explain what has happened and how we might get around our problem.

5.7 Constructors

When an attempt is made to output an unset date (as above) the output, from the first call to print(), will be undefined because m_type has not been given a value. It may be zero, or any other value, depending on your compiler. This obviously is not very satisfactory. What we really need is to be able to give m_type an initial value, as soon as a object of type date is declared (or instantiated, or created). We can do this by using a *constructor* function. Constructors have the same name as the class object and there can be more than one of them – in other words we can create overloaded constructors, just as we can create any other overloaded function. For the moment we will just add one constructor to our date class. This will be inserted into the public section of the class definition could look like this:

```
    date() { m_type = -1;} // constructor to trap unset dates
```

Remembering that we need to be able to distinguish, not only between dates which have been given a value and dates which haven't, but also between the two date formats (DD/MM/YYYY and DD/MONTH/YYYY) suggests that an enumerated data type might be used for m_type. This might consist of three integer values with names such as `numeric`, `text` and `invalid`. The constructor function (which doesn't set the date) will therefore set `m_type` to invalid, as is illustrated in the following definition of our `date` class.

```
class date {
    enum {              // help to clarify the code!
        numeric,
        text,
        invalid         // used to prevent garbage being
                        // output if date not set
    } m_type;
    char day;
    union {             // anonymous union
        int mm;
        char month[9];
    };
    int year;
public:
    date() { m_type = invalid; }
            // constructor - used to initialise
            // m_type so that unset dates can
            // be trapped
    void set(char d, int m, int y);
    void set(char d, char pm[], int y);
    void print();
};
```

Since we will not require any other instances of the enumerated type we can append the `m_type` variable name to the end of the `enum` definition, thus creating an untagged enumeration.

There are various improvements we could make to this `date` class, some of which are left as exercises, however before leaving you to try some out for yourself it would be useful to add a function to enable the user to enter a date from the keyboard. The simplest solution is to tell the user to enter the date in numeric form and then read in the date in that form. (We could if we wish add error trapping so that an invalid date format is disallowed.) One solution is:

```
void date::get() {
    cout << "Enter a date in the form 25 12 1996 > ";
    cin >> day >> mm >> year;
}
```

However this, on its own is not sufficient, as although this appears to work correctly, when we try to display the date we entered we get the message

```
*** DATE NOT SET ***
```

The reason for this is because the month flag (`m_type`) is still set to invalid. There are two ways round this, one is to set `m_type` explicitly inside our new function (i.e. `m_type = numeric`) the other is to call `set()` which will do that task for us.

There are still more problems lurking in this function. We need to remember the definition we have used for our date class. In the earlier discussion we decided that since day could be no bigger than 31 we could use a char type for it. So even if we add the explicit setting of m_type to our get() function we will get the wrong day from our keyboard input. Taking this last consideration into account indicates that using the set() function is the better of the two options we discussed above – it sets the date up correctly and sets m_type. It is also better from the point of view of data hiding. We have a function set() (actually two functions) which is used solely for the purpose of setting the date up, so why not use it? There is then less likelihood of incorrect values being passed or the function behaving incorrectly. So our new function get() becomes:

```
void date::get() {
    int d, m , y;

    cout << "Enter a date in the form 25 12 1996 > ";
    cin >> d >> m >> y;
    set(d, m, y);
}
```

As promised above you will get a chance to improve the date class – you will find suggestions in the exercise at the end of the chapter.

Whilst constructors are often used for initialising important data members, as in the example we have been discussing, they are also frequently used to enable objects themselves to be initialised. Consider the class oblong, which has two attributes – height and width – and take a look at the following two constructors:

```
oblong(){}
```

and

```
oblong(int h, int w){ height = h; width = w; }
```

In the first of these we have a constructor which can be used to create an uninitialised object when it is declared, via

```
oblong o1;
```

In the second constructor we use two arguments to the constructor so that initialisation is possible when an object is declared, e.g.:

```
oblong o2(2, 6);
```

We could even create another constructor which uses one argument and so sets up a square, for example:

```
oblong(int h) { ht = width = h; } // create a square
```

which might be used like this:

```
oblong o3(4);
```

All three of the above constructors are used in Program 5.2, try it out before reading on.

▢ Program 5.2

```
//: OBLONG.cpp
//. overloading constructors

#include <conio.h>
#include <iostream.h>
// ..........................................................
// class definition of oblong
class oblong {
    int height, width;
public:
    oblong(){} // constructor for oblong
    oblong( int h, int w) { height = h; width = w; }
            // another constructor
    oblong( int h){ height = width = h; }
            // overload again - create a square
    void set( int h, int w) { height = h; width = w; }
    int area(){ return height * width; }
};
// ..........................................................
void main() {
    oblong o1;        // an uninitialised oblong
    oblong o2(2, 6);   // an oblong 2 x 6 units
    oblong o3(8);     // create a square of side 8 units

    clrscr();
    cout << " OBLONG " << endl;
    cout << " ====== " << endl;

    cout << endl << " o1: area = " << o1.area() << endl;
    cout << endl << " o2: area = " << o2.area() << endl;
    cout << endl << " o3: area = " << o3.area() << endl;
    o1.set(5, 9);
    cout << endl << " after: o1.set(5.9); " << endl;
    cout << endl << " 01: area = " << o1.area() << endl;
    o1 = o2;
    cout << endl << " after: o1 = o2; " << endl;
    cout << endl << " o1: area = " << o1.area() << endl;
    cout << " Press any key to Quit ";
    getch();
}
```

5.8 Destructors

The proper management of memory by a program is of vital importance if we are not going to run the risk of running out of storage space or causing other undesirable mishaps! Whenever we declare an object we use a constructor member function to allocate storage. Once we have finished with the object we ideally want the storage used by that object to be released so that other elements in the program can use it. This is achieved in C++ by using a destructor function. As with constructor functions, a destructor does not have a data type specifier, not even void, but it differs from a constructor function in tat it cannot have any arguments. The general form of a destructor declaration is:

```
~myclass();
```

and its definition is:

```
myclass::~myclass(){ // body of destructor }
```

Notice that the tilde (~) is used to denote a destructor function.

In the absence of any explicit definition of a destructor C++ will use a default destructor when an object goes out of scope. In many cases this may be sufficient, but there are times when you will need to write your own destructor function to ensure that objects are destroyed correctly and memory is released properly. To illustrate the use of a destructor we will look at a simple example of setting up a dynamic array.

We can construct an array class consisting of an int (size) which holds the number of elements in the array and a pointer to an int (*pn), i.e.

```
class intarray() {
   int size, *pn;
...
}
```

A constructor `intarray(int n);` can then be used to create objects of any size we wish, e.g.

```
intarray(int n) {
   size = n;
   pn = new int[size];
   if (!pn) {
      cout << "** Insufficient memory available **" << endl;
      size = 0;
      exit(1);
   }
}
```

This constructor member function assigns `size` to the `int` argument n and attempts to allocate storage for the `int` array. We have included in this function a primitive form of error trapping to stop the program in a controlled manner if we run out of memory while trying to set up an array. It is advisable to include something similar to this (usually it would be more sophisticated to enable the program to continue) to prevent an uncontrolled crash of the program. Now take a look at the Program 5.3 (`INTARR1.cpp`).

Program 5.3

```
//: INTARR1.cpp
//. illustrating a constructor function

#include <conio.h>
#include <iostream.h>
#include <stdlib.h>
// .........................................................
class intarray {
    int size, *pn;  // size - no. of elements
            // pn used to point to first
            element
public:
    intarray(int n);   // constructor
    void print(char *mess);
};

intarray::intarray(int n) {
    size = n;
    pn = new int[size];
    if (!pn) {
      cout << " *** Insufficient memory to create array *** " << end
      size = 0;
      exit(1);
    }
}

void intarray::print(char *mess) {
    cout << mess;
    cout << "   size = " << size << endl;
    cout << " &pn[0] = " << &pn[0] << endl;
    for ( int i = 0; i < size; i++ )
       cout << pn[i] << " ";
    cout << endl;
}
// .........................................................
void main(void) {
    intarray a(8);
    clrscr();
    cout << " INTARR1 " << endl;
    cout << " ======= " << endl << endl;

    a.print(" a:");
    cout << " &a: " << &a << endl;
    // start another block
    {
```

```
        intarray b(5);
        b.print(" b:");
        cout << " &b: " << &b << endl;
    }
    intarray c(3);
    c.print(" c:");
    cout << " &c: " << &c << endl;
    cout << " Press any key to Quit ";
    getch();
}
```

This program simply creates three objects a, b and c of different sizes. It then displays the addresses of these intarray objects together with the contents of the uninitialised elements. Test run 5.1 shows a sample run.

🖳 **Test run 5.1**

```
INTARR1
=======

a: size = 8
&pn[0] = 0x369b103e
-11516 17387 -15988 -13565 -15997 -29664 15304 29640
&a: 0x369bfff2

b: size = 5
&pn[0] = 0x369b1052
-25567 -29178 1286 -5981 -8938
&b: 0x369bffea

c: size = 3
&pn[0] = 0x369b1060
1907 -17913 -26820
&c: 0x369bffee

Press any key to Quit
```

The different (uninitialised) values given to each element of the three arrays should be sufficient to show that different portions of memory are allocated when the objects are created, however the program also displays the starting address of the array created by intarray and you can check that these are also all different. Note in addition that the objects also each have different base addresses.

Now let's add the destructor function to the program. The definition for this is:

```
intarray::~intarray() {
    delete [] pn;
    cout << "destructor called" << endl;
}
```

Including this function in the above program and running it produces Test run 5.2 (some blank lines have been omitted to save space).

```
INTARR2
=======
a: size = 8
&pn[0] = 0x36a01050
-16701 129 30143 13213 13257 -5934 -765 -195
&a: 0x36a0fff2

b: size = 5
&pn[0] = 0x36a01064
0 20597 16000 -20619 29958
&b: 0x36a0ffea

destructor called

c: size = 3
&pn[0] = 0x36a01064
0 20597 16000
&c: 0x36a0ffee
Press any key to Quit
destructor called
destructor called
```

Now if you take a close look at the output from this program you will notice that the three elements of array c are the same as the first three elements of array b. Again, as a check the address of the first element of pn is also the same for arrays b and c. What has in fact happened is that the destructor has released the memory used by b (after exiting the block in which b is declared) which has then been used by c.

Notice also in the output from this program that the message "destructor called" appears twice more right at the end of the output. The reason for this is that objects a and c are destroyed on exit from the main() block (i.e. after passing the last }).

These two program also include one further useful construct. Namely the way the print() function is written. When using classes, and especially when checking output with numerous objects of the same class, it is useful to know which object we are looking at! The print() function we use here illustrates one way of doing that. We pass a pointer to a char into the print() member function, this message is then displayed whenever print() is called. Then each time we use print() we include a suitable argument so we know which object is being referred to (e.g. a.print("a:");).

5.9 Class name scope

The scope (i.e. availability) of a class name is local but with some exceptions! A class name comes into scope at the point of declaration and ends at the end of the enclosing block. A class name hides any class, object, enumerator, or function with the same name in the enclosing block. If an object, enumerator, or function is declared within the same block (i.e. having the same scope) then the relevant elaborated type specifier (class, struct, or union) is required when declaring new objects. For example:

```
struct a{...};  // declaration of some struct a

int a(struct a *aptr); // function declaration -
   // different from struct a

void main(void) {
   a t; // Illegal declaration - elaborated
      // type specifier missing and function
      // a in scope
   struct a t; // this is OK - elaborated with
         // struct (class key)
   a(&s);  // also OK - a function call
}
```

In the above extract there is obviously a name clash between the structure a and the function a. This becomes apparent when we try to declare a variable t (a t) but it can be overcome by including the class key (in this case struct) in the declaration of t.

A further illustration is given in Program 5.4 (SCOPEC2A.cpp).

Program 5.4

```
//: SCOPEC2A.cpp -- the scope of classes
//. using class to prevent the clash of identifiers

#include <iostream.h>
#include <conio.h>

int num;        // global scope
// .............................................
class num {             // class declaration
   int a;
public:
   num(int i){ a = i;}
   int print() { return a; }
};
// .............................................
void main(void)
{
   class num j(2); // declare object j of type num & set to 2
      // note that the elaborated type specifier 'class'
      // is required to prevent the clash between
      // the int variable num and the class num

   clrscr();

   cout << " Classes and scope - scopec2a" << endl;
   cout << " ============================" << endl;
```

```
        cout << " outside main(): " << endl;
        cout << " int num;        // num declared as int" << endl;
        cout << " class num {     // class num also declared"
                        << endl;
        cout << "     int a; " << endl;
        cout << " public: " << endl;
        cout << "        num(int i){ a = i; } // constructor "
                        << endl;
        cout << "     int print() { return a; } " << endl;
        cout << " }; " << endl << endl;
        cout << " within main(): " << endl;
        cout << " class num j(2); // j declared of type class num &
                initialised " << endl;
        cout << "                  // variable num can still be seen
                because " << endl;
        cout << "                  // class is used in the
                declaration of j " << endl;
        cout << " j.print() = " << j.print();
        cout << "    // uses member function print to return a(=2)";
        cout << endl;

        cout << "                       // can still access the int
                variable num, e.g. " << endl;
        cout << " num = 99; " << endl;
        num = 99;

        cout << " .. so int variable num = " << num << endl;
        cout << " *** now remove class from the declaration of j
                ***";
        cout << endl;
        cout << " *** recompile and see what happens ***" << endl;

        cout << " \nPress any key to Quit ";
        getch();
}
```

If you try this program out will find that both the `class num` and the `int num` can be accessed even though they are both in scope, provided that the `class` keyword is used in the declaration of `j`. However if the `class` keyword is removed from the declaration of `j` then a compilation error will result – actually two errors one indicating that a semi-colon is expected after the `j`, in the line `num j(2);`, and a second when (the intended object) `j` is used to call the `print()` where we get a message of the form "undefined symbol j".

Normally such problems as have been illustrated above should not arise since good programming practice dictates that sensible and unique names are used for identifiers (and user-defined types such as classes). However it is possible that when using or reusing libraries of classes or functions such clashes may occur. In which case this discussion will hopefully prove to be of some use!

5.10 Using static class members

Whenever an object is created of a particular class all the data members in that class have storage space allocated to them. Thus if a class includes data members `char day`, `char month` and `int year` and two objects are created, `date1` and `date2`, say, then both `date1` and `date2` will have independent storage for `day`, `month` and `year`. Sometimes it is useful, or necessary, to have only one instance of a data member created no matter how many objects of that type there are. A simple example might be if we wish to keep track of how many objects have been created. We can achieve this by declaring the data member as static. Take a look at Program 5.5 (`STATDM.cpp`) which creates a number of instances of the class `some_class` and uses a member function (`how_many()`) to check on the number currently "alive". Test run 5.3 shows a sample run.

📋 **Program 5.5**

```
//: STATDM.cpp
//. using a static data member in a class

#include <conio.h>
#include <iostream.h>
// ..........................................................
class some_class {
   static int count;
public:
   some_class() { count++; // increment count when
              // constructor called
      cout << " create an object " << endl; }
   ~some_class() { count--;  // decrement count when
              // destructor is called
      cout << " destroy an object " << endl; }
   void how_many() {
      cout << " No. of objects of 'some_class' = "
                  << count << endl;
   }
};
// ..........................................................
int some_class::count = 0; // initialise (and define) count
// ..........................................................
void main(void) {

   clrscr();
   cout << " STATDM " << endl;
   cout << " ====== " << endl << endl;

   some_class a;
   a.how_many();
   { // start another block
     some_class b;
     b.how_many();
     {  // and another block
```

```
        some_class c;
        a.how_many();
      }
      // c no longer exists
      b.how_many();
    }
    // b no longer exists
    a.how_many();
    some_class d;
    d.how_many();
    cout << " Press any key to Quit " << endl;
    getch();
}
```

```
create an object
No. of objects of 'some_class' = 1
create an object
No. of objects of 'some_class' = 2
create an object
No. of objects of 'some_class' = 3
destroy an object
No. of objects of 'some_class' = 2
destroy an object
No. of objects of 'some_class' = 1
create an object
No. of objects of 'some_class' = 2
Press any key to Quit
destroy an object
destroy an object
```

This output shows that count is keeps track of the number of objects created. Now take a closer look at the program. In particular notice the way we have declared (not defined) count in the class some_class:

```
static int count;  // declaration
```

this simply tells the compiler to retain the value of count between uses. However we don't initialise count at this point – this has to be done outwith the class definition and before any objects of some_class have been created. This is done globally (i.e. outside main()):

```
int some_class::count = 0; // global definition
                           // (and initialisation)
```

We need to use the scope resolution operator otherwise the compiler won't be able to access count. Notice that it is essential that the type qualifier is included in the initialisation statement (i.e. int). However the presence of int in the class definition (`static int count;`) is in fact optional, although it is as well to retain it for purposes of clarity. Note also that it is illegal to use `static` in the global definition of `count`. Any attempt to do so results in the compiler error "`Storage class "static" is not allowed here`" or something similar.

This program uses a private data member for `count`. What if we use a public data member? If you have entered this program then modify it so that `count` is a public data member instead of a private one. You should find that the output is the same as before.

So why use private rather than public static data members? The reason can be illustrated by inserting the statement:

```
some_class::count = 99;
```

in the middle of the main program (with `count` being a public data member), e.g. after the statement `a.how_many()`. Although the resulting program compiles and runs it has, in this case, the undesirable effect of resetting `count` to 99! Inserting this same statement in the original program (`private count`) will produce different compilation errors depending on where it has been inserted. If you insert the statement in the same place you will get the error: `some_class::count not accessible`. If you insert it immediately after the first initialisation of `count` (outside `main()`) then you get the error message: `Member "some_class::count" is initialised more than once`. The moral is that private static data members can only be initialised once, and that must be globally (outside `main()`).

So, to sum up, you should use private static data members when you wish to make a variable available to all instances of the class, retain its value and only wish the variable to be initialised once. If you require a variable to be reset globally, but only be declared once no matter how many instances are created then use a public data member. By judicious use of these two types of static data members you should be able to eliminate any need for global variables. This in turn means that the principle of encapsulation, which is fundamental to OOP, will not be violated.

5.10.1 Static member functions

In addition to creating static data members we can also create static member functions. Such functions would normally be created if we wish to perform operations on the class *as a whole* rather than on each instance of the class individually. A simple illustration uses the previous example but in it we create a static member function to carry out the initialisation of `count`. We create a member function `init_count()` in the definition of `some_class`:

```
static void init_count() { count = 0; }
```

and then call this function *before* creating any objects of type `some_class`, e.g.

```
some_class::init_count();
some_class a;
```

One important point to note concerning static member functions is that they can only access static data members – for an example see Exercise 5.12.7.

Notice how we call this static member function – we use the scope resolution operator (`::`) together with the class name. This is obviously necessary in this instance since it is the only way we can refer to `init_count()`. However, once an object is declared of type `some_class` any subsequent call to `init_count()` could be as for any other member function call (e.g. `a.init_count()` or `b.init_count()`). Having said that it makes sense to stick to the first method especially bearing in mind that a static member function can only operate on a static data member which by definition is common to all objects of that class. It only confuses matters to use a specific instance of a class in such cases.

When using static member functions and data it is important to remember that static data members must always be defined, although they need not necessarily be initialised. So, for example, we see that the static data member `count` must still be defined as a global `int`, but in this case not initialised. Forgetting to do this results in an error message, this time from the linker, of the form "`Undefined symbol some_class::count in module ...`". Try commenting out the global definition of `count` in your program and see what message you get.

5.10.2 A final comment

It may see rather messy to have to place the global definition before the beginning of `main()` and tedious to remember to do so. However remember that all the class definitions, their associated member function definitions and any global definitions will normally be in one file and once debugged will/can/should be invisible to the user.

5.11 Summary

This concludes chapter 5, where we have delved a little deeper into C++ and hopefully you now have more of a feel for how C++ differs from languages like Pascal, COBOL and even C! A number of new ideas have been introduced, together with some additional terms common to other object-oriented languages.

Topics covered:

- *Why classes*?
- Class member functions
- The structure pointer operator (->)
- Classes – the keyword `class`
- Unions and sharing `storage`
- Using `public` and `private` in classes
- Data abstraction
- Constructors and constructor overloading
- Releasing memory – destructors
- Constructors with default arguments
- The scope of class names
- Classes with `static` data members
- `static` member functions

5.12 Exercises

5.12.1 Make sure that you have tried out all the programs discussed in Section 5.4. You can then usefully make some modifications to them as follows:

a) Modify the `next()` function so that it works correctly – i.e. it returns 1st June after 31st May and it moves to a new year and sets day and month to 1 when passed 31st December.

b) You can also allow for leap years. Remember that a leap year occurs when the year is divisible by 4 but not if the year is divisible by 100 except when it is divisible by 400. Thus 1900 was not a leap year but 2000 will be.

c) Modify the `prev()` function so that it also works correctly.

d) Write a member function for the `date` class to enable a tighter check to be made on invalid dates. For example nothing prevents 0 or negative integers from being entered or days greater than the number of days in the month. Similarly months outside the range 1 to 12 can be entered at present. *Hint*: since we need the month in order to validate the day and we need the year to check for leap years, it is best to read in the complete date (e.g. as 21 5 1999) before validating.

5.12.2 Take a look at Program 5.6 (ENUM.cpp). This illustrates the points discussed in Section 2.7. Try the program out in its current form – you will find that it will not compile. Make a note of any error or warning messages. Then follow the instruction in the comments in the definition of the darray class and try recompiling and running it.

Program 5.6

```
//: ENUM.cpp
//. enum and array dimensions
//. as it stands this shouldn't work!
//. - see the comments in the definition of darray

#include <conio.h>
#include <iostream.h>
// ...........................................................
class darray {
   const dsize = 10;  // comment this line out
// enum {dsize = 10};  // and uncomment this one to get it
                  // working!
   double darray[dsize];
public:
   darray();
   void get_dsize(){ cout << " In darray: " << endl;
      cout << "   using const, won't compile! " << endl;
      cout << "   using enum, dsize = " << dsize << endl;
   }
};
// ...........................................................
void main(void) {

   const fsize = 20;    // can use const here to set array size
   float farray[fsize];

   clrscr();
   cout << " ENUM " << endl;
   cout << " ==== " << endl << endl;

   cout << " In main:" << endl;
   cout << "   using const, fsize = " << fsize << endl;

   // now declare an object of type darray
   darray da;

   // and check its size
   da.get_dsize();

   cout << " Press any key to Quit ";
   getch();
}
```

5.12.3

    a) Modify the oblong class so that it incorporates the following member functions:

```
inc_width()    – increase width by 1 unit.
dec_width()    – decrease width by 1 unit.
inc_height()   – increase height by 1 unit.
dec_height()   – decrease height by 1 unit.
```

Thoroughly test these new functions.

b) How might you improve the class so that an integer other than 1 could be added to or subtracted from the width or the height? Try out your proposed solution(s).

c) Add a member function (called `print_details()`) to print the height, width and area of an object of the class `oblong`. The output should be in the form:

```
height = 10width = 12    area = 120
```

5.12.4

a) Create an overloaded date member function which allows a date to be declared and initialised and sets `m_type` correctly. For example a date can be declared as `date christmas_day(25, 12, 1996)` with `m_type` set to `numeric`. Incorporate this function in the latest date program and test it out.

b) Create another overloaded function which allows a date such as `hogmanay(31, "December", 1996)` to be declared. Again make sure that `m_type` is correctly set.

5.12.5 Construct a class `roman` which uses the enumerated data type `roman_num` discussed in Chapter 2. The class should have member functions:

```
roman()              – a basic constructor function.
roman(int dec_num)   – to initialise a roman number.
set(int dec_num)     – to set/reset a roman number.
display()            – to display the number in its roman form.
```

Remember that it is not possible to output enumerated types directly to produce the name tag – use an `if`, or `switch()` statement for this purpose. This illustrates one of the tedious aspects when using enumerated types, as mentioned in the chapter.

5.12.6

a) The program STATDM.cpp can be modified to illustrate the use of the static member function init_count(). Carry out the following changes to STATDM.cpp:

i) Add the inline definition to the some_class definition

```
static void init_count(){ count = 0; };
```

ii) Change the global initialisation of count to a definition only

```
int some_class::count;          // define count
```

iii) Insert just before the creation of a the call of init_count()

```
some_class::init_count();
        // set count to 0 before creating
        // any instances of 'some_class'
```

b) Make count a non-static member of some_class and check what happens when you try to access it with the static member function init_count().

5.12.7   Now rewrite the last program so that it consists of a main program and a header file stat.h which contains the class definition and associated declarations. Check that it still works.

5.12.8   Create a class called particle which has private data members (double) mass, xvelocity (v_x), yvelocity (v_y) and zvelocity (v_z). Write member functions so that:

i)   Uninitialised objects can be created.
ii) Objects can be created of a given mass but undefined velocities.
iii) Objects can be created with a given mass and given velocities.
iv) Already declared objects can have their mass and velocities set (or reset).
v)   The mass and all three velocities can be displayed.
vi) The momenta (mass * xvelocity, etc.) can be displayed.
vii) The kinetic energy can be stored and displayed –

$$KE = \frac{1}{2} \times mass \times \left(v_x^2 + v_y^2 + v_z^2 \right)$$

5.12.9   In a traffic simulation program a class `traffic_light` is required which has the (simplified) states red and green. An object of such a class will remain in each state for a set number of seconds (`red_period` and `green_period` respectively). Construct suitable member functions to create and control the settings of objects of type `traffic_light`. You will need to create constructor and destructor member functions, a function or functions to enable the (red–green) periods to be set, a function to set the light to a specific colour, and a means of cycling the light through its stages. For the purposes of this exercise use an integer counter which is assumed to be counting in seconds.

5.13 References

[1]   Quoted from Stroustroup in an article by Al Stevens C for C++ Programmers, Dr Dobbs Journal, July 1997, pp 99-102.

6 | Extending Functions

6.1 Introduction

In this chapter we look in detail at some C++ enhancements, in particular, as they apply to functions. We will be considering the use of default arguments, inline functions, reference variables as return values, function overloading and operator overloading.

Operator overloading, which forms the bulk of the material in this chapter, represents one of the most important concepts in object oriented programming and is therefore of central importance to our discussion of C++. Having the ability to use standard operators (such as +, −, /, *, =, ++, etc.) with objects of our own design greatly increases the flexibility of C++ and can help significantly in improving the legibility and readability of programs. Of course giving the programmer the power to redefine operators can also be fraught with danger − it is always possible to overload an operator so that it does something really bizarre or completely the opposite to its normal use, so be warned! The other important topic in this Chapter deals with *friend classes* and *friend functions*. By using the idea of friends we can provide means of granting non-member functions access to the private elements of a class. Although, on the surface, this may appear a retrograde step − for example we seem to be moving away from the idea of data abstraction − there are circumstances when such constructs are useful. For example, friends can be useful when overloading certain types of operators (see Section 6.5); friends can also make the construction of some I/O interfaces easier; and friends may also be useful when two or more classes contain members that are related to one another.

6.2 Default arguments

We saw in Chapter 2 that the static facility could be used to initialise variables within a function. One other method in C++ is to use default arguments. This has limited value until we introduce classes but it can at times be useful.

Default values are given to arguments when a function is declared (or prototyped). This means that a function can be called with fewer arguments than are in the parameter list of the defined function. So for example a function defined as:

```
void f(float x, int i, char c) { … }
```

may be declared as:

```
void f(float x, int i = 0, char c = 'a');
```

and used with one, two or three arguments, as Program 6.1 illustrates; Test run 6.1 shows a sample run.

Program 6.1

```
//: FUNDEFL1.cpp
//. simple program illustrating of the use of default arguments
#include <iostream.h>
#include <conio.h>
// .......................................................
void main()
{
    void f(float x, int i = 0, char c = 'a');
    //function declaration with default arguments
    clrscr();
    cout << " Functions with default arguments";
    cout << " (i = 0, c = 'a') " << endl;
    cout << endl << " calling f(3.2, 5, 'h') gives : ";
    f(3.2, 5, 'h');
    cout << endl << " calling f(-8.9, 20) gives : ";
    f(-8.9, 20);
    cout << endl << " .. and f(5.7) gives : "
    f(5.7);
    cout << endl << "End of FUNDEFL1 " << endl;
}
// .......................................................
// function definition
void f( float x, int i, char c)
{
    cout << endl;
    cout << " x = " << x << " i = " << i;
    cout << " c = " << c << endl;
}
```

The first call of f, which uses three parameters, overrides the default arguments. In the second call only two arguments are used (-8.9 and 20) and so the missing third argument is given the default value 'a'. Then in the third call of f, with only one parameter (5.7) the default values are used for the two remaining arguments. As this program illustrates, when calling a function which has been given default arguments the argument list begins with the first argument, if there is one, which is matched by the first parameter in the function definition – arguments and parameters are then paired off in sequence until no arguments are left, at which point the default arguments take over and are used for any remaining parameters. So it is not possible to miss arguments out by for example attempting a function call such as f(3.1, , 'z') – once an argument is missed out then any remaining arguments must be left out of the function call.

```
Functions with default arguments (i = 0, c = 'a')

 calling f(3.2, 5, 'h') gives :
 x = 3.2 i = 5 c = h

 calling f(-8.9, 20) gives :
 x = -8.9 i = 20 c = a

 .. and f(5.7) gives :
 x = 5.7 i = 0 c = a
 End of FUNDEFLT
```

Notice also that in the declaration of f (in the main body of the program) once a parameter is given a default value the remaining parameters in the function declaration must also be given default values. Thus declarations such as:

```
void f(int i = 0, float x, char c);
```

and

```
void f(int i = 10, float x, char c = 'a');
```

are both illegal.

The declaration(s) of a function assign default values to function arguments and as such can vary from declaration to declaration. The function definition, however, remains the same – i.e. as always, there is only one definition. Multiple declarations of a function can however only occur if these declarations are in different blocks, as is illustrated by Program 6.2.

📋 **Program 6.2**

```
//: FUNDEFL2.cpp
//. simple program illustrating of the use of default arguments
//. This time showing how different default arguments
//. can be used, provided the function declarations
//.are in different blocks (in this case functions)

#include <iostream.h>
#include <conio.h>
// .................................................................

void main()
```

```
{
    void f1(float x, int i, char c);
    void f2(float x, int i, char c);

    //function declaration with default arguments

    clrscr();
    cout << " FUNDEFL2 " << endl;
    cout << " ======== " << endl << endl;

    cout << " Functions with default arguments";
    cout << " (i = 0, c = 'a') " << endl;
    cout << " calling f1(3.2, 5, 'h') gives : ";
    f1(3.2, 5, 'h');
    cout << " .. and f2(5.7) gives : ";
    f2(5.7);
    cout << " End of FUNDEFLT2 \n";
    cout << " Press any key to Quit ";
    getch();
}
// ..........................................................
// function definition
void f( float x, int i, char c)
{
    cout << endl;
    cout << " x = " << x << " i = " << i;
    cout << " c = " << c << endl;
}
// ..........................................................
// function definition for f1
void f1(float x, int i, char c)
{
    void f(float x, int i = 0, char c = 'a');
}
// ..........................................................
// function definition for f2
void f2(float x, int i, char c)
{
    void f(float x, int i = 99, char c = 'z');
}
```

6.2.1 Default arguments used with constructors

There is one further variation on constructors that we can use – one that provides default values for data members of a declared object. Thus:

```
oblong (int h = 1, int w = 2){ height = h; width = w;}
```

will allow objects of type oblong to be declared with a default height of 1 and width of 2. So declarations of objects which do not specifically initialise either the height or the width will be given these default values. Examples are:

```
oblong o1;          // o1 has h = 1, w = 2
oblong o2(3);       // o2 has h = 3, w = 2
oblong o3(5, 8);    // o3 has h = 5, w = 2
```

Note however that we cannot use both this overloaded constructor and the 'empty' constructor `oblong(){}`. Why not?

You cannot have both `oblong(){}` and `oblong(int h = 1, int w = 2){height = h; width = w;}` since there will be an ambiguity when objects are declared and not initialised –, e.g. `oblong o4;` the compiler has no way of distinguishing between the constructor `oblong()` and the constructor with default initialisers (`oblong(int h = 1, int w = 2)`).

6.2.2 Use and misuse of default arguments

It is important to know when and when not to use default arguments to functions. The first point to note is that one reason for using them is to improve the efficiency of a function. This means that we only use default arguments if in the majority of cases these values will be required. Obvious examples arise in screen output – maximum no. of characters per line (possibly 80); placement of tabs on a line (perhaps 5 for a program, 10 for normal text); and maximum no. of lines on screen of text (normally 25). So, if a particular value is normally associated with a function (e.g. 90% or more of the time) then use a default argument, otherwise don't.

6.3 Function overloading

In C we can only define one function with a given name. In C++ we have the facility to define a number of functions with the same name, the only provisos being that the parameter types are different, or the number of parameters is different. Function overloading provides one of the main means of implementing polymorphism (literally many forms) which is a key concept in object-oriented programming (OOP).

6.3.1 Overloaded functions – parameter types different

We begin by considering the overloading of a function where the parameter types are different. As an example suppose we wished to write the `arith()` function used earlier in this book to compute results of simple arithmetic calculations for both real and integer arithmetic (i.e. when both parameters are either real numbers (e.g. `float`) or both are integer). The float version of the function is the same as before – with the addition of an output line to identify the function:

```
// function definition
void arith( float x, float y)
{
    cout << " FLOAT arith function " << endl;
    cout << " Sum       = " << x + y << endl;
    cout << " Difference = " << x - y << endl;
```

```
   cout << " Product   = " << x * y << endl;
   cout << " Ratio     = " << ( y != 0 ? x / y :
             (x > 0 ? 1e20 :
             ( x < 0 ? -1e20 : 0.0)))
             << endl;
}
```

The integer version simply uses int parameters instead of float:

```
// function definition
void arith( int x, int y)
{
   cout << " INT arith function " << endl;
   cout << " Sum       = " << x + y << endl;
   cout << " Difference = " << x - y << endl;
   cout << " Product   = " << x * y << endl;
   cout << " Ratio     = " << ( y != 0 ? x / y :
             (x > 0 ? 1e20 :
             ( x < 0 ? -1e20 : 0.0)))
             << endl;
}
```

Here the division will be integer division because both x and y are int variables and so the result will be a truncated version of the correct value. These
two functions can be used as necessary – the exact one being called depending
on the type of the arguments used.

A program which incorporates the two arith functions might contain the
following lines of code:

```
float x = 5.6, y = 8.0;
arith(x, y);
x = 6.8;
y = 0.0;
arith(x, y)
arith(5, 8);
arith(7, 0);
```

A couple of interesting points arise out of this example, so let's take a closer
look at it. You will notice that we declared two float variables x and y and
after assigning them values used them as arguments to the function call. You
might think that we could use the constants directly in the function call as we
have done for the int version. The reason that we cannot use a call such as
arith(5.6, 8.0); or one such as arith(6.8, 0.0); is that the constants
5.6, 8.0, 6.8 and 0.0 are are stored as doubles, not floats. If such calls are attempted then they will result in compilation errors. The compiler finds an ambiguity between the two functions and cannot decide which to call – i.e.
whether to call arith(int, int) or arith(float, float). By assigning the
float variables x and y to (double) constants we avoid this ambiguity and the
compiler automatically selects the arith(float, float) function.

Apart from the use of `float` variables there are two other ways of getting around this problem. One is to write a version which uses parameters of type double. This is left as an exercise for the reader. The other is to use *casting*. This is a method which forces type conversion on a data type. Thus we can force the double constants into type `float` and thereby make sure the correct function is used. The method is illustrated in the following two function calls:

```
arith( (float) 5.6, (float) 8.0);
arith( (float) 6.8, (float) 0.0);
```

Make these amendments and check that they work as intended.

6.3.2 Overloaded functions – number of parameters different

The above functions have all been void functions and they have all had the same number of parameters. Let's have a look at functions with varying numbers of parameters. The two date functions given below allow a date to be output in the form DD-MONTH or DD-MONTH-YYY depending on the number of arguments in the function call.

```
date( int day, char *month)
{
   // short date form
   cout << day << "-" << month << endl;
}

date( int day, char *month, int year)
{
   // long date form
   cout << day << "-" << month << "-" << year << endl;
}
```

These functions might then be called using statements such as these:

```
date(21, "JAN");
```

or

```
date(day, month);
```

to output the short form, or

```
date(21, "JAN", 1997)
```

or

```
date(day, month, year);
```

to output the date in its long form.

Functions can be overloaded even if they return values. So we might have:

```
int max( int x, int y);
```

and

```
float max( float x, float y);
```

which can be used to return the `int` maximum of two integer arguments or the `float` maximum of two `float` arguments. However we cannot have two (or more) functions with the same name returning different data types unless their arguments differ in number or type. For example `int h( int x)` and `float h( int x)` are illegal (in the same block of code).

6.4   Inline functions

Inline functions can also be defined within the body of a class as, for example, the constructor function `date()` (see Section 5.7). As it only consists of one simple statement there is no need to go to the trouble of prototyping it within date and then defining the function elsewhere. Constructor functions are often of this type since their body is generally quite simple and can therefore save the overhead of function calls if written as inline functions. Note, by the way, that it is not necessary to write the function on one line – C++, like C, is a 'free format' language – so we could legitimately write the date constructor in this form:

```
date() {
        m_type = -1;
}       // constructor to trap unset dates
```

This function is still treated as an inline function within the class date, even though the layout suggests that it is not.

6.4.1 Use of inline functions

Inline functions are functions which are expanded *in situ* – the function call is replaced by the necessary code at compilation time, so there is no need to call the function, which means transfer of control to the function code and then a return back to the code following the function call. Inline functions are typically used for very small functions which for aesthetic or other reasons are best written as a function, rather than the equivalent code.

An obvious example might be a function which returns the maximum value of two integers. This would be defined as:

```
inline int max(int n,int m) {return ( n > m ? n: m);}
                // inline max
                // function definition
```

and might then be used in a program as follows:

```
largest = max(num, 10);
i = j * max(num, 1);
etc.
```

Both of these statements are (marginally) clearer than the equivalent code, i.e.
:

```
largest = num > 10 ? num : 10;
i = j * (num > 1 ? num : 1);
```

The inline function is introduced by use of the keyword `inline` – the remainder of the function is then defined in the usual manner.

Another example of an inline function is a function to convert an uppercase letter to its lowercase equivalent. This uses the fact that, in a normal ASCII character set, each of the lowercase letters is displaced a fixed number from its uppercase equivalent. Rather than work out what this is we can simply use 'A' - 'a' to provide the offset and let the computer do the arithmetic. The inline function is:

```
inline char lowcase( char c) {
return ((c >= 'A' && c <= 'Z')?c-'A'+'a': c); }
```

Only characters between A and Z are affected by this function, any other character is return unaltered. An extract from a program which uses this function might be as follows:

```
...
cout << " Enter a string of characters -
    end with <ENTER> " << endl;
cin >> s;
int i = 0;
cout << " Converted to lowercase - " << endl;
while (s[i] != '\0')
    cout << lowcase(s[i++]);
count << endl;
...
```

6.4.2 Macros

Inline functions are new to C++ and so are not available to C programmers. However pre-processor macros can be used for the same purpose. You will come across macros in C code and may still find them used in C++ programs, although inline functions are preferable. The `max()` function described above can be written as a macro as follows:

```
#define max(n,m)  (n > m ? n : m)
```

This would then be used in the same way as the equivalent inline function.

There is one important difference between inline functions and macros. If you attempted to use the `max inline` function (which uses `int` arguments) in a program you will find that if an attempt is made to call the function with arguments other than `int`, then errors will occur. Whereas using the macro version will allow any numeric data type as its arguments. So macros have no type checking , whereas inline functions do allow (even force) type checking.

6.5   Member access – a recap

Before moving on to look at friends, in Section 6.6, we will briefly recap what we already know about access to the attributes and methods of a particular class.

So far we have allowed classes to have public or private members. Public members of an object are accessible anywhere that object is in scope. They can also by accessed even if the (global) object is hidden by a local variable of the same name.

6.5.1 A note on I/O

We will see later, once we have introduced operator overloading, that input and output functions are generally better written so that they can be used directly with `cin` and `cout` (or other appropriate streams). So that instead of displaying the `circle` statistics as above via a call to the function `display_circle_stats()` we use `cout << c1;`. Until we reach the point where we are in a position to describe the overloading of `<<` and `>>` we will continue to use functions such as `show()`, `print()`, `enter()`, etc. Once operator overloading, as it applies to the shift operators, has been covered (Section 6.16.3) we will use these methods in preference to the ones we use at present whenever the context suggests that we should. At that point you are encouraged to review all previous programs and examples and replace the older function calls with the use of overloaded shift operators for each class.

In order to be able to overload these two operators we first need to understand the concept of friends. We saw in our earlier discussions, and previously, that whilst public data and function members are available outside the class definition private members are only accessible by member functions of objects of that class. But, now read on ...

As we have just been reminded all the classes and member functions which we have been looking at so far restrict the access of members of other classes to the public members. Sometimes we may wish to allow other functions to have access to private variables or functions. This is where friends come in! Friends have the same access privileges as member functions, but they are not associated with an object of the host class (i.e. the class of which they are a designated friend). Friends come in a variety of forms – *classes*, *functions* and *operators*. In other words, a whole class can be a friend of another class, a function can be a friend of (one or more classes), or an operator can be a friend of another (or more than one) class. We will look at examples of each of these types of friend in the following subsections.

6.6.1   Friend classes

If a class is a friend of another class then the member functions of the friend can read and write the private data members of the first class. A simple application of a friend class is given in Program 6.3 (FRIEND0.cpp).

Program 6.3

```
//: FRIEND0.cpp
//. illustrating a friend class

#include <conio.h>
#include <iostream.h>
#include <math.h>
// ........................................................
class circle;          // forward reference

class point {          // a simple point class
   float x, y;
public:
   point(){}
   point(float x1, float y1){ x = x1; y = y1;}
   void show(){ cout << " x = " << x << " y = " << y << endl;}
   friend circle;  // tell point that circle is a friend
};
// ........................................................
class circle {    // ... and a simple circle class
   float x, y, radius;
public:
   circle(){}
   circle(float xr, float yr, float r)
            { x = xr; y = yr; radius = r;}
   circle(point p1, float r)
            { x = p1.x; y = p1.y; radius = r;}
   void set_rad(float r){ radius = r;}
   void show(){ cout << " centre: x = " << x
                << " y = " << y;
   cout << endl << " rad = " << radius << endl;}
```

```
};
// ..........................................................
void main(void) {
  point p(0,0), p2(5,12);
  circle c(4,3,6);
  float d;

  clrscr();
  cout << " FRIEND0 " << endl;
  cout << " ======= " << endl << endl;
  cout << " Point p : ";
  p.show();
  cout << " Circle c : ";
  c.show();
  cout << " Point p2 : ";
  p2.show();

  circle c1(p2, 10);
  cout << endl << " After circle c1(p2, 10); " << endl;
  cout << " Circle c1 : ";
  c1.show();
  cout << " Press any key to Quit ";
  getch();
}
```

The above program begins with a forward reference to the class point (class point;) this informs the compiler that a class point will be defined later on but will be referenced before that – similar to the idea of prototyping functions before they are defined.

Next, in the class point, we declare circle to be a friend of point:

```
friend circle;
```

Then, in the class circle itself, we use an object of class point as an argument to the (overloaded) constructor circle to enable us to centre a circle on a previously initialised point. Thus:

```
circle(point p1, float r) { x = p1.x; y = p1.y; rad = r;}
```

Program 6.4 (IMPERIAL.cpp) illustrates another similar use of a friend class.

Program 6.4

```
//: IMPERIAL.cpp
//. an example of a friend class

#include <iostream.h>
#include <conio.h>
// ...........................................................
class metric; // declare metric so that imperial can see it

// the imperial class
class imperial{
```

```
      int gallon;
      float pint;
public:
   imperial() {}
   imperial(int g, float p) { gallon = g; pint = p; }
   void display() { cout << gallon << " gals " << pint
                         << " pints" << endl; }
   friend metric;  // allows metric member functions to see
           // imperial private members
};
// ..........................................................
// the metric class
class metric {
   float litre;
public:
   metric(float l) { litre = l; }
   void display() { cout << litre << " litres" << endl; }
   operator imperial();
};

// member conversion function ( metric to imperial )
const float LITRE_PER_PINT = 0.567;
metric::operator imperial(float l) {
   imperial imp;
   imp.pint = litre / LITRE_PER_PINT;
   imp.gallon = imp.pint / 8;
   imp.pint = imp.pint - 8 * imp.gallon;
             // canÕt use % as pint is float
   return imp;
}
// ..........................................................
void main(){
   imperial i_vol;
   metric m_vol(1.0); // give m_vol a value of 1 litre

   clrscr();
   cout << " IMPERIAL " << endl;
   cout << " ======== " << endl;
   cout << " converting metric to imperial " << endl;
   cout << " using a friend class " << endl << endl;
   i_vol = m_vol;

   cout << " Metric   : ";
   m_vol.display();   // metric vol e.g. 1.0 litre
   cout << " Imperial : ";
   i_vol.display();      // imperial volume e.g. = 1.76 pints
   cout << " Press any key to Quit ";
   getch();
}
```

Before taking a detailed look at the above program let's see what it is supposed to do. In this simple form it just allows a metric volume (measured in
litres) to be converted to an imperial volume (for simplicity restricted to gallons and pints). It can easily be modified to enable a metric volume entered by
the user to be converted to imperial measure. This is left as an exercise for the
reader.

Now to see how the program works. Notice first of all the declaration of the class metric:

```
class metric;
```

This is simply to inform the compiler that this class will be defined later but a reference will be made to it before it is defined – this is sometimes known as 'forward referencing'. (We will see an alternative method which avoids the need for this particular method of prototyping a class later – see Program 6.5.) Next we have the definition of the class imperial. This consist of, what by now should be familiar elements to you: two private data members to hold the volume in gallons and pints, a constructor with no initialisation (imperial()), a constructor with initialisation (imperial(float g, float p)) and a function to display the volume in imperial form (display()). Finally we have another new construct:

```
friend metric;
```

which declares the whole class metric to be a friend of the imperial class. This means that the class metric is given access to all the member functions and data members of the imperial class.

The next definition is that of the class metric. There is nothing unusual in this except for the statement:

```
operator imperial(float l);
```

which declares a conversion function to enable a volume, passed in its metric form (i.e. in litres) to be converted into an imperial volume (in gallons and pints). In the definition of this function:

```
const float LITRE_PER_PINT = 0.567;
metric::operator imperial(float l) {
    imperial imp;
    imp.pint = litre / LITRE_PER_PINT;
    imp.gallon = imp.pint / 8;
    imp.pint = imp.pint - 8 * imp.gallon;
                    // can't use % as pint is float
    return imp;
}
```

we begin by defining the conversion factor 0.567 representing the number of litres in one pint. Then, in the body of the function, we create a local object (imp) which will hold the volume converted from the metric volume. The conversion is then carried out by first converting the volume in litres (litre) into pints and then working out the number of gallons. Notice that we can't use the % operator to compute the remaining pints as pint is a float variable not an int. Finally we return the volume as an imperial measure.

In the main program we invoke this member function simply by assigning an imperial volume to a metric one (i.e. i_vol = m_vol;).

As we mentioned above there is an alternative method of letting the compiler know that the class metric is to be referenced before it is defined. This uses the following construct in the definition of metric where we declare metric to be a friend of imperial:

```
friend class metric;
```

So the definition of the imperial class becomes:

```
// the imperial class (ver 2.0)
class imperial{
    int gallon;
    float pint;
public:
    imperial() {}
    imperial(int g, float p) { gallon = g; pint = p;}
    void display() { cout << gallon << " gals " << pint
                        << " pints" << endl; }
    friend class metric; // allows metric member functions to
                         // see imperial private members
};
```

6.6.2 Friend functions

It is quite rare to have a whole class as a friend of another class, more often we simply want member function(s) of some other class(es) to have access to the data members, or private functions of our class. One way is to make the data members and functions public – but this is going too far, we don't want every Tom, Dick and Henrietta to have access to the data members and functions. So again we simply state in the definition of our first class that a particular function of another class is a friend.

Program 6.5 (IMPERIA2.cpp) illustrates this use of friends.

Program 6.5

```
//: IMPERIA2.cpp
//. an example of a friend function

#include <iostream.h>
#include <conio.h>
// ...................................................................
class metric;// declare metric so that imperial can see it

// the imperial class
class imperial{
    int gallon;
    float pint;
public:
    imperial() {}
    imperial(int g, float p) { gallon = g; pint = p;}
```

```
    imperial(metric m);
    void display() { cout << gallon << " gals " << pint
                         << " pints" << endl; }
};
// ...........................................................
// the metric class
class metric {
   float litre;
public:
   metric(float l) { litre = l;}
   void display() { cout << litre << " litres" << endl;}
   friend imperial::imperial(metric m);
};

// member conversion function ( metric to imperial)
const float LITRE_PER_PINT = 0.567;
imperial::imperial(metric m) {
   pint = m.litre / LITRE_PER_PINT;
   gallon = pint / 8;
   pint = pint - 8 * gallon;
}
// insert main() code here
```

It is instructive to compare the function definitions given in Program 6.4 and 6.5 (IMPERIAL and IMPERIA2), i.e. between the example when a whole class is declared as a friend and one where one (or more) member functions are declared as friends. First of all take a look at the differences between the definitions of the two imperial classes. In Program 6.5 (IMPERIA2) instead of declaring metric a friend of imperial, we declare a function imperial which takes a parameter of type metric – this will eventually be defined so that it converts an imperial volume into a metric one.

Next, in the definition of the metric class, we declare imperial(metric m) to be a friend:

```
    friend imperial::imperial(metric m);
```

And then, finally, we have the definition of this friend function (a member of the imperial class). Within this function we now no longer need to set up a local imperial object, as we did in the first version, since, because this is a member of imperial, we have direct access to both gal and to pint. However when accessing the imperial measure (litre) we do this via m (i.e. m.litre). Note also in this function that there is no return statement. The reason for this is that this new function is actually a constructor function – it constructs an imperial volume out of a metric one. This means that we can create an imperial volume and initialise it with a metric volume all in one go. For example

```
    imperial i_vol1(10.0);
```

will create an object i_vol1 with gallon equal to 2 and pint equal to 1.64...

6.6.3 Bridge friend functions

One final use of friends is encountered when we want a function to have access to elements from two different classes. In such cases the function will need to be a friend to both classes. To illustrate this use of friends we return to our two geometrical classes `point` and `circle`. We wish to be able to find the distance between the centre of a, previously defined, circle and a point. We can use a function called `distance()` which will have as arguments an object of the class circle and a point object. The function then returns the distance from the point to the centre of the circle. Since this function needs to access the private data members of both `circle` and `point` (i.e. the x and y coordinates) then it must be a friend to both class `circle` and class `point`. So in both of these class definitions we will have a declaration such as:

```
friend float distance( circle c1, point p1);
```

The definition of distance then follows and this will be a normal (global) function – it cannot be a member of either `circle` or `point` since it is a friend of both.

Program 6.6

```
//: FRIEND1.cpp
//. illustrating a friend of two classes

#include <conio.h>
#include <iostream.h>
#include <math.h>
// ...........................................................
class circle;

class point {            // a simple point class
   float x, y;
public:
   point(){}
   point(float x1, float y1){ x = x1; y = y1;}
   void show(){ cout << " x = " << x << " y = " << y << endl;}
   friend float distance(point p1, circle c1);
};
// ...........................................................
class circle {          // ... and a simple circle class
   float x, y, rad;
public:
   circle(){}
   circle(float xr, float yr, float r){
                  x = xr; y = yr; rad = r;}
   void set_rad( float r){ rad = r;}
   void show(){ cout << " centre: x = " << x << " y = " << y;
       cout << endl << " rad = " << rad << endl;}
   friend float distance(point p1, circle c1);
};
// ...........................................................
```

```
// "global" function - friend of both point and circle
float distance(point p1, circle c1) {
    return sqrt((p1.x - c1.x)*(p1.x - c1.x) +
                (p1.y - c1.y)*(p1.y - c1.y));
}
// ..............................................................
void main(void) {
    point p(0,0);
    circle c(4,3,6);
    float d;

    clrscr();
    cout << " FRIEND1 " << endl;
    cout << " ======= " << endl << endl;
    p.show();
    c.show();
    d = distance(p, c);
    cout << " Distance between centre of circle and point p "
                            << endl;
    cout << " = " << d << endl;
    cout << " Press any key to Quit ";
    getch();
}
```

Notice that since the declaration of distance() in class point refers to the class circle we must forward reference circle before defining point. Instead of the statement class circle; before the definition of point we could include the keyword class in the declaration of distance within point, i.e.

```
friend float distance(point p1, class circle c1);
```

Finally it is also possible to make our distance() function in the previous example both a friend of circle and a member function of point (or vice versa). We do this by making minor modifications to the declarations in both the classes point and circle as well as changing the definition of distance().

First of all, since we want distance() to be a member function of point, we don't need to pass a point as a parameter to the function – distance() will already have access to the elements of point (i.e. x and y). Thus in point we declare distance() as:

```
float distance(circle c1); // member function of point
```

However in circle we need to declare distance() as a friend, whilst remembering that it is a member function of point, thus:

```
friend float point::distance(circle c1);
             // still a friend of circle
```

It is obviously important to include the reference to point (through the use of the class name and scope resolution operator – point::) otherwise circle will not know where to find the function even though it is a friend!

Finally, in the definition of distance() we no longer need to refer to a point variable – we can obtain access to the x and y co-ordinates directly:

```
return sqrt((x-c1.x)*(x-c1.x)+(y-c1.y)*(y-c1.y));
```

It is instructive to make these changes and check that the program still works – see the Exercises at the end of the chapter.

Before moving on we summarise the various methods of using friends in Table 6.1.

Table 6.1 Summary of friend usage

	In Class C1	In Class C2
Class C2 friend of C1	friend class C2	can use member functions of C1 and access data members of C1
Member function (f) of C2 a friend of C1	friend type C2::f()	type f() f() has access to private data and functions of C1
Function (f) a friend of C1 and C2	friend type f() f() then defined globally	friend type f()

6.7   Operator overloading

Operator overloading is really another aspect of function overloading and it provides a very powerful tool for making C++ code more readable and intuitive (as well as providing scope for the exact opposite – so beware!).

Operator overloading enables the majority of binary and unary operators to be given alternative uses – see Table 6.2. Note however that the precedence rules for operators (see Table 1.7) cannot be over-ridden – except in the usual way with the use of brackets. A couple of obvious examples of operator overloading are:

i)   overloading of the binary arithmetic operators so that they can be used to manipulate objects belonging to a complex number class, and

ii)   using overloaded operators with a string class.

Thus in case i) we want to be able to write x = y + z, instead of x = add(y, z), where x, y and z are all objects of type complex. And in the case of a string class we might prefer writing s = "Example of " + "operator over-loading" instead of using the built-in string functions strcpy and strcat (i.e. strcpy(outs, "Example of ");strcat(outs,"operator overloading")).

Table 6.2 Overloadable operators

+	–	*	/	%	^	&	|	++	– –	=
+=	–=	*=	/=	%=	^=	&=	|=	~	!	<
>	<=	>=	==	!=	<<	>>	<<=	>>=	&&	||
,	–>	–>	*	()	[]	new	delete			

Let's begin by looking at ways in which we can overload some binary operators, for example +, -, *, /, +=, etc. We will use the complex class referred to earlier:

```
class complex {
   float real, imag;
public:
   complex() { real = 0.0; imag = 0.0; }
   complex( float re, float im)
           { real = re; imag = im; }
   void set( float re, float im)
           { real = re; imag = im; }
   void print( char * mess);
};
```

So how do we go about overloading the addition operator (+)? The general form for overloading a binary operator as a member of a class is:

```
classname   operator#( classname identifier );
```

where *classname* is the name of the class for which this operator is being overloaded, operator is a C++ keyword, # is the desired operator and *identifier* is an identifier of type *classname*. Program 6.7 illustrates the definition and use of the overloaded + operator.

Program 6.7
```
//: COMP1.cpp
//. example of operator overloading using a member function
#include <conio.h>
#include <iostream.h>
// ...............................................................
class complex {
   float real, imag;
public:
   complex(){ real = 0.0, imag = 0.0; }
   complex(float re, float im){ real = re; imag = im; }
   void set(float re, float im){ real = re; imag = im; }
   void print(char * mess);
   complex operator+(complex operand2);
};
```

```
void complex::print(char * mess){
   cout << mess << " " << real;
   if (imag > 0)
      cout << " + " << imag << "i" << endl;
   else
      cout << " - " << -imag << "i" << endl;
}

// operand1 + operand2
complex complex::operator+(complex operand2){
   complex cm = *this;
   cm.real += operand2.real;
   cm.imag += operand2.imag;
   return cm;
}
// ...................................................
void main() {

   complex a(4.0,-5.0), b(-2.4,6.9), c;

   clrscr();
   cout << " COMP1 " << endl;
   cout << " ===== " << endl << endl;
   a.print("a:");
   b.print("b:");
   c.print("c:");
   cout << endl << " Now c = a + b;" << endl;
   c = a + b;
   c.print("c:");
   cout << " Press any key to Quit ";
   getch();
}
```

Test run 6.2 gives the output of the Program 6.7 (after `c = a + b`).

🖳 **Test run 6.2**
```
c: 1.6 + 1.9i
Press any key to Quit
```

Notice how the function `operator+()` is declared in the definition of complex:

```
complex operator+(complex operand2);
```

and then how the function is defined:

```
// operand1 + operand2
complex complex::operator+(complex operand2){
   complex cm = *this;
   cm.real += operand2.real;
   cm.imag += operand2.imag;
   return cm;
}
```

The first statement in the `operator+()` member function uses the keyword this. This (i.e. this!) is a built-in pointer to the object which the operator has as its first operand. So in the case of c = a + b this will point to the address of a. Thus, by declaring a variable as complex cm = *this; we are setting cm equal to the object pointed to by this – i.e. a bit by bit copy is made of (say a) and placed in cm.

The next two statements complete the normal arithmetic operation of addition by using the += operator to add the separate parts of the complex number (making up operand2) to cm. Finally the new value held in cm is passed back from the function using the return statement.

6.7.1 A problem

It is interesting to see what happens if we dispense with the additional declaration and therefore the temporary (automatic) variable cm. Instead we can access the components of the complex object (e.g. a) by means of *this and update them using similar statements to the original ones, and then finally returning a pointer to the updated object (by means of *this). Why won't this work as intended? What will it do? Take a look at the following fragment, which codes the above process, and try to work out answers to these two questions before reading on.

```
complex::operator+( complex operand2) {
        // incorrect solution, but why?
    (*this).real += operand2.real;
    (*this).imag += operand2.imag;
    return *this;
}
```

to be used for example in the statement:

```
c = a + b;    // where a, b and c are all
              // complex objects
```

If you write a program which implements the above modifications, when you run it you will find that not only has c changed, as intended and as happened before, but the value of a has also been changed and is also equal to c. This is not what was intended! So we cannot overload + (or its companions) in this way.

6.7.2 Overloading +=

Although the previous example reveals a problem it also suggests a way in which the += operator might be overloaded. We declare within the complex class our overloaded += operator:

```
complex operator+=(complex operand2);
```

and then our definition becomes:

```
// operand1 += operand2
// (i.e. operand1 = operand1 + operand2)
complex::operator+=( complex operand2) {
    // ok for +=
    (*this).real += operand2.real;
    (*this).imag += operand2.imag;
    return *this;
}
```

We do not need to use *this to access the real and imaginary parts of the first operand of +=, we already have access to these (that is real and imag) because they are private members of the class complex. We can therefore rewrite the function as:

```
complex::operator+=( complex operand2) {
    // alternative method for +=
    real += operand2.real;
    imag += operand2.imag;
    return *this;
}
```

Notice however that we still need to return *this. Without *this we would have no way of returning the updated value of the complex object.

6.7.3 Overloading + again

After that brief diversion we return to our discussion of the overloaded + operator. As a member function we only require one parameter for the operator+() function. This may seem a little strange since after all we are dealing with a binary operator which requires two operands. A little thought, following on from our previous diversion, should reveal why only one argument is required.

If we look at this question by considering the function we are writing to achieve operator overloading then it should become clear. What we are in fact doing when we overload the + operator is to write a function called operator+() to simulate the operation of addition. This function is then used in the normal way – remember that the function has a type complex and so returns an object of type complex. Instead of c = a + b which we have used to perform complex addition we could have written:

```
c = a.operator+(b);
```

We can do this since the function operator+() is a member function of complex and so we can use it just like set() and print() with any object of type complex. Since the object which is effectively the first operand is already known (i.e. a) we only need one argument to the function (e.g. b). This also confirms our earlier discussion about the need for a temporary variable (cm) in the overloaded + function. Incidentally this also shows that operator overloading is just a special case of function overloading.

6.8 Using a friend for operator overloading

In addition to using member functions for operator overloading we can also use friend functions. But since we have seen member functions working satisfactorily why do we need friends? Well we would be very lonely otherwise, but ... there are other reasons! Consider the class date which might have the form:

```
class date {
    int day, month, year;
public:
    // usual constructor and member functions
}
```

We can construct an overloaded + operator in the usual way to enable a number of days to be added on to a date. For example:

```
friend date operator+(int days, date &dt);
```

declares our date operator + as a member of the date class, and this is then defined as:

```
date date::operator+( int days) {
    date d = *this;

    d.day += days;
    while( d.day > days_in_month[d.month]) {
        d.day -= days_in_month[d.month];
        d.month++;
        if (d.month > 12) {
            d.year++;
            d.month = 1;
        }
    }
    return d;
}
```

Within our main program or another function we can then write statements like:

```
d1 = d2 + 28;     // add 4 weeks onto d2
days = 100;
d3 = d2 + days;   // add 100 days to d2
```

Suppose we would also like to be able to write:

```
    d1 = 28 + d2;
or  d3 = days + d2;
```

Given our current overloaded + operator this is not possible. The reason is clear when you recall the alternative method of writing an overloaded operator call. For example `d1 = d2 + 28;` can also be written as `d1 = d2.operator+(28);`. Now what happens when we attempt to write `d1 = 28 + d2;`? We cannot write `d1 = 28.operator+(d2);`!! since 28 is not an object of type `date`, it is an integer constant.

⬚ Program 6.8

```cpp
//: OVLDATE.cpp
//. overloading + with a date class as a member function
#include <conio.h>
#include <iostream.h>
// ..........................................................
class date {
   int day, month, year;
   static int days_in_month[] = {31, 28, 31, 30, 31, 30, 31, 31,
                                 30, 31, 30, 31};
public:
   date(){};
   date(int d, int m, int y) { day = d; month = m; year = y;}
   void set(int d, int m, int y) {
                 day = d; month = m; year = y;}
   void print(char * mess) { cout << mess << " " << day
         << " / " << month << " / " << year << endl; }
   date operator+(int days);
};

date date::operator+( int days) {
   date d = *this;

   d.day += days;
   while( d.day > days_in_month[d.month]) {
      d.day -= days_in_month[d.month];
      d.month++;
      if (d.month > 12) {
         d.year++;
         d.month = 1;
      }
   }
   return d;
}
// ..........................................................
void main() {

   date d1(4,6,96), d2;

   clrscr();
   cout << " OVLDATE " << endl;
   cout << " ======= " << endl << endl;
```

```
d1.print(" d1 = ");

d2 = d1 + 30;
d2.print(" d2 = d1 + 30: ");
d1.print(" d1 = ");   // to check that d1 hasn't changed

cout << " Press any key to Quit ";
getch();
}
```

In Program 6.8 (OVLDATE.cpp) you will see that we have declared a static array days_in_month which holds the number of days in each month for a 'normal' year. If you wish you can modify the program to take account of leap years. This program should compile and run correctly, but what happens if we replace d1 = d2 + 28; with d1 = 28 + d2; ? What will happen is that the compiler will object and give a compilation error of the form "Illegal structure operation".

Now let's see how friends can help. We declare a friend operator within the public section of our class as follows:

```
friend date operator+(int days, date dt);
```

and define it as:

```
date operator+(int days, date dt) {
    ...
}
```

We could have as the body of this function a suitably modified version of the member operator+ function, however there is a simpler and more elegant alternative. Can you see what it is?

Remember all we are trying to do is provide a suitable structured function call to allow expressions of the type date_variable = int + date_variable to be correctly computed. We already have a function which computes date_variable = date_variable2 + int (the original operator+() function), so we can use that to carry out the addition, as follows:

```
date operator+(int days, date dt) {
    date d;
    d = dt + days;
    return d;
}
```

In this function we simply declare a temporary object d of type date, perform the addition and return the new value of d. The statement d = dt + days calls our original overloaded + operator and carries out the arithmetic correctly. Obviously if we hadn't already defined operator+() then the body of this function would be slightly more complicated.

6.9 Non-member and non-friend operator overloading

So far we have looked briefly at overloading an operator by means of a member function (e.g. overloaded + for complex numbers – COMP1.cpp) and using a friend function (e.g. overloaded + for use with dates – FRIEND1.cpp), however we can also overload operators in another way so that the operator is more generally available outside the class definition. Consider again the overloaded + operator as applied to our complex class. We still need to use the operator keyword, but this operator function isn't a member of the class complex. The prototype for this function is then:

```
complex operator+(complex operand1, complex operand2);
```

The body of the function requires access to the real and imaginary components of operand1 and operand2, but as yet, in our class definition, we have no means of accessing these components. We therefore a need a function such as get_comp() which will extract real and imag from a complex object to which it is applied. The function looks like this (defined within the class complex):

```
get_comp(float &re, float &im) { re = real; im = imag;}
```

and so our definition of the complex operator+() function becomes:

```
complex operator+(complex operand1,
            complex operand2) {
    operand1.get_comp(r1, i1);
        // get real & imag components of operand1
    operand2.get_comp(r2,i2);
        // ... and of operand2
    return complex( r1+r2, i1+i2);
}
```

This operator can now be used with any objects of type complex, just as before.

6.10 Summary ... so far

We have now looked at three ways of overloading an operator and it is worth reminding ourselves of each one (Table 6.3).

Notice that the function header for both the friend and global functions are the same: the difference arises in where, if at all, and how, they are prototyped, as Table 6.4 shows.

Table 6.3 Overloading operator definitions

Function type	Example definition for +
Member	`complex operator+( complex op2){ ... }`
Friend	`complex operator+( complex op1, complex op2){ ... }`
Global	`complex operator+( complex op1, complex op2){ ... }`

So binary operators, as member functions have one argument, as friend and global functions they have two arguments. For the global function to work we need access to the components of the class which is being operated upon (e.g. by using `get_comp()` to obtain `real` and `imag`).

The exercises at the end of this chapter will give you further opportunities to experiment with other binary operators but we now take a look at how unary operators can be overloaded.

Table 6.4 Overloading operator declarations

Function type	Example declaration for +	Location
Member	`complex operator+(complex op2);`	class `complex`
Friend	`Friend complex` `    operator+ (complex op1,complex op2);`	class `complex`
Global	`Complex operator+(complex op1,` `    complex op2);`	global

6.11 Overloading unary operators

The simplest unary operator to consider is the unary - operator which is used to change the sign of an object. Again we will discuss this with reference to the `complex` class. We want to construct the - operator so that we can create expressions such as:

```
c = -a
```

Once we have this unary operator defined we can use it, together with the binary + operator, to define the binary - operator. So how do we define the unary - operator? First let's consider the member function operator. Extending our previous discussion it seems logical that if a binary member function operator requires only one argument then a unary member function operator will not require any arguments. Thus our definition for this unary - operator will be (defined inline):

```
complex operator-(){ return complex( -real, -imag); }
```

A few simple modifications can be made to the COMP1.cpp program to implement and test this new operator. This is left as an exercise for the reader. As mentioned above, once this operator has been written, we can use it together with the + operator to define the unary - operator:

```
complex operator-( complex op2) { complex cm = *this;
                        return cm + -op2; }
```

Again you should try out this for yourself.

6.11.1 Overloaded auto-increment operator

On the face of it the auto-increment operator (++) is a unary operator and so we can define this operator using the method just discussed for overloading unary operators. Since the auto increment operator is perhaps more useful when dealing with dates rather than with complex numbers we will use the former to illustrate the overloading of this operator.

The definition of the overloaded ++ operator is:

```
date date::operator++() {
    day++;
    if( day > days_in_month[month]) {
       day -= days_in_month[month];
       month++;
       if (month > 12) {
          year++;
          month = 1;
       }
    }
    return *this;
}
```

In this (member) function we simply increment day and then check the range and change the month and year if necessary. Notice the difference between this function and the overloaded operator+() function which needs a local declaration (date d = *this). Once we have compute the correctly incremented date we return the pointer to this date (i.e. *this). Compare this overloaded operator with the overloaded += operator discussed earlier. Program 6.9 gives a complete program which uses this operator.

⬛ Program 6.9

```
//: OVLDATE2.cpp
//. overloading + and ++ with a date class as a member function
#include <conio.h>
#include <iostream.h>
// ........................................................
const int days_in_month[] =
     {31, 28, 31, 30, 31, 30, 31, 31, 30, 31, 30, 31};
class date {
    int day, month, year;
```

```
public:
   date(){};
   date(int d, int m, int y) { day = d; month = m; year = y; }
   void set(int d, int m, int y)
            { day = d; month = m; year = y; }
   void print(char * mess) { cout << mess << " " << day
        << " / " << month << " / " << year << endl; }
   date operator+(int days);
   date operator++();
};

date date::operator+( int days) {
   date d = *this;
   d.day += days;
   while( d.day > days_in_month[d.month]) {
      d.day -= days_in_month[d.month];
      d.month++;
      if (d.month > 12) {
         d.year++;
         d.month = 1;
      }
   }
   return d;
}

date date::operator++() {     // prefix

   day++;
   if( day > days_in_month[month]) {
      day -= days_in_month[month];
      month++;
      if (month > 12) {
         year++;
         month = 1;
      }
   }
   return *this;
}
// ..............................................................
void main() {

   date d1(4,6,96), d2;

   clrscr();
   cout << " OVLDATE2 " << endl;
   cout << " ======== " << endl << endl;

   d1.print(" d1 = ");

   d2 = d1 + 30;
   d2.print(" d2 = d1 + 30: ");
   d1.print(" d1 = ");   // to check that d1 hasn't changed
   cout << endl << " Now using auto-incrementing" << endl;
   ++d2;
   d2.print(" ++d2: ");
   cout << " Press any key to Quit ";
   getch();
}
```

Notice in the program we have used the prefix notation to call this operator (i.e. ++d2). What happens if we change this to the postfix notation. If you entered this program and tried it out with the postfix ++ you should have found, depending on your compiler, a warning message saying that a prefix operator is being used as a postfix operator. This leads us to suspect that it ought to be possible to define a postfix operator as well as a prefix operator, and this is indeed the case. Earlier versions of C++ used the same overloaded operator in both prefix and postfix operations, but later ones allow different operators to be defined. We define a postfix operator in a similar way to binary operators, i.e. by including a single int parameter in the function parameter list – this is a 'dummy' parameter and simply serves to distinguish between the two overloaded ++ operators. This new function has the form:

```
date date::operator++(int) { // postfix ++

    date d = *this;
    (*this).day++;

    if( (*this).day > days_in_month[(*this).month]){
        (*this).day -=
            days_in_month[(*this).month];
        (*this).month++;
        if ((*this).month > 12) {
            (*this).year++;
            (*this).month = 1;
        }
    }
    return d;
}
```

Notice in this function that we create a local variable d, to store the initial value of the object, and then operate on the object pointed to by this. Once all the computations have been completed we return the original object (d).

The above overloaded function definition contains a number of instances of the form (*this).day, etc. Since the de-referencing of pointers within structures is quite a common occurrence an alternative notation is available. (You may remember this from Chapter 5 where we introduced the structure pointer operator (i.e. ->).) We can therefore replace an expression such as:

```
(*this).day++
```

with:

```
this->day++
```

We will come, in a moment, to more operator overloading and, in particular, to the overloading of the assignment operator. Before tackling the issue of assignment overloading however, it is worth spending a little time discussing the topic of object copying. We will look at initialisation of objects, which should serve as revision, and at copying of objects, which has not so far been covered explicitly in this book.

Consider the following declarations.

```
sometype a;           // simple object declaration
sometype b(45);       // declaration and initialisation
sometype c = b;       // declaration of c and copy of b into c
sometype d = 67;      // declaration and initialisation (C style)
```

When an object (e.g. a) is declared one thing that happens is that space in the free store is reserved for the new object. This is achieved by calling the constructor function for objects of that class (in this case the class sometype). The constructor for new objects may be defined very simply as:

```
sometype(){}
```

or it may carry out some initialisation, for example:

```
sometype (){ n = 0;}
```

where sometype consists of a single int data member (n), or:

```
sometype(){day = 1; month = 1; year = 1900;}
```

where sometype represents a date class.

We may also have an overloaded constructor function which allows us to initialise a new object on declaration, as will be the case for the second and fourth examples given above. In both cases the overloaded constructor will look something like this:

```
sometype(int m){ n = m;}
```

In the third example we are copying a complete class; the object b is being copied to the new object c. The data members of object b are copied 'bit-by-bit' into the new object c. This will work fine for simple classes, which contain no pointers, such as a date class consisting of simple data types for the day, month and year. Program 6.10 (ASSIGN1.cpp) illustrates this method of initialisation.

Program 6.10

```
//: ASSIGN1.cpp
//. example of bit-by-bit copying

#include <iostream.h>
#include <conio.h>
// ...........................................................
// the date class
class date {
    int da, mo, yr;
public:
    date(){}
    date(int d, int m, int y) { da = d; mo = m; yr = y;}
    void display() { cout << da <<" / "<< mo <<" / "<< yr
                            << endl;}
    void addresses() { cout << &da << " " << &mo << " "
                            << &yr << endl;}
};
// ...........................................................
void main(void) {

    date d1, christmas(25,12,95);

    clrscr();

    cout << " ASSIGN1 " << endl;
    cout << " ======= " << endl;
    cout << " illustrating bit-by-bit copying" << endl;

    d1 = christmas;    // copy christmas into d1

    cout << " d1 : ";
    d1.display();

    cout << " Addresses " << endl;
    cout << " --------- " << endl << endl;
    cout << " Christmas - " << &christmas << endl;
    christmas.addresses();
    cout << endl << " d1 - " << &d1 << endl;
    d1.addresses();
    cout << " Now date d2 = d1; " << endl << endl;

    date d2 = d1;
    cout << " d2 : ";
    d2.display();

    cout << " Addresses " << endl;
    cout << " --------- " << endl << endl;
    cout << " d1 - " << &d1 << endl;
    d1.addresses();
    cout << endl << " d2 - " << &d2 << endl;
    d2.addresses();

    cout << " Press any key to Quit ";
    getch();
}
```

A copy constructor could be written for this class, which would have the following form:

```
date(date &dt) {da = dt.da; mo = dt.mo; yr = dt.yr;}
```

If this function is added to the date class in Program 6.10 (ASSIGN1.cpp) and the program rerun then there should be no difference in the output from the two programs. This is because bit-by-bit copying is sufficient for a simple class like date that is used in these programs. However, we need to consider what might happen if we use a rather more complicated class. Suppose that as well as the month being represented as an integer we also use an array of characters (or a pointer to a character). So the data members for this class are:

```
int   da;
int   mo;
int   yr;
char  *ms;
```

Using the default bit-by-bit copying we obtain a 'shallow copy' of the date in the new object.

☐ **Program 6.11**
```
//: ASSIGN2.cpp
//. example of bit-by-bit copying - the default 'shallow copy'

#include <iostream.h>
#include <conio.h>
#include <string.h>
#include <stdio.h>
// ...........................................
// the date class
class date {
   int da;
   int mo;
   char *ms;
   int yr;

public:
   date(){da = 0;  mo = 0; yr = 0; ms = 0; }
   date(int d, int m, int y);
   void display() { cout << da <<" / "<< ms <<" / " << yr
                         << endl;}
   ~date() { delete ms; }
   void addresses();
};

void date::date(int d, int m, int y) {
   static char *month[] =
   {"January","February","March","April", "May","June","July",
   "August","September","October","November","December"};
   da = d;
   mo = m;
```

```
        ms = new char[strlen(month[m-1])+1];
        strcpy(ms, month[m-1]);
        yr = y;
}

void date::addresses() {
        printf(" da : %u \n", &da);
        printf(" mo : %u \n", &mo);
        printf(" ms : %u -> %u contains %s\n", &ms, ms, ms);
        printf(" yr : %u \n", &yr);
}
// ...........................................................
void main(void) {

        date christmas(25,12,95);

        clrscr();

        cout << " ASSIGN2 " << endl;
        cout << " ======= " << endl;
        cout << " the default 'shallow copy'" << endl;

        date d1 = christmas; // declare d1 & copy christmas into it
        cout << " d1 : ";
        d1.display();

        cout << " Addresses " << endl;
        cout << " --------- " << endl << endl;
        cout << " Christmas - " << &christmas << endl;
        christmas.addresses();
        cout << endl << " d1 - " << &d1 << endl;
        d1.addresses();
        cout << " Press any key to Quit ";
        getch();
}
```

The integer value of month (mo) is copied correctly into new space, as is the
address of the pointer to the character array version of the month, but the
pointer which is copied still points to the same address in memory where the
original value resides, as Test run 6.3 illustrates.

Notice the contents of ms in the two cases, although the addresses themselves
are different (65522 and 65514) the contents (4322) is the same.

What we really want to happen is for new space to be reserved for ms itself
and for the pointer to ms to address the relevant area thus created. What is required therefore is a copy constructor of our own which will perform a 'deep
copy' rather than a 'shallow copy'. The function required is:

```
date::date(date &dt) {
        da = dt.da;
        mo = dt.mo;
        yr = dt.yr;
        ms = new char[strlen(dt.ms)+1];
        strcpy(ms, dt.ms);
}
```

```
ASSIGN2
=======
the default 'shallow copy'
d1 : 25 / December / 95
Addresses
---------

Christmas - 0x3ad2ffee

da : 65518
mo : 65520
ms : 65522 -> 4322 contains December
yr : 65524

d1 - 0x3ad2ffe6

da : 65510
mo : 65512
ms : 65514 -> 4322 contains December
yr : 65516
```

Test run 6.4 shows the test run with the new function.

🖥 **Test run 6.4**

```
ASSIGN2B
========
example of 'deep copying'
d1 : 25 / December / 95
Addresses
---------

Christmas - 0x3ad7ffee

da : 65518
mo : 65520
ms : 65522 -> 4322 contains December
yr : 65524

d1 - 0x3ad7ffe6
da : 65510
mo : 65512
ms : 65514 -> 4336 contains December
yr : 65516
```

A close examination of the output given above indicates that now the address pointed to by ms is different in the two objects Christmas and d1. From this we deduce that ms has been copied into a new location, having first reserved space for it.

The above discussion has concentrated on the use of a copy constructor when an object is declared, or instantiated. However copying can also occur when using functions; for example when an object is passed as an argument to a function, or when an object is returned from a function, a copy of the object is made. (Unless of course we pass a reference to the object, in which case no extra memory is required and no copying need occur.) Whenever any such copying occurs a copy constructor is required. Whether the programmer supplies the function or whether the default bit-by-bit copy constructor will be adequate depends on the make-up of the class being copied. Remember that if pointers are involved then normally the default constructor will not be sufficient and you will need to write one to carry out the desired operation.

6.13 A class as a function parameter

It should not surprise you that objects can be passed as arguments to a function call in the same way that any other data types can be passed. (In fact we have already used this in our discussion of the imperial and metric classes in Chapter 3.) Recall that 'call by value' is used in C and C++ when passing arguments to a function. So, under normal circumstances, a copy of the argument is generated as a local variable inside the function (see Chapter 2). Now, what happens when an object is passed as an argument to a function? Well, it looks as if a second (local) object is created, but if this is the case then when an object is created its constructor is called and when it goes out of scope its destructor is called. So far, so good. But what if the constructor initialises a data member? We may then not get an exact copy of the original object since a, possibly unwanted and unintended, initialisation will take place in the copying process. Take a look at Program 6.12 (OBASPAR1.cpp). This provides a simple example where an object is passed to a function. Test run 6.5 gives a sample run.

Program 6.12

```
//: OBASPAR1.cpp
//. passing an object to a function

#include <conio.h>
#include <iostream.h>
// ........................................................
class a_class {
   int n;
public:
   a_class(){ n = 0;}    // constructor - initialises n to 0
   ~a_class(){};         // destructor
   void set(int num) { n = num; }
   void print() { cout << " n = " << n << endl;}
};
// ........................................................
// a function which uses a_class
void func( a_class a) {
```

```
      cout << "   In func - ";
      a.print();
}
// ........................................................
void main(void) {
   a_class i;
   clrscr();
   cout << " OBASPAR1 " << endl;
   cout << " ======== " << endl << endl;

   cout << " Before changing n:" << endl;
   cout << "   In main - ";
   i.print();
   func(i);

   i.set(12);   // give i a new value
   cout << " After changing n:" << endl;
   cout << "   In main - ";
   i.print();
   func(i);
   cout << " Press any key to Quit ";
   getch();
}
```

⌨ Test run 6.5

```
OBSAPAR1
========

Before changing n:
   In main -  n = 0
   In func -  n = 0
After changing n:
   In main -  n = 12
   In func -  n = 12
Press any key to Quit
```

Now this program works as we would wish, but not as how I led you to believe above. Obviously the analysis was wrong. When a local copy of the object is made, inside func(), the constructor cannot be called since if it had then the value of n would be 0 in both calls of func(), not just the first where it has been given, correctly, the value 0. So the constructor function is not called when the copy is made, but what about the destructor? How many times is that called?

Try to work out what should happen with regard to the calling of ~a_class() inside the function func(), then read on.

```
a_class(){ n = 0; cout << " Constructor called " << endl;}
      // constructor - initialises n to 0
~a_class(){ cout << " Destructor called " << endl;};
      // destructor
```

If we make the above changes to the constructor and destructor functions in

OBSPAR, compile and run the program, then we should obtain the result given in Test run 6.6.

```
Constructor called
OBASPAR2
========
Before changing n:
   In main -   n = 0
   In func -   n = 0
Destructor called
After changing n:
   In main -   n = 12
   In func -   n = 12
Destructor called
Press any key to Quit   Destructor called
```

This confirms our recent analysis of when the constructor function is called. It also reveals that whilst there is only one call of the constructor function there are three calls of the destructor function – one for each of the calls of func() and one when the program is finished. A moment or two's reflection should show why this has to be the case. Within the function a local object is created, which must be of the actual object as passed (not a new instantiation of an object) so no call to the constructor function is made. But when control passes from the function there is still the need to clear up and release storage. Therefore the destructor member function needs to be brought in to play to accomplish this task.

6.14 Returning an object

Since we can use an object as a parameter to a function then equally we should be able to return an object from a function. This is done in the usual way by:

i) Declaring the function to be of type some_class (say) and then
ii) Using the return statement in the function body to return the object.

Consider the following example. We define a class employees which among other things contains an employee name, their initials, their staff identity number and their salary. We have member functions which allow us to set the salary, and display their staff number and salary. Suppose that we frequently require to compare the salary of two employees and select the one with the lower salary. This could be done using code such as:

```
if (emp1.get_salary() < emp2.get_salary()) {
   // use emp1 ...
}
else {
   // use emp2 ...
}
```

However if this operation is to be carried out more than once or twice then it becomes rather tedious. Instead we could write a function which takes two objects of type `employees` and returns the one with the smaller salary. Inside the function, which is not a member function of `employee`, we need to compare the salaries of two employees. We can do this so long as we have a public member function which returns the value of the salary of an employee (e.g. `get_salary()`). Thus the function is:

```
// function which uses objects of type employee as
// parameters and as a return value

employee is_smaller_salary(employee emp1, employee emp2){
   if (emp1.get_salary() < emp2.get_salary())
      return emp1;
   else
      return emp2;
}
```

and we can use this function in the main program to assign to another object of type `employee` the details of the employee with the smaller of the two salaries, e.g:

```
e3 = is_smaller_salary(e1,e2);
```

We can even use the return value directly, as in:

```
cout << is_smaller_salary(e2,e3);
```

but now we don't know which of `e2` or `e3` has the smaller salary. However what we can't do, although the compiler won't complain – at least mine didn't – is to try to find out who has the smaller salary and given them a rise all in one go, i.e:

```
is_smaller_salary(e2,e3).give_salary(30000);
```

doesn't do what we might expect. The reason for this is that what `is_smaller_salary()` returns is not actually `e2` or `e3` but a copy – the one with the smaller salary. So we can give this copy a pay rise but it will get lost – happens all the time I think! If you want to check this then take a look at Program 6.14 (`RETOBJ1.cpp`) in exercise 6.15.18 at the end of this chapter.

Suppose that we still want a statement like

```
is_smaller_salary(e2,e3).give_salary(30000);
```

to work. Is there any way of doing this? The clue is in the paragraph before the previous exercise. In that paragraph I said that the function returns 'a copy' of the employee with the smaller of the two salaries. We don't want a copy but the real thing! We can do that by using references to the employees in our function is_smaller_salary(), as follows:

```
employee &is_smaller_salary(employee &emp1, employee &emp2){
   if (emp1.get_salary() < emp2.get_salary())
      return emp1;
   else
      return emp2;
}
```

Notice that the only places we need to include the reference operator is before the function name and in the parameter list before the variables emp1 and emp2. All other elements in the function remain the same. The function call also remains the same.

6.14.1 A problem and a benefit

Although the above method solves our current problem it does have a dangerous side effect – in fact we have used that side effect in solving the problem. By passing references to the two employee objects and returning a reference we allow direct modification of the details for the employee with the smaller salary. Care needs to be taken with such code as inadvertent modification could occur. If we want to ensure that modification cannot take place then we simply pass and return objects by value. If, on the other hand, we do want to allow modification to take place then we use references.

One benefit of using references is that local copies of the objects are not made. This means that, particularly when large structures are being used, we can drastically reduce unnecessary memory usage.

One last point, before moving on to consider overloading the assignment operator, concerns classes which contain classes. How, you might ask, are objects such as these copied? The answer is that 'member wise copying' takes place – which means that if a member class contains a copy constructor(s) then it will be used in the copying process, if not then bit wise copying will take place as for a simple class.

6.15 Overloading =

The assignment operator may be overloaded in the same way as other operators. Cases when we might wish to overload this operator include improving readability (such as `m1 = m2`, where `m1` and `m2` are both objects of type `matrix`, say; or `str1 = str2`, where `str1` and `str2` are strings (arrays of char)). Sometimes there will be no need to overload the assignment operator, for example when a straightforward bit-by-bit copy is sufficient, however when objects allocate memory or contain pointers to other objects or data types then more care needs to be taken and an overloaded = operator may need to be written.

As an example we will return to the date class discussed in Section 6.16. We can use an overloaded assignment operator in a statement such as

```
d2 = christmas;
```

where the function itself looks like this:

```
// overloaded =
void date::operator=(date &dt) {
   da = dt.da;
   mo = dt.mo;
   yr = dt.yr;
   delete ms;
   // create space for ms
   ms = new char[strlen(dt.ms)+1];
   strcpy(ms, dt.ms);
}
```

A comparison of this function with the copy constructor discussed earlier shows only one difference, namely the presence of the `delete ms;` statement. Before reading on try to work out why the `delete` statement is required in one function but not in the other.

The reason that the `delete` statement is needed in the overloaded = operator function is that `ms` may already have been assigned to another value. The memory set aside must therefore be released before allocating new memory. Without the delete, especially where large arrays or structures are involved, would mean that the program could run out of memory.

6.16 The date class revisited

As a means of gathering together the topics discussed so far in the chapter we provide a complete example which illustrates the use of both operator overloading and friends. Many of the overloaded operators have already been introduced so much of the material in this section (and the corresponding pro-gram) should be little more than revision! However this example also contains some new overloaded operators and we will look at these during our discussion of the program.

We require a date class which will allow us to manipulate dates given in the form 22/10/97. We wish to be able to enter and display dates in this form. (However in order to be able to deal with 'the millennium problem' we need to be able to clear up ambiguous dates, e.g. 22/10/04 could mean 22nd October 1904 or 22nd October 2004, or the fourth year of any century for that matter. We have elected to do this by storing the year in its full form – so if a one- or two-digit year is entered the century is also requested to remove any ambiguity.)

In addition we want to be able to add or subtract one day from a date as well as add or subtract any integral number of days. We also wish to be able to use constructs of the form:

```
d1 = 14 + d2;
```

as well as:

```
d1 = d2 + 14;
```

The program DATEOPS.cpp (given in Appendix A) contains the necessary class definition and member function definitions required to achieve the operations just described. In this program a couple of additional operators are overloaded which haven't so far been discussed – we will take a brief look at them shortly. The class definition is given next:

```
#include <iostream.h>
#include <conio.h>
#include <string.h>

#define TRUE 1
#define FALSE 0

static int days_in_month[] =
    {31, 28, 31, 30, 31, 30, 31, 31, 30, 31, 30, 31};

static char *months[] = {     "January",
            "February",       "March",
            "April",          "May",
            "June",           "July",
            "August",         "September",
            "October",        "November",
            "December"
};

class date {
    int date_set; // date_set = TRUE if date has
            // valid value, otherwise FALSE
```

```
         int day;
         int mm;           //  range 1 - 12
         int year;         //  must be complete i.e. 1996 =
                           //  1996 not 96)
                           // private member functions
         long day_num(date dt);
         isleap(int y);

public:
         // constructor - used to initialise date_set
         // so that unset dates can be trapped
         date() { date_set = FALSE; }
                                     // overloaded constructor
         date(int d, int m, int y)
           { day = d; mm = m; year = y; date_set = TRUE; }
         void set(int d, int m, int y);
         void next();
         void prev();
         void print_long_date();
         void operator=(date &dt);

         date operator+(int n);   // add n days e.g. d1 + n
         friend date operator+(int n, date &dt);// n + d1

         long operator-(date dt);// e.g. d1 - d2
         date operator-(int n);   // e.g. d1 - n
         date operator++();       // prefix ++
         date operator++(int);    // postfix ++
         date operator--();       // prefix --
         date operator--(int);    // postfix --
         date operator+=(int n); // d1 = d1 + n
         date operator-=(int n); // da = d1 - n
               // comparison operators for date
         int operator<(date &dt);
         int operator>(date &dt);
         int operator<=(date &dt);
         int operator>=(date &dt);
         int operator==(date &dt);
         int operator!=(date &dt);
                     // overloaded << and >>
         friend ostream &operator<<(ostream &stream, date dt);
         friend istream &operator>>(istream &stream, date &dt);
};
```

We will examine various aspects of this class by taking a look at the uses of
the functions and overloaded operators in the program.

First of all the declarations for d1, d2 and christmas.

```
date d1, d2(23,10,1996);
date christmas(25,12,1996);
```

These use respectively the constructor functions date() and date(int d,
int m, int y). Notice that for d2 and christmas although we have used the
four-digit year there is nothing in the definition of date(...) to prevent us
using a two-digit date. Also there is nothing to prevent us initialising invalid

dates. A complete solution should prevent illegal initialisations. (The same criticism also applies to set() and the overloading of >>, see later.) One way around the year problem is to force a four-digit year to be entered (including leading zeros); an alternative is to use four parts for a date – day, month, two-digit year and century.

6.16.1 Overloading =

The first overloaded operator in the program is the assignment operator:

```
// overloaded assignment operator

void date::operator=(date &dt) {
    day = dt.day;
    mm = dt.mm;
    year = dt.year;
}
```

which is used in the statement d1 = d2;. This should present no problems for you as we have already looked at similar uses.

6.16.2 Overloading postfix--

The next overloaded operator is the postfix decrement operator:

```
// decrement date - postfix
date date::operator--(int) {

    if (!date_set) {
        cout << endl << " *** Attempt to decrement an invalid date **
            << endl;
        return *this;
    }
    int d_in_m[12];

    for(int m = 0; m < 12; m++)
        d_in_m[m] = days_in_month[m];
    if (isleap(year))
        d_in_m[1]++;

    date dt = *this;
    day--;
    if ( day < 1) {
        mm--;
        if (mm < 1) {
            mm = 12;
            year--;
        }
        day = d_in_m[mm-1];
    }
    return dt;
}
```

There are three points worth noting about this function.

1) Since this is intended to mimic the normal postfix operator (i.e. --) we need some way to distinguish it from the prefix operator. This is achieved by simply using a *dummy* parameter for this operator – the parameter is never used so there need be no variable in the parameter list simply the `int` data type.

2) Again, because we want to mimic the normal operation of postfix --, we return the original date, even though on subsequent use it will have been decremented. This is achieved through the two statements `dt = *this;` and `return dt;` and by applying the decrement operation to `*this` rather than to `dt`. (Compare this function with that for the prefix -- operator given in the program.)

3) We have utilised a *private member function* `is_leap()` so that we can correctly cater for leap years. Again, take a look at how `is_leap()` is defined.

6.16.3 Overloading the left shift operator <<

The third overloaded operator which we need to discuss is the left shift operator which, in this case, enables dates to be output directly to the screen using, for example `cout << d1`. The function looks like this:

```
// overloaded left shift allows cout to be used directly
// with a date e.g. cout << d1;

ostream &operator<<(ostream &stream, date dt) {
    stream << dt.day << " / " << dt.mm << " / " << dt.year;
    return stream;
}
```

This operator (<<) is often referred to, in C++, as the *insertion operator*. This name is derived from the fact that it is used to insert characters into a stream. Analogously the right shift operator (>>), associated with `cin`, is also known as the *extraction operator*.

The first point to note about this function is that is a friend function. It cannot be a 'normal' member function because it does not return a date (see below) but it must have access to the private data members of date so that they can be shifted to the output stream.

Notice the form of this function. It must begin with the predefined class name `ostream` which is the stream, derived from `ios`, used for outputting characters. The function must return a reference to the output stream, so after `ostream` we have `&operator`, and the last thing the function must do is to return `stream` – this enables our overloaded inserter to be used in a chain of insertions (e.g. `cout << " d1= " << d1 << " d2 = " << d2 << endl; `). Next there are just two parameters to the function; the first being a reference to the output stream (`ostream &stream`), and the second being the object being inserted (`date dt`). Within the body of the function we can place any operations we choose but, following good programming practice, it is sensible to only allow operations which are associated with outputting information to a stream.

To recap, then, the general form of an overloaded insertion operator is:

```
ostream &operator<<( ostream &stream, class_type object) {
    // body of inserter function
    return stream;
}
```

where items in italics are programmer-defined identifiers. A similar structure is used for the extractor function:

```
istream &operator>>( istream &stream, class_type &object) {
    // body of inserter function
    return stream;
}
```

Refer to the program DATEOPS.cpp (in Appendix A) for an example of this overloaded operator. Remember that since, in this function, we need to read new values into our object we must pass a reference to the object (i.e. the second parameter becomes: *class_type &object*).

As mentioned earlier (Section 6.5.1) these two overloaded operators should be used whenever direct input or output of a class is required instead of the (clumsier) functions such as `read()`, `enter()`, `show()` or `print()`. By doing this we provide an interface for our class(es) which is 'cleaner' and closer to the way in which the built-in data types are manipulated in C++. From now on, wherever possible, we will therefore use these overloaded operators for input and output and you should adopt the same philosophy in your programming.

6.16.4 The comparison operators

Our next overloaded operators are used to compare dates – two of these operators are used in the program, i.e.

```
if (d3 > christmas)  // use overloaded > to  compare dates
    cout << " Sorry - Christmas is over "  << endl;
else if (d3 < christmas)    // ... and <
    cout << christmas - d3
         << " days to Christmas " << endl;
else
    cout << " HAPPY CHRISTMAS! " << endl;
```

The overloaded greater than operator (>) looks like this:

```
int date::operator>(date &dt)
{
    if (day_num(*this) > day_num(dt))
```

```
      return TRUE;
   else
      return FALSE;
}
```

and uses the private member function `day_num()` to make the comparison of dates easier. We will look in detail at `day_num()` in a moment, but first take a look at the > overloaded operator. Since it is a binary operator it will have one parameter (`date &dt`). The first operand is accessed via `this`. So we pass the contents of `this` (i.e. via `*this`) to the `day_num()` function and then compare this value with the equivalent day number of our parameter, returning TRUE or FALSE as appropriate. (Obviously both TRUE and FALSE will need to be defined earlier in the class definition.)

The `day_num()` function is defined as follows:

```
// convert date to a day number
// day 0 is 1/1/0 A.D.
// note - this assumes that y is the four digit year


long date::day_num(date dt) {
   long d;
   int y;

   y = dt.year-1;

   d = 365 * (long) y + (y/4) - (y/100) + (y/400);
   for (int m = 1; m < dt.mm; m++)
     d += days_in_month[m];

   d += dt.day;

   if (isleap(dt.year))
      if (dt.mm > 2)
         d++;
      else
      if (dt.mm == 2)
         if (dt.day == 29)
            d++;

   return d;
}
```

This function assumes day 1 is 1st January 0 A.D. and then works out a unique day number for the date passed to it. The most important point to note about this function is that we need to use a `long int` for the day number otherwise we would get truncation and therefore an incorrect value for the day number. This means that we need to cast `y` into a `long int`. An alternative method would be to declare both `y` and `d` to be of type `long`.

6.16.5 The overloaded + operator

The final operator we will be discussing in this section is the addition operator as it is used in expressions of the form `12 + christmas`, or, as in the program, `60 + today`. Take a look at these two similar functions:

```
// add n days to a date e.g. d1 + 5
date date::operator+(int n) {
   int d_in_m[12];

   for(int m = 0; m < 12; m++)
      d_in_m[m] = days_in_month[m];
   if (isleap(year))
      d_in_m[1]++;

   date dt = *this;
   n += dt.day;

   while( n > d_in_m[dt.mm-1]) {
      n -= d_in_m[dt.mm-1];
      if (++dt.mm == 13) {
         dt.mm = 1;
         dt.year++;
      }
   }
   dt.day = n;
   return dt;
}

//    add n days to a date e.g.  5 + d1
// note - this uses the previous operator

date operator+(int n, date &dt) {
   return dt + n;
}
```

The first of these function is the more complicated of the two since it contains the necessary operations to account for leap years as well as converting the resulting date (after adding n) in the correct form. This first function will deal happily with any expression of the form `d1 + n`, where `d1` is a date and `n` is an integral number of days, but it will not work with expressions of the form `n + d1`. We therefore need the second overloaded + operator which has two parameters (`int n` and `date &dt`). This function just calls the previous overloaded + operator, taking care to place the number of days being added last in the return statement, i.e. `return dt + n;`. This illustrates a useful precept – if you already have a function (which has been thoroughly tested!) then use it to simplify other functions.

We will leave our discussion of the DATEOPS.cpp program at this point, however it would be worthwhile spending further time looking over the program and checking that you understand how it works.

In Section 6.6 we illustrated how friend classes and friend functions could be used in the conversion of a date given in one form into another form. This is a particular application of the idea of class conversion which we shall go on to discuss in this section.

You will, by now, be aware of the fact that automatic conversion occurs between different fundamental data types in the C and C++ languages. Thus if an expression involves a mixture of int and long types a built-in function will be invoked to convert the ints to longs. Similarly if a function expects a double as an argument but is passed as float then an automatic conversion to a double will take place. Another example might be when we wish to force conversion, in which case we use the idea of casting, as when for example we write an expression like x = 1 / (float) n; where n is an int and x is a float. We wish to be able to mimic these conversion processes for our own classes. In this section we look at how conversion functions can be written to enable conversions to be made to and from the C++ types as well as how conversion functions can be written which enable a whole class to be converted from one to another.

6.17.1 Conversion to a built-in type

Program 6.13 (CONV1.cpp) illustrates some basic principles of type conversion. In this program we have one class called radian which provides two type conversion functions int() and double(). These two functions use the appropriate built-in types as their names – int() to convert (or cast) a radian to an int and double() to convert a radian to a double!

Thus in the program, where we have assignments from objects of type radian to int or double then the appropriate type-conversion operator will be called. So int i = r1; calls radian::operator int() and double d = r1; calls radian::operator double(). A second class radian2 allows for conversion from an object of type radian2 to an object of type radian and this would be called whenever an object of type radian is expected but an object of type radian2 is found. Thus:

```
r1 = r2;   and
show(r2); // calls radian2::operator radian()
```

both call the radian2::operator radian() function to achieve the required type-conversion.

Program 6.13
```
//: CONV1.cpp
//. type conversions using casting functions
#include <conio.h>
```

```
#include <iostream.h>
// ..................................................................
class radian {
float rad;
public:
    radian(float angle = 0.0) { rad = angle; }
    operator double() { return (double) rad;} //convert to double
    operator int() { return (int) (rad+0.5);} // convert to int
    friend ostream &operator<<(ostream &stream, radian r){
        stream << r.rad;
        return stream;
    }
};
// ..................................................................
class radian2 {
    int a;
public:
    radian2(int angle = 0) { a = angle;}
    operator radian(){ return radian((float) a); }
    friend ostream &operator<<(ostream &stream, radian2 r){
        stream << r.a;
        return stream;
    }
};

void show(radian r) {
    cout << " using show : " << (double) r << endl;
}

void main(void) {
    radian r1(2.6);
    radian2 r2(4);
    clrscr();
    cout << " CONV1 " << endl;
    cout << " ===== " << endl << endl;
    cout << " Illustrating type-conversions " << endl;

    int i = r1;      // calls radian::operator int()
    double d = r1;   // calls radian::operator double()

    cout << " i = " << i << endl;
    cout << " d = " << d << endl;
    cout << " r1 = " << r1;
    cout << endl;
    show(r1);        // no conversion

    r1 = r2;
    cout << " r2 = " << r2;
    cout << endl;
    show(r2);                   // calls radian2::operator radian()
    cout << " Press any key to Quit ";
    getch();
}
```

Before leaving this example take a look at the function show() which illustrates a second use of the type-conversion function – that of casting.

```
void show(radian r) {
```

```
    cout << " using show : " << (double) r.rad << endl;
}
```

You may wonder why we have to explicitly cast r to a double in this function. The reason is that since we have two conversion functions `int()` and `double()` an ambiguity arises when attempting to output r – enter this program, remove the `(double)` from the function and compile it to check. This raises an important issue regarding conversion functions which we will discuss at the end of this section.

6.17.2 Constructor conversion

In the examples which we have looked at so far conversions are performed by calling an appropriate function which is to be found in the source class (i.e. in the class `radian` for `int()` and `double()` and in class `radian2` for `radian()`). It is also possible to write constructor functions to carry out such conversions, as we have already seen. However in order to do this the source class either has to give the destination class explicit access privileges (by declaring the destination class constructor function to be a friend) or provide suitable (public) member functions so that the destination's object constructor can access the relevant data. In Program 6.14 (`CONV2.cpp`) we illustrate both of these techniques.

The two classes in this program `radian` and `degree` provide the necessary functions to allow conversion from one unit of angular measurement to the other. In the `radian` class we provide a function `get_rad()` which returns the `radian` value. This is a public member function and so is available to member functions of the `degree` class. We use this function in the function `degree( radian &r)` to enable conversion from radians to degrees. In the `degree` class we have constructed a friend function: `radian( degree &d)` which converts degrees to radians. Since this is a `friend` function it has direct access to the data members of `degree`.

Two other functions are used (`show_deg()` and `show_rad()`) which are invoked in the program as a means of illustrating when the various conversion constructor functions are called. So, for example, if `show_deg()` is called with an object of class `degree` then no conversion is required, but if we call the function with a `radian` argument then a conversion is required and so the conversion constructor function `degree::degree( radian &r)` is called to carry out this process.

Finally we have used casting operator functions so that objects of type `radian` and `degree` can be output directly by `cout`. These functions are `operator float(){return rad;}` and `operator float(){return deg;}`.

⬒ **Program 6.14**
```
//: CONV2.cpp
//. constructor type conversions
```

```
#include <conio.h>
#include <iostream.h>

#define PI 3.141592
// ..........................................................
class degree;               // declare degree so radian can see it

class radian {
        float rad;
public:
   radian(float angle = 0.0) { rad = angle; }
   radian(degree &d);        // type-conversion constructor
   float get_rad(){ return rad;}    // for use with degree

   operator float(){return rad;}
                    // so r can be used directly with cout
   friend ostream &operator<<(ostream &stream, radian r){
      stream << r.rad;
      return stream;
   }
};
// ..........................................................
class degree {
   float deg;
public:
   degree(float angle = 0.0) { deg = angle;}
   degree(radian &r);

   friend radian::radian(degree &d);
   operator float(){return deg;}
                    // so deg can be used directly with cout

   friend ostream &operator<<(ostream &stream, degree d){
      stream << d.deg;
      return stream;
   }
};

radian::radian(degree &d) {
   cout << " ** radian::radian degree( &d) called **" << endl;
   rad = d.deg * PI / 180.0;
}

degree::degree(radian &r){
   cout << " ** degree::degree radian( &r) called **" << endl;
   deg = r.get_rad() * 180.0 / PI;
}

// ..........................................................
void show_rad(radian r) {
   cout << "    using show : " << r << " radians " << endl;
}

void show_deg(degree d) {
   cout << "    using show : " << d << " degrees " << endl;
}
// ..........................................................
void main(void) {
```

```
radian r1, r2(2.0);
degree d1, d2(60.0);

clrscr();
cout << " CONV2 " << endl;
cout << " ===== " << endl << endl;
cout << " Illustrating type-conversions " << endl;
cout << " ... using constructor functions " << endl << endl;

r1 = d2;                 // calls radian::radian(degree &d)
d1 = r2;                 // calls degree::degree(radian &r)

cout << " r1 = " << r1;
cout << " radians " << endl;
show_rad(r1);    // no conversion
show_deg(r1);    // o/p value in degrees
                 // calls degree::degree(radian &r)

cout << endl;
cout << " d1 = " << d1;
cout << " degrees " << endl;
show_rad(d1);    // calls radian::radian(degree &d)
show_deg(d1);    // no conversion

cout << " Press any key to Quit ";
getch();
}
```

6.17.3 Example

As a final example of the use conversion functions take a look at Program
6.15 (CONVFUN2.cpp). This program uses two classes imperial and metric
(variations on classes with the same name used earlier when we looked at
friends – in Section 6.6). The imperial class stores a linear measure in feet and
inches whilst the metric class stores the measure in centimetres. A conversion
function (operator imperial(metric)) is used to convert measurements
from metric to imperial.

This program illustrates four ways in which a conversion function may be
called:

- An implicit call when an object of type imperial is assigned to a metric
  object (iht = mht;),
- An explicit cast (iht1 = (imperial) mht1;),
- An explicit call of the imperial conversion function (iht = imperial(
  mht);), and
- An implicit call when an argument of the wrong type is passed to a function (display(mht3)).

Program 6.15

```
//: CONVFUN2.cpp
//. using a friend class to enable class conversion
//. also illustrating casting
```

```
#include <iostream.h>
#include <conio.h>
// ...........................................................
class metric;

class imperial {
   int feet;
   float inches;
public:
   imperial(){}
   imperial(int f, float i){ feet = f; inches = i; }
   friend ostream &operator<<(ostream &stream, imperial imp);
   friend metric;
        // give imperial access to private members of metric
};

ostream &operator<<(ostream &stream, imperial imp){
    stream << imp.feet << "ft " << imp.inches << "in " << endl;
    return stream;
}
// ...........................................................
class metric {
   float cms;
public:
   metric(){}
   metric(float c){ cms = c; }
   friend ostream &operator<<(ostream &stream, metric met);
   operator imperial();// conversion function
};

ostream &operator<<(ostream &stream, metric met){
   stream << met.cms << "cms " << endl;
   return stream;
}

metric::operator imperial() {
   imperial imp;              // object imp - instance of class im-
perial
   float ins = cms/2.54;

   imp.feet = ins/12;// since imperial is a friend of metric we
   imp.inches = ins-12*(imp.feet); // can access feet & inches
   return imp;               // return the imperial object
}
// ...........................................................
// global function with imperial class as a parameter
void display(imperial imp){
   cout << imp;
}
// ...........................................................
void main(void) {
   imperial iht;
   metric mht(254.0), mht1(25.4), mht2(2.54), mht3(0.254);

   clrscr();
   cout << " CONVFUN2 " << endl;
   cout << " ======== " << endl << endl;
```

```
        cout << " Four ways in which the conversion function "
                    << endl;
        cout << "  metric::operator imperial(metric) " << endl;
        cout << " may be used: " << endl;

        cout << "implicit call of metric::operator imperial(metric) "
                    << endl;
        cout << " iht = mht: ";
        iht = mht;
        cout << iht << " = " << mht;;

        cout<<"explicit cast-call of metric::operator imperial(metric)
                    << endl;
        cout << " iht = (imperial) mht1: ";
        iht = (imperial) mht1;
        cout << iht << " = " << mht1;

        cout << "explicit call of metric::operator imperial(metric) "
                    << endl;
        cout << " iht = imperial(mht2): ";
        iht = imperial(mht2);
        cout << iht << " = " << mht2;

        cout << "implicit call of metric::operator imperial(metric) "
                    << endl;
        cout << " display(mht3): ";
        display(mht3);
        cout << " = " << mht3;
        getch();
}
```

6.18 Summary

Having reached the end of Chapter 6 you should have a reasonable grasp of
the fundamental elements of C++ programming. As was mentioned in the introduction to this chapter the concept of operator overloading – another aspect
of polymorphism – is central to many applications of object-oriented programming. You should therefore, perhaps even more than usual, check that
you have understood this chapter before moving on.

Topics covered:

• Recap on member access.
• Friend classes and functions.
• Friends of more than one class – bridge friend functions.
• Operator overloading.
• Overloading the binary addition operator (+).
• Overloading +=.

- The keyword `this`.
- Friend functions and operator overloading.
- Non-member and non-friend operator overloading.
- Overloading unary operators.
- Overloading auto-increment (++) operators.
- Postfix and prefix ++ and --.
- Using the arrow operator (->).
- Copying objects – shallow and deep copying.
- Using classes as function parameters.
- Functions returning an object.
- Assignment operator overloading (=).
- Overloading left shift (<<) and right shift (>>) operators.
- Overloading comparison operators (==, !=, <, >, etc.).
- Class conversion to a built-in type.
- Class conversion using constructors.
- Casting operator functions.
- Functions with default arguments and function overloading
- Inline functions.

6.19 Exercises

6.19.1 Write a program to test the `arith` functions, both the `int` and `float` version, as discussed in 6.3. Check that calling the function using constants –, e.g. `arith(5.6, 8.0)` – won't work. Note the error message obtained. Now try casting the arguments to `floats`, i.e. `arith( (float) 5.6, (float) 8.0);` and `arith( (float) 6.8, (float) 0.0);` and see that these work correctly.

6.19.2 Write a program to test the `max` inline function described in the text (Section 6.4).

6.19.3 Complete the program illustrating the `lowcase` function described in Section 6.4.

6.19.4

a) Write overloaded functions to return the absolute value of either an `int`, `long int`, `float` or `double`. So `abs(5.8)` returns 5.8, as does `abs(-5.8)`. As usual write a suitable test program to check that the functions all work correctly and are correctly called. What alternative is there in C where we don't have the overload facility. (This can also be used in C++ but because function overloading is available it is rarely needed.)

b) Write the above functions as inline functions.

6.19.5 Two functions have been overloaded as follows:

```
int pos(int num); // returns num as a positive number
int pos(char c, char *s);
                  // returns the position of c in the
                  // string s or -1 if none found
```

Why should such declarations never be made (in the same program, or libraries, or ... ever!)? What alternatives are there to such bad programming style?

6.19.6 Code the second function in the previous exercise. Remember to return -1 if the character c does not occur in s.

6.19.7 How would you modify the function so that it returned the next occurrence of the character in the string? Carry out this modification and test it.

6.19.8 Write a program which uses two classes, the date class discussed in this chapter and a `julian` class which represents a date as a day number in the year (1 – 365/6) and the year. So 1/1/1996 is 1 1995 and 1/3/1995 is 60 1995. Write a function so that dates initially given in the standard form (1/6/1999) can be converted to a Julian date.

6.19.9 Construct a class `imp_length` which stores a length as yards, feet and inches (both yards and feet should be of type `int` but inches should be of type `float`). Write member functions `set(int y, int f, float i)` and `show()` to allow the user to give values to an object of type `imp_length` and to display on the screen the values for a given object.
Create overloaded operators to allow for addition, subtraction and multiplication of objects of type `imp_length`.

6.19.10 Enter the program `FRIEND1.cpp` (Program 6.6) and try it out.

6.19.11 Modify program `FRIEND1.cpp` to incorporate the modifications discussed at the end of Section 6.6 – so that the `distance()` function is a friend of `circle` and a member function of `point`.

6.19.12 As an exercise in logic rewrite the friend `operator+` function without using the other overloaded + operator (see Program 6.8 and the discussion that follows).

6.19.13 Modify the program `COMP1.cpp` (Program 6.7) by replacing `c = a + b;` by `c = a.operator+(b);` and check that it still works correctly.

6.19.14 Write a program to implement the class complex. This should provide overloaded operators for the arithmetic operators, as defined next.

Operator	Definition	Example of use
+	r1+r2, i1+i2	c3 = c1 + c2;
−	r1-r2, i1-i2	c3 = c1 - c2;
*	r1*r2-i1*i2, i1*r2+i2*r1	c3 = c1 * c2;

Provide two constructor functions one with no initialisation and one where the imaginary component is initialised to zero.

Write a function `float mod()` which returns the number $real^2 + imag^2$.

Further define the function `complex conj()` which returns the complex conjugate of a complex number, which for a complex number c `= real + i * imag`, is `real - i * imag`, i.e. the complex conjugate simply changes the sign of the imaginary part. Use these functions in your definition of complex division as defined here:

```
c1 / c2   = c1 * c2.conj() / c2.mod()
```

This will also require an overloaded operator / which allows a complex number to be divided by a float i.e. `c1 / x = c1.real/x, c1.imag/x`.

6.19.15

a) Modify program `COMP1.cpp` so that it incorporates the += overloaded operator discussed in the text.

b) This is not the only way in which we could code this function. Can you think of an alternative?

6.19.16 Write overloaded operators for >> and << to allow for the direct input and output of complex numbers.

6.19.17 Modify OVLDATE2.cpp (Program 6.9) to include the postfix ++ operator discussed in Section 6.11.

6.19.18 a) Enter Program 6.16 (RETOBJ1.cpp) and try it out.

📋 **Program 6.16**

```
//: RETOBJ1.cpp
//. returning an object from a function call

#include <conio.h>
#include <iostream.h>
// ..........................................................
// class employee - partial definition only
class employee {
   char name[20];          // allow for longish names!
   char initials[4];       // allow max. 4 initials
   char staff_no[5];
   long int salary;        // plenty big enough!
public:
   employee(){ salary = 0; } // constructor - set salary to 0
   ~employee(){};
   friend istream &operator>>(istream &stream, employee &emp);
   void give_salary( long int sal){ salary = sal;}
   long int get_salary(){ return salary;}
   friend ostream &operator<<(ostream &stream, employee emp);
};

istream &operator>>(istream &stream, employee &emp){
   cout << "Enter details below for the employee " << endl;
   cout << "  Surname : "; stream >> emp.name;
   cout << " Initials : "; stream >> emp.initials;
   cout << " Staff no : "; stream >> emp.staff_no;
   return stream;
}

ostream &operator<<(ostream &stream, employee emp){
   stream << " Staff no " << emp.staff_no;
   stream << "   Salary = " << emp.salary << endl;
   return stream;
}
// ..........................................................
// function which uses objects of type employee as
// parameters and as a return value

employee is_smaller_salary(employee emp1, employee emp2){
   if (emp1.get_salary() < emp2.get_salary())
      return emp1;
   else
      return emp2;
}
// ..........................................................
void main(void) {

   employee e1, e2, e3;
```

```
    clrscr();
    cout << " RETOBJ1 " << endl;
    cout << " ======= " << endl << endl;

    cout << " Enter details for 1st employee " << endl;
    cin >> e1;          // give e1 a name
    e1.give_salary(15000);   // ... and a salary

    cout << " Enter details for 2nd employee " << endl;
    cin >> e2;          // give e2 a name
    e2.give_salary(20000);   // ... and a salary

    clrscr();

    cout << " Current State " << endl;
    cout << " e1: " << e1;
    cout << " e2: " << e2;

    cout << " Now find out who should have a pay rise!" << endl;
    e3 = is_smaller_salary(e1,e2);
    cout << " The smaller salary is: " << endl << e3;

    // give the lowest paid a rise to 22000
    e3.give_salary(22000);

    cout << endl;
    cout << " After giving her a rise she has: " << e3;
    cout << " and the smaller salary is now: ";
    cout << is_smaller_salary(e2,e3);

    // now give the smaller of these a rise!
    // won't work - modify the function so that it does!
    cout << " After a rise for the new samllest - to 30000 "
                << endl;
    is_smaller_salary(e2,e3).give_salary(30000);
    cout << " e2: " << e2;
    cout << " ... that should have been 30000! " << endl;
    cout << " e3: " << e3;

    cout << " Press any key to Quit ";
    getch();
}
```

This illustrates the function is_smaller_salary() discussed in Section 6.14 in action.

b) Now modify the program so that it does work.

6.19.19 Enter the program CONVFUN2.cpp (Program 6.15). Add an output statement of the form cout << " imperial conversion function called " << endl; to the metric::operator imperial(metric) function to verify that this function is called in all four cases mentioned in the text.

6.19.20 A `boolean` class has the following form:

```
enum condition {FALSE, TRUE };
class boolean {
   condition cond;
public:
   boolean(condition c = FALSE) { cond = c; }
   boolean operator&&(boolean b);
   boolean operator||(boolean b);
   boolean operator!(void);
   friend ostream &operator<<( ostream &stream,
                boolean b);
   friend istream &operator>>( istream &stream,
                boolean &b);
};
```

Write the definitions for the above and test them.

6.19.21 In the class `boolean` we wish to be able to form expressions such as:

```
b = (6 > 9)
b = (8 <= i)
b = (i == j)
```

where b is an object of type `boolean` and i and j are `int`s.

Write an additional assignment operator (i.e. =) to allow such expressions to be used.

7 | Manipulating Objects

7.1 Introduction

In this short, but nevertheless important, chapter we move from dealing with single instances of a class to multiple instances, in the form of arrays of objects and pointers to objects. We illustrate how dynamic objects can be created (at run-time) and therefore how dynamic arrays can be set up to hold objects.

7.2 Arrays of simple objects

You will already be familiar with the use of arrays with the fundamental data types and you will not be surprised that we can also build arrays of objects. So, for example, we can create a simple integer class with a member function `get_i()` and a constructor function `int_class()` which allows an array made up of objects of `int_class` to be declared and initialised.

There is nothing particularly new in this use of classes with arrays, however there are a couple of points worth drawing to your attention. First we must provide initial values for all the elements of the array `a` (of type `int_class`) and this is done in the usual way by enclosing the list of initial values in braces (`{}`) when the array is declared. Secondly in order to gain access to the elements of the object `a` we need to call the member function `get_i()` for each element for which we require the value and this is achieved, as usual, by separating the element required and the member function with the `.` operator.

The program, as it stands, is not particularly useful as we are unable to declare uninitialised arrays. For example, commenting out the initialisation part of the int_class declaration to give `int_class a[2]; // = { 4, 12};` will result in a compilation error which will read something like:

```
Cannot find default constructor to initialise array element
of class int_class
```

Program 7.1

```
//: ARRAYOB.cpp
//. an array of objects - initialised
#include <conio.h>
#include <iostream.h>

class int_class {
    int i;
public:
    int_class(int j) { i = j;}
    int get_i(){ return i;}
};
// ................................................
void main(void) {

    int_class a[2] = {4, 12};
    clrscr();
    cout << " ARRAYOB " << endl;
    cout << " ======= " << endl << endl;
    cout << "a[0] = " << a[0].get_i() << endl;
    cout << "a[1] = " << a[1].get_i() << endl;
    cout << " Press any key to Quit ";
    getch();
}
```

The reason for this is that the only constructor function we have at this stage is one which also initialises an int_class object and therefore, when used to instantiate an array, the array elements. To overcome this we need to overload the constructor function with another constructor function which allows for arrays to be created but doesn't require them to be explicitly initialised. The constructor function required will look something like this:

```
int_class(){ i = 0;}
```

which, because it takes no arguments, will deal with missing initialisers. In this case we set the data member (i) to zero – this is not necessary, but is desirable since we can now rely on the fact that all array elements of this class will be set to zero unless explicitly initialised.

Now that we have two constructor functions available we can declare an array of objects in a number of different ways:

1 `int_class a[3] = {4, 7, 9};` all elements initialised explicitly
2 `int_class b[5];` all elements initialised to 0
3 `int_class c[5] = {1, 9};` c[0] = 1, c[1] = 9, all other elements set to 0

The use of simple classes to create arrays of objects should now present no problems to you, but what if we wish to create and initialise arrays of rather more complex objects? We will look at some examples in the Section 7.3.

7.3 Arrays of more complex objects

Consider the class `vector` with data members representing the position of a point on a two-dimensional plane:

```
class vector {
   double x;
   double y;
public:
   vector(){ x = 0.0; y = 0.0; }    // constructor 1
   vector(double xval){ x = xval; y = 0.0; }
                     // constructor 2
   vector(double  xval, double yval)
      { x = xval; y = yval; }    // constructor 3
   vector( vector &v){ x = v.x; y = v.y; }
                     // constructor 4
   double get_x(){ return x; }
   double get_y(){ return y; }
};
```

In this class we have four overloaded constructors which enable us to create and initialise objects of type `vector` in a variety of ways:

```
vector v1;           // v1.x = 0.0, v1.y = 0.0
vector v2(4.5);      // v2.x = 4.5, v2.y = 0.0
vector v3(2.8, -8.9);// v3.x = 2.8, v3.y = -8.9
vector v4(v2);       // v4.x = v2.x = 4.5, v4.y = v2.y = 0.0
```

Program 7.2 (VECTOR1.cpp) illustrates the vector class in use.

▯ Program 7.2

```
//: VECTOR1.cpp
//. using multiple constructors

#include <conio.h>
#include <iostream.h>

class vector{
   double x;
   double y;
public:
   vector(){ x = 0.0; y = 0.0;}                     // constructor 1
   vector(double xval){ x = xval; y = 0.0;}         // constructor 2
   vector(double xval, double yval){ x = xval; y = yval;}
                                                    // constructor 3
   vector(vector &v){ x = v.x; y = v.y;}            // constructor 4
   double get_x(){ return x; }
   double get_y(){ return y; }
   friend ostream &operator<<(ostream &stream, vector v){
      stream << v.x << ", " << v.y;
      return stream;
   }
};
```

```
// .................................................................
void main(void) {

    vector v1;                // v1.x = 0.0, v1.y = 0.0
    vector v2(4.5);           // v2.x = 4.5, v2.y = 0.0
    vector v3(2.8, -8.9);     // v3.x = 2.8, v3.y = -8.9
    vector v4(v2);            // v4.x = v2.x = 4.5, v4.y = v2.y = 0.0

    clrscr();
    cout << " VECTOR1 " << endl;
    cout << " ======= " << endl << endl;

    cout << " v1 = " << v1 << endl;
    cout << " v2 = " << v2 << endl;
    cout << " v3 = " << v3 << endl;
    cout << " v4 = " << v4 << endl;

    cout << " Press any key to Quit ";
    getch();
}
```

We can use similar methods of initialisation when we create an array of vectors. So for example, the declaration

```
vector v[3] = { vector(), vector(4.5), vector(2.8, -8.9) };
```

creates a three-element array v, with the same values as given to the individual variables v1, v2 and v3 in the previous example.

Program 7.3

```
//: VECTOR2.cpp
//. using arrays with multiple constructors
#include <conio.h>
#include <iostream.h>

// vector class definition goes here
// .................................................................
void main(void) {
    vector v[3] = { vector(), vector(4.5), vector(2.8, -8.9)};
    vector v4(v[1]);// v4.x = v[1].x = 4.5, v4.y = v[1].y = 0.0

    clrscr();

    cout << " VECTOR2 " << endl;
    cout << " ======= " << endl << endl;

    for( int i = 0; i < 3; i++)
        cout << " v[" << i << "] = " << v[i] << endl;
    cout << " v4 = " << v4  << endl;
    cout << " Press any key to Quit ";
    getch();
}
```

In this example we created a vector v4 equal to the second element of v (i.e. v[1]). However we could also have created a fourth element of v and assigned it to v[1]:

```
vector v[4] = { vector(), vector(4.5),
              vector(2.8, -8.9), v[1] };
```

Thus, provided the element referred to has already been created (declared), we can use that element in our initialisation list.

7.4   Pointers to objects

Pointers play such an important part in the C and C++ languages that we obviously will need to examine how they work with objects – this we will be doing in this section. Normally we use the .(dot) operator when accessing members of classes, however when accessing class members given a pointer to an object we use the arrow operator (->). Program 7.4 (PTTOOB.cpp) illustrates one use of a pointer to an object.

Program 7.4
```
//: PTTOOB.cpp
//. a pointer to an object

#include <conio.h>
#include <iostream.h>

class int_class {
   int i;
public:
   int_class(int j) { i = j;
      cout << "constructor 1 called " << endl;
   }              // constructor for initialised objects
   int_class(){i = 0;
      cout << "constructor 2 called " << endl;
   }              // constructor for uninitialised objects
   int get_i(){ return i;}
   ~int_class(){
      cout << "destructor called " << endl;
   } // destructor
};
// ....................................................
void main(void) {
   clrscr();
   cout << " PTTOOB " << endl;
   cout << " ====== " << endl << endl;

   int_class a(27), *p; // object a - value 27 and
                        // pointer to an int_class object (p)
```

```
p = &a;                     // address of a

cout << "a.i = ";
cout << p -> get_i() << endl;
            // use -> to call get_i()

cout << " Press any key to Quit ";
getch();
}
```

In this example an object (a) is declared, and initialised, and a pointer (p) is declared, in the usual way, to be of type int_class, through the statement:

```
int_class a(27), *p;
```

The pointer p is then assigned the address of the object a:

```
p = &a;
```

and finally the value of the data member i of a is displayed using the member function get_i() and the arrow operator:

```
p -> get_i()
```

We can also assign a pointer (of the correct type) to an array of objects, thus allowing us to use pointer arithmetic to access different elements of the array. In Program 7.5 (PTTOOB1.cpp) a pointer to an object is created :

```
int_class *p;
```

this in turn is assigned to the address of a previously created array of objects of type int_class:

```
p = a;      // equivalent to p = &a[0];
```

then within a loop the value of the data member i is displayed using

```
p -> get_i()
```

after which the pointer is incremented so that it points to the next object in the array, using:

```
p++;
```

This example illustrates that pointer arithmetic works in the expected manner even for objects – i.e. incrementing the pointer allows us to access the next element in the array of objects.

Program 7.5

```
//: PTTOOB1.cpp
//.a pointer to an array of objects

#include <conio.h>
#include <iostream.h>

// int_class definition goes here
// .............................................................
void main(void) {
    clrscr();
    cout << " PTTOOB1 " << endl;
    cout << " ======= " << endl << endl;

    int_class a[4] = {1, 5, 9};
    int_class *p;

    p = a;      // address of array a

    for(int j = 0; j < 4; j++){
        cout << "a[" << j << "].i = ";
        cout << p -> get_i() << endl;// use -> to call get_i()
        p++;                          // increment pointer
    }
    cout << " Press any key to Quit ";
    getch();
}
```

7.5 Creating dynamic objects

In this section we will be extending our use of arrays of objects to *dynamic arrays* of objects. You will recall that we introduced the C++ dynamic allocation operators in Chapter 3 (Section 3.10) and looked briefly at dynamic arrays in 3.11 – before reading on it would be well worth your while checking back over that material to remind you of the processes involved.

Creating an object dynamically means that first space must be allocated for the object (on the heap) and second that a pointer is returned which points to the newly created object. As with other created objects (i.e. through declaration) at creation time the relevant constructor function is called and when the object is released (i.e. when the block in which the object is declared is left) the appropriate destructor function is called.

Program 7.6

```
//: STORE.cpp
//. heap and stack
```

```cpp
#include <conio.h>
#include <iostream.h>
class makeroom {
    int i;
public:
    makeroom(int j = 0){
        cout << " constructor called " << endl;
        i = j;
    }
    ~makeroom() {
        cout << " destructor called " << endl;
    }
    void show() {
        cout << " makeroom::show() i = " << dec << i <<
        " address = " << hex << &i << endl;
    }
};
// .....................................................
void a() {
    int li = -1;     // create local int
    makeroom local(5); // create local object
    makeroom *heap = new makeroom(12);
                // create object on heap

    cout << " ** in call to a()... " << endl;
    cout << "                          li = " << li;
    cout << " address = " << hex << &li << endl;
    cout << " a:local"; local.show();
    cout << "   a:heap"; heap->show();
}
// .....................................................
void b() {
    int li = 9;     // create local int
    makeroom local(20);  // create local object
    makeroom *heap = new makeroom(10);
                // create object on heap

    cout << " ** in call to b()... " << endl;
    cout << "                          li = " << li;
    cout << " address = " << hex
    << &li << endl;
    cout << " b:local"; local.show();
    cout << "   b:heap"; heap->show();
}
// .....................................................
void main(void) {

    void (*func_ptr)();     // pointer to a function return void

    clrscr();
    cout << " STORE " << endl;
    cout << " ===== " << endl << endl;

    func_ptr = a;     // assign func_ptr to address of a()

    a();              // call a()
    cout << " address of a() = " << hex
            << (unsigned long)(*func_ptr) << endl;
```

```
    cout << " address of func_ptr = " << hex << &func_ptr
         << dec << endl;
    func_ptr = b;

    b();
    cout << " address of b() = " << hex
         << (unsigned long)(*func_ptr) << endl;
    cout << " address of func_ptr = " << hex << &func_ptr
         << dec << endl;
    cout << " Press any key to Quit ";
    getch();
}
```

Program 7.6 (STORE.cpp) illustrates the creation of a simple dynamic object. This program introduces a number of new ideas and so we will take a little time working through it. As well as looking at the creation (and deletion) of objects we will take this opportunity to mention briefly the differences between the stack and the heap (or free store) and will need to use pointers to functions. It would be instructive if you entered the above program and tried it out before reading on. If you do this, make a careful note of the output so that you can refer to it during the following discussion. We will look at the output from this program (and you can compare your output with mine) in a while, but before that we need to investigate what the program is doing!

First of all we have a class definition which will be used in the creation of dynamic objects. This class definition provides a simple member i and three member functions: makeroom() to construct an object (and give it a default value if none is provided); the destructor ~makeroom(); and a function to display both the value of the variable i and its address. Note how we have used the dec and hex manipulators to ensure that the data (value of i) and address of i are output in the correct format.

This class is then used in two very similar functions a() and b() both of which create: a local int variable (li); a local object (local); and a dynamic object (heap). Each of the three variables is initialised, with different values, and then the value and address of each is output. Notice how in both the functions a() and b() the object heap is created. Since this is a dynamic object (we create a pointer to the object) we need to allocate storage, so we use:

```
makeroom *heap = new makeroom(12);
```

makeroom *heap creates a pointer to an object of type makeroom which points to the newly allocated memory through assignment to new makeroom(12). Finally makeroom(12) calls the constructor for makeroom and initialises i to 12.

Next we have the main program. The first point to notice about this is the declaration of the variable func_ptr. Since we wish to keep track of the address of the functions a() and b() we need to declare a pointer to a function – which is done like this:

```
void (*func_ptr)();
```

We require the brackets around the variable otherwise we would be declaring a function which returns a pointer to a void.

Most of the remaining statements should require no further explanation except, perhaps, for the statement:

```
cout << " address of a() = " << hex
     << (unsigned long)(*func_ptr) << endl;
```

As you will see from the context we are attempting to output the address of the function a(). This cannot be done like this:

```
cout << " address of a() = " << hex
     << *func_ptr << endl;   // incorrect
```

since *func_ptr returns a void and we require the address of a(), we therefore need to cast the pointer into an unsigned long before attempting to output the value.

Having had a quick look at the program and its structure let's now take a look at the output. Test run 7.1 shows a sample run.

🖳 **Test run 7.1**
```
STORE
=====
constructor called
constructor called
** in call to a()...
                        li = -1 address = 0x39b6ffee
a:local makeroom::show() i = 5 address = 0x39b6ffec
 a:heap makeroom::show() i = 12 address = 0x39b6111e
destructor called
address of a() = 36580291
address of func_ptr = 0x39b6fff4
constructor called
constructor called
** in call to b()...
                        li = 9 address = 0x39b6ffee
b:local makeroom::show() i = 20 address = 0x39b6ffec
 b:heap makeroom::show() i = 10 address = 0x39b61126
destructor called
address of b() = 3658034a
address of func_ptr = 0x39b6fff4
Press any key to Quit
```

The first thing to notice about the output from this program is that whenever function a() or b() is called we get two calls to the constructor function of makeroom. The first call is made when the local object local is created, the second when the dynamic object heap is created.

Next we have the addresses of the variables li, local and heap. These all refer to addresses on the heap (free store), and in my implementation, build downwards. Thus li is stored at 0x39B6FFEE, local (i) at 0x39B6FFEC, and heap (i) at 0x39B6111E. Notice that because funct_ptr is given space on the heap before a() or b() are called its address is above that of li (i.e. 0x39B6FFF4). Now compare the addresses of the same variables when b() is called:

variable	in a()	in b()
li	0x39B6FFEE	0x39B6FFEE
local(i)	0x39B6FFEC	0x39B6FFEC
heap (i)	0x39B6111E	0x39B61126

Although the variables li and local(i) have the same address in the call to a() and the call to b() the address of heap(i) is different. Before reading on see if you can account for this difference.

A clue can be found by checking on the number of times the destructor function is called. You will see that it is only called once for each call of a() and for each call of b(). The reason for the addresses being different is that the memory allocated to heap in a() is still allocated even when control is passed back from a() to the main program. However since the address of the pointer to heap is lost on exit from a() we have no way of releasing the storage assigned to the dynamic object (heap). This illustrates an important aspect of dynamic memory allocation – that the user must clear up after the work is done! This can be achieved in this case by adding the statement

```
delete heap;
```

before exiting the function a() (and, for that matter b()). If this modification is made to the program then we will find that the destructor is called twice for each call of a() and b() and that now the address for the dynamically allocated object heap is the same in both function calls. This is left as an exercise for the reader.

Finally take a look at the addresses of the functions a() and b(). In my case they are respectively 36580291 and 3658034A. In other words a() is stored lower in memory than b() – in fact their addresses are stored on the stack, which in my implementation builds up, towards the heap.

7.6 Interim summary

Before moving on to consider dynamic arrays we will summarise when dynamic memory allocation is necessary. Dynamic memory allocation will be necessary:

- When you don't know how many objects you will need until run-time.
- When you don't know what the lifetime of an object will be.
- When you don't know how much memory the object will need until run-time.

Finally an important point to remember:

- When an object is created using new then it is your responsibility to remove it (using delete).

7.7 Dynamic arrays of objects

The creation of dynamic arrays of objects is quite straightforward provided that you have followed the discussion so far! A simple illustration is given in Program 7.7 (DYNARR.cpp). This creates a dynamic array of int_class objects and, for comparison, an auto array of the same objects. To achieve this we have two functions create_auto_objects() and create_dynamic_ objects().

📋 **Program 7.7**
```
//: DYNARR.cpp
//. auto arrays of objects and dynamic arrays of objects

#include <conio.h>
#include <iostream.h>

class int_class {
   int num;
public:
   int_class(int j) { num = j;
      cout << "constructor 1 called " << endl;
   } // constructor for initialised arrays

   int_class(){num = 0;
      cout << "constructor 2 called " << endl;
   } // constructor for uninitialised arrays

   int get_num(){ return num; }

   ~int_class(){
      cout << "destructor called " << endl;
   } // destructor
};
// ................................................................
void create_auto_objects() {
   int_class a[4];
   int_class b[] = {12, 9, 44};
```

```
   cout << " a: ";
   for(int i = 0; i < 4; i++)
      cout << a[i].get_num() << " ";
   cout << endl;

   cout << " b: ";
   for( i = 0; i < 3; i++)
      cout << b[i].get_num() << " ";
   cout << endl;
}
// ..............................................................
void create_dynamic_objects() {
   int_class *a = new int_class[2];
   int_class *b = new int_class[4];
   int_class *pa, *pb; // declare pointers so we can step
                       through a & b

   pa = a;
   pb = b;
   *pb = 5; pb++;      // two ways of getting next element!
   *pb++ = -7;
   *pb = 2; pb++;
   *pb = 99;
   pb = b;             // reset pb to point to start of b

   cout << " a: ";
   for(int i = 0; i < 2; i++)
      cout << pa++->get_num() << " ";
   cout << endl;

   cout << " b: ";
   for( i = 0; i < 4; i++)
      cout << pb++->get_num() << " ";
   cout << endl;

   delete []a;
   delete []b;
}
// ..............................................................
void main(void) {

   clrscr();
   cout << " DYNARR " << endl;
   cout << " ====== " << endl << endl;

   cout << "calling create_auto_objects() " << endl;
   create_auto_objects();

   cout << " Press any key to continue ";
   getch();

   cout << endl;
   cout << "calling create_dynamic_objects() " << endl;
   create_dynamic_objects();
   cout << " Press any key to Quit ";
   getch();
}
```

The function `create_auto_objects()` creates two arrays of `int_class`, one (a) with default initial values (`i = 0`) and the other with explicitly initialised values for `num` (12, 9 and 44). Notice that the destructor for `int_class` is called automatically on exit from this function – this is because the arrays which have been created are auto arrays – local to `create_auto_objects()`.

The second function, `create_dynamic_objects()`, also creates an array (this time using pointers) which has its elements initialised to the default value (i.e. 0) and a second array of `int_class` objects which are explicitly set within the function. Notice here how we use pointer arithmetic to access the elements of a and b. First of all we create space for the two arrays:

```
int_class *a = new int_class[2];
int_class *b = new int_class[4];
```

we then create two `int_class` pointers (pa and pb) to allow us to access the elements of these arrays just created.

Why can't we simply use the pointers a and b to access the various elements using pointers? We cannot use a or b as pointers to access the individual elements of a and b because if we did we would lose the original addresses of a and b. For example if we incremented a (via a++) then this would now point to the next element in a. So by the time we had accessed all elements of a we would have lost our way! We could of course decrement but that would mean keeping a careful track of where we were. It is simpler and safer to use another pointer.

Take a close look at the way in which pointer arithmetic is used to access the various elements of a and b.

For illustrative purposes I have provided two ways of assigning a value and moving to the next element of b:

```
*pb = 5;  pb++;
*pb++ = -7;
```

The first line uses two separate statements, one to do the assignment and a second to move the pointer to the next object. The second obviously combines the previous two statements into one.

When we come to output the value of i for the various elements of a and b there are two important points to note. First we must remember to reset pb to a and pb to b otherwise we will be starting at the wrong place in memory. Second, as we saw in Section 7.6, we use the arrow operator to access the member function `get_num()` and thus display the value of num:

```
pa++->get_num()
```

etc.

Finally after we've finished with a and b we delete them so that the heap (or free store) is released to the system. We do this through the statements:

```
delete []a;
delete []b;
```

Note it is important not to get confused between a and pa or b and pb. We don't delete pa or pb (we didn't use new to create them!).

We can use dynamic arrays to allow an array of objects to be created at run-time. This is obviously useful when we the number of objects we need to create may vary from run to run.

In Program 7.8 (DYNARRAY.cpp) we use a class int_array which allows us to do just that.

Program 7.8

```
//: DYNARRAY.cpp
//. a dynamic array of integers size entered at run-time

#include <conio.h>
#include <iostream.h>
#include <process.h>     // for exit()

class int_array {
   int *num;
   int size;
public:
   int_array(int s);
   ~int_array(){
      delete [] num;
   }                              // destructor
   int &operator[](int index);
   friend ostream &operator<<(ostream &stream, int_array &a){
      for(int i = 0; i < a.size; i++)
         stream << a.num[i] << " ";
      return stream;
   }
   friend istream &operator>>(istream &stream, int_array &a){
      //& doesn't work either!
      for(int i = 0; i < a.size; i++){
         cout << "a[" << i << "] = ";
         stream >> a.num[i];
   }
      return stream;
   }
};
// constructor for uninitialised arrays
int_array::int_array(int s) {
   size = s; num = new int[size];
   if (!num) {
      cout << " *** Unable to create array [ " << size << "] ***"
           << endl;
   exit(1);
   }
```

```
        for(int i = 0; i < size; i++) num[i] = 0;
}
// overloaded [] operator
int &int_array::operator[](int index){
    if (index < 0 || index > size-1){
        cout << endl << " Index out of bounds = " << index << endl;
        exit(1);
    }
    return *(num+index);
}
// ..........................................................
void main(void) {

    clrscr();
    cout << " DYNARRAY " << endl;
    cout << " ======== " << endl << endl;

    cout << " How many elements? > " << endl;
    int n;
    cin >> n;

    int_array a(n);

    cout << " Uninitialised: " << endl << a << endl;

    cout << "Now enter some values: " << endl;
    cin >> a;

    cout << " Initialised: " << endl << a << endl;
    cout << " Adding 1 to each element: " << endl;
    for( int i = 0; i < n; i++)
        a[i]++;

    cout << a << endl;

    cout << " Press any key to Quit ";
    getch();
}
```

This program introduces a few new features so we will take a few minutes to examine them before moving on. First notice how we have created the array. The size of the array is passed when the constructor is called, size is set to s and then an attempt to create space for the array made. The pointer num will return 0 if this fails – we therefore have a means of ensuring that we don't overwrite other parts of memory. Here we simply halt the program using a call to exit(). The second new element is the overloading of the [] operator. This enables us to use square brackets in the usual way. Overloading [] as reference (int &operator[](int index)) means that we can use on both the left and right hand side of assignment expressions. Without the & we could only use the overloaded [] (with objects of type int_array) on the right hand side of assignment expressions. Finally in this overloaded function we have include bounds checking to ensure that a call using [] does not index outside the array bounds.

7.8 Summary

This chapter provided the basic elements required for the manipulation of objects, using arrays and pointers.

Topics covered:

- Arrays of simple objects
- Arrays of more complex objects
- Pointers to objects
- Pointers to arrays of objects
- Dynamic objects
- Dynamic arrays of objects

7.9 Exercises

There is only one exercise in this Chapter, however it would be instructive to enter all the programs discussed and try them out before moving on to the next Chapter.

7.9.1 Modify Program 7.2 (VECTOR1.cpp) by creating a pointer to an object of type vector and use this to access the x and y values of v3.

8.1   Introduction

This chapter deals with the very important topic of inheritance. Much of the material dealt with so far has been presented in order that you will be able to use and understand inheritance, as it applies to C++. It is therefore important that you are fully conversant with the material covered in the previous chapters. We look first of all at single inheritance, where one class inherits attributes and methods from another (base) class. In our discussion of single inheritance we take a look at the different levels of access provided by the private, protected and public keywords. We examine when name clashes between functions can occur and how to resolve them. In sections 8.3 and 8.7 we look at how classes can be descended from more than one base class and see when multiple inheritance might be required. Sections 8.4 and 8.5 deal with the important topics of virtual functions and abstract classes.

8.2   Single inheritance

We have now dealt with most of the fundamental elements of C++ programming and are ready to move to more general topics of relevance to object-oriented programming. We have looked at how to create both simple and complex classes and we will now go on to consider how we can create hierarchies of classes. Inheritance enables a general class (the base class) to be constructed which contains member data and member functions relevant to a certain general task (e.g. graphic objects). This class may then be used as a basis for more specific classes (e.g. circle, rectangle, triangle, line). Only those elements of the base class which are necessary for the more specific class (i.e. the derived class) need be inherited.

One important point to note about the relationship between a base class and the derived classes which inherit the former's data members and member functions is that inheritance is defined by the derived class, not by the base class. All C++ structures and classes have the potential for being base classes – other classes can be inherited from them. As well as inheriting the traits (data members & member functions) from just one class (known as single inheritance) classes can be constructed which inherit traits from a number of classes (multiple inheritance). Finally a base class may be abstract (or virtual) in which case it is designed only as a base class – without inheritance it could do nothing. So for example we might create a general-purpose list processing class which includes all the member functions required for list processing (`get_head()`, `get_tail()`, `no_in_list()`, `sort()`, etc.) but does not specify any data types. A class can then be derived from this abstract base class which includes the details of the concrete data which serve to make up the list.

In order to be clear about inheritance it is useful to compare it with composition. Consider the case of fruit. Fruit is a base class for the derived classes apples, oranges, plums, bananas, grapes, to name only a few. The class `fruit` has characteristics such as colour, weight and is edible. A specific class of `fruit` may have additional characteristics, for example apples have a core, oranges have pips, grapes (may or may not) have pips. What parts of a fruit are eaten may differ in each case, for example all but the core of an apple might be eaten, but we don't normally eat the skin of an orange or a banana! Thus whilst the method is-edible is inherited the details of what is edible in a particular class may vary.

Consider another example. We might construct a base class `bicycle` which can then be used to derive particular classes of bicycle – penny farthing, boneshaker, touring, racing, mountain. Now each class of `bicycle` is made up of a number of different elements, some present in all cases (frame, handlebars, wheels) and some not always present (gears, brakes, chain). Some of these may themselves be describable as classes. Take for example wheels, these have characteristics such as diameter, number of spokes, and we can derive at least two types of wheel from the base class – pneumatic (on most modern bikes) and solid (on penny farthings and boneshakers). Similarly we might have a class `handlebars` which could lead to the derived classes dropped and straight, to name but two. Now bicycles do not inherit the class `wheels` nor the class `handlebars` but they are made up of, constructed from, wheels and handlebars, amongst other things.

So, when considering building classes from other classes it is important to remember the difference between construction and inheritance. Classes can be constructed from other classes in the sense that they are made up of other classes but a class may also inherit certain attributes from a more abstract, or more general class. One final example, the class `car` describes a particular class of the more general class `vehicle` and it will therefore inherit the characteristics of the `vehicle` class – colour, dimensions, number of wheels, etc. However a car is also made up of an engine, body and wheels which themselves might be described by classes. However neither engine, body nor wheels are *inherited* from the base class, rather objects of type engine, body, wheels are *contained* within the `car` class.

In the discussions that follow always keep in mind the difference between inheritance and composition and don't be tempted to overuse inheritance. When considering whether to use inheritance a useful question to ask is "Is the derived class essentially similar to another class?" If it is then consider using inheritance, otherwise composition may be more appropriate.

After this general discussion we now turn to the specifics of inheritance in C++. First of all we will take a look at how classes can be constructed from other classes, in other words we need to look at base class access.

8.2.1 Base class access

When one class inherits another we use this general form for its definition (for single inheritance):

```
class derived_class_name : access base_class_name {
    // body of derived class
};
```

where access is one of the three keywords:

```
private     protected     public
```

Which data members and which member functions of the base class are inherited by the derived class depends on the value of access and the status of the members which make up the base class (private, protected or public). We will go on to discuss the various combinations shortly, but let's first take a look at a simple example which uses just public and private members.

Program 8.1 (INHER1.cpp) contains a base class defined as:

```
class base {
    int i, j;
public:
    void setij(int n, int m){ i = n; j = m;}
    base(){ i = 0; j = 0;}   // constructor
    base( int n, int m){ i = n; j = m;} //overloaded constructor
    void showij(){ cout << " i = " << i << " j = " << j << endl;}
};
```

which contains member functions to access i and j. We then have a derived class which inherits the data members and member functions from base:

```
class derived : public base{
    int k;
public:
    void set(int p){ k = p;}
    derived(){ k = 0;}
    derived(int p){ k = p;}
    void showk(){ cout << " k = " << k << endl;}
};
```

This includes one additional data member (private to derived) and the member functions needed to access k. Within the main program the member functions of base are available for use by objects of type derived, thus we can display i & j for u and v and set i and j:

```
u.showij();   // can access showij()
v.showij();
v.setij(9, 3);
```

as well as use member functions of derived in the usual way:

```
u.set(77);
u.showk();
```

The complete program, indicating where the base classes are defined, is given in Program 8.1.

Program 8.1

```
//: INHER1.cpp
//. simple single inheritance
#include <conio.h>
#include <iostream.h>
// base class definition goes here

// derived class definition goes here
// ...................................................
void main(void) {
   base x, y(5,-8);
   derived u, v(-12);

   clrscr();
   cout << " INHER1 " << endl;
   cout << " ====== " << endl << endl;
   cout << " base " << endl;
   cout << "  x: "; x.showij();
   cout << "  y: "; y.showij();
   cout << endl << " derived" << endl;
   cout << "  u: "; u.showk();
   u.set(77);
   cout << " after u.set(77)" << endl;
   cout << "  u: "; u.showk();
   u.showk();
   u.showij();   // can access showij()

   cout << "  v: "; v.showk();
   v.showij();
   v.setij(9,3);
   cout << " after v.setij(9,3)" << endl;
   cout << "  v: "; v.showij();

   cout << " Press any key to Quit ";
   getch();
}
```

You will have noticed that we used a function called setij() in base and a function set() in derived. What if both functions have the same name? If you have entered the above program you can try this out by removing the ij from all references to setij(). What happens, or what do you think will happen? Can you think of any solutions? If you can then try them (it) out! ... or read on.

When the same name is used for the two set() functions and the program is compiled, a compilation error will result with a message something like:

```
Extra parameter in call to derived::set(int)
```

The compiler cannot distinguish between the two functions called set(), one in base and one in derived. We can overcome this problem in three ways:

1. As in the original program, by giving the two functions different names (e.g. setij() and set() or set_ij()), or
2. By explicitly calling the base function through the use of the scope resolution operator (::). Thus we can call set() in base with:

```
v.base::set(9,3);
```

or

3. By writing a derived set() function which itself calls explicitly the base set() function, e.g.

```
set(int n, int m){ base::set(n, m);}
```

Before moving on it is worth looking briefly at what happens when objects of the derived class are created. First of all any data members belonging to the base class are created and where appropriate initialised. Then the derived data members are created. How might you check this? Program 8.2 (INHER1A.cpp) illustrates how this can be done.

Test run 8.2 shows the most important part of the output, for our present discussion.

This shows quite clearly that when a derived object is instantiated the base constructor is called first, followed by the relevant constructor for the derived class itself. Notice also which base constructor function is called when a derived object is created. It is the default (no parameters) constructor, which illustrates an important point concerning inheritance, namely that a base class must contain a default constructor (containing no parameters), or one constructor which has default values for all its parameters, otherwise any class inheriting the base class will be unable to create their base object(s). You can check this out for yourself by commenting out the default base constructor and then try recompiling the program.

Program 8.2

```
//: INHER1A.cpp
//. simple single inheritance
//. illustrating constructor calls
#include <conio.h>
#include <iostream.h>
class base {
   int i, j;
public:
   void setij(int n, int m){ i = n; j = m;}
   base(){ i = 0; j = 0;
      cout << " base constructor 1 called" << endl;
   } // constructor
   base( int n, int m){ i = n; j = m;
      cout << " base constructor 2 called" << endl;
   } // overloaded constructor
   void showij(){ cout << " i = " << i << " j = " << j << endl;
   }
};
// .........................................................
class derived : public base{
   int k;
public:
   void set(int p){ k = p;}
   derived(){ k = 0;
      cout << " derived constructor 1 called " << endl;
   }
   derived(int p){ k = p;
      cout << " derived constructor 2 called " << endl;
   }
   void showk(){ cout << " k = " << k << endl;}
};
// .........................................................
void main(void) {
   clrscr();
   cout << " INHER1A " << endl;
   cout << " ======= " << endl << endl;
   // remainder of program as for INHER1
}
```

🖥 Test run 8.1

```
INHER1A
=======

declare x and y:
base constructor 1 called
base constructor 2 called
declare u and v:
base constructor 1 called
derived constructor 1 called
base constructor 1 called
derived constructor 2 called
base
  x:  i = 0 j = 0
  y:  i = 5 j = -8
.....
```

One final point, suppose we wish to set i and j as well as k. How might this be achieved? See if you can suggest a solution before moving on.

Hopefully you didn't think of modifying set() in derived to directly set i and j, e.g. like this:

```
void set(int p, int q, int r)
    { k = p; i = q; j = r;} // won't work
```

This is incorrect because i and j are private to the base class – any derived class doesn't have direct access to them. However, a moment's thought tells us that derived does have access to the public member functions of base. So we can have the following:

```
void set(int p, int q, int r)
    { k = p; setij(q, r);} // will work
```

If you didn't get this, or something similar, then try it out now.

The example we have been discussing up till now treated the base class as public for the derived class. What would happen if we change the access to private? If you try this out you will find that you obtain compilation errors such as "base::showij() is not accessible" etc. Thus, giving the derived class only private access to base means that all members of the base class are only accessible by member functions of derived – they cannot be accessed even by objects of the derived class.

So it looks as if we cannot set i and j since v.setij(), u.showij() won't now work. However there are ways around it as we shall now see. One solution is to write public member functions of derived which themselves set and show i and j. This cannot be done by directly accessing i and j, e.g. by writing a function:

```
set(int n, int m){ i = n; j = m;}
```

since i and j are private to base and therefore cannot be accessed by derived. However the public member functions of base are accessible. So we can write functions in derived such as:

```
set(int n, int m){ setij(n,m);}
```

which uses the public member function of base setij(). Remember that if we use the same name (e.g. set() in both base and derived classes then within the derived set() we need to use the class scope operator (::) to ensure that the base set() function is called and not the derived set() function.

Program 8.3 (INHER2.cpp) illustrates the above: in this solution set() is used in both base and derived, but we have two names for showij - showij() in base and show_ij() in derived – in order to illustrate the two possible approaches just mentioned.

There is one further level of accessibility which we can use – namely protected – and we will go on to discuss how this can be used in the Section
8.2.2..

📋 **Program 8.3**

```cpp
//: INHER2.cpp
//. private access of base class given to the derived class
#include <conio.h>
#include <iostream.h>
class base {
    int i, j;
public:
    void setij(int n, int m){ i = n; j = m;}
    base(){ i = 0; j = 0;
        cout << " base constructor 1 called" << endl;
    } // constructor
    base( int n, int m){ i = n; j = m;
        cout << " base constructor 2 called" << endl;
    } // overloaded constructor
    void showij(){ cout << " i = " << i << " j = " << j << endl;
    }
};
// ..............................................
class derived : public base{
    int k;
public:
    void set(int p){ k = p;}
    derived(){ k = 0;
        cout << " derived constructor 1 called " << endl;
    }
    derived(int p){ k = p;
        cout << " derived constructor 2 called " << endl;
    }
    void showk(){ cout << " k = " << k << endl;}
    show_ij() { showij(); }
    // no conflict so don't need base ::
    // . . . but do need base :: here
    void set(int n, int m) { base::set(n,m); }
};
// ..............................................
void main(void) {
    base x, y(5,-8);
    derived u, v(-12);
    clrscr();
    cout << " INHER2 " << endl;
    cout << " ====== " << endl << endl;

    cout << " base " << endl;
    cout << " x: "; x.showij();
    cout << " y: "; y.showij();
    cout << endl << " derived" << endl;
    cout << " u: "; u.showk();
    u.set(77);
    cout << " after u.set(77)" << endl;
    cout << " u: "; u.showk();
    u.showk();
```

```
    u.show_ij(); // can access showij()

    cout << " v: "; v.showk();
    v.show_ij();
    v.setij(9,3);
    cout << " after v.setij(9,3)" << endl;
    cout << " v: "; v.show_ij();

    cout << " Press any key to Quit ";
    getch();
}
```

8.2.2 Using protected access and protected members

The `protected` keyword provides an additional level of accessibility between private and public and it can be applied to both member data and functions as well as to whole classes through stating the access level. The three levels of access for class members can be summarised as follows:

- *private*. The member's name can be used only by member functions and friends of the class in which it is declared.
- *protected*. The member's name can be used only by member functions and friends of the class in which it is declared and by member functions and friends derived directly from this class.
- *public*. The member's name can be used by users of objects of this class.

Perhaps the simplest way to think about the difference between public and the other two levels of access is that public members of a class act as the interface between objects of that class and users of the class. Unless inheritance is being used then there is no difference between private and protected members of a class – they can both be considered to be private.

Inherited member access depends upon the accessibility specified for the member in its base class and on the access allocated to the base class given in the definition of the derived class. The basic rule is:

The accessibility of an inherited member is given by the most restrictive of the sequence of gradings generated by its base class specification and its inheritance path.

Suppose we have a class x defined as follows:

```
class X{
    int a;
protected:
    int b;
public:
    int c;
    X(){ a = 0; b = 0; c = 0;}
    set(int i, int j, int k){ a = i; b = j; c = k;}
```

```
        show () {
          cout << a << " " << b << " "
                   << c << endl;
        }
    };
```

and that we derive three class Y1, Y2 and Y3 from X as follows:

```
class Y1 : private X { };
class Y2 : protected X { };
class Y3 : public X { };
```

The accessibility of a, b and c in Y1, Y2 and Y3 are given in Table 8.1. Before moving on to discuss multiple inheritance we will look at a few examples of single inheritance so that you can see in practice how inheritance works.

Table 8.1 Accessibility gradings for derived classes

	a	b	c
In base class X	private	protected	public
in Y1 (private)	private	private	private
in Y2 (protected)	private	protected	protected
in Y3 (public)	private	protected	public

8.2.3 An example: point and line classes

We will begin by defining a point class for a two-dimensional surface – e.g. a VDU screen.

```
class point {
protected:
   float x, y;      // x and y coordinates
public:
   point(){};                  // constructor
   ~point(){};                 // destructor
   point(float u, float v){ x = u; y = v;}
      // constructor with
      // initialisation
   void setxy(float u, float v){ x = u; y = v; }
   friend ostream &operator<<(ostream &stream, point &p){
      stream << " x = " << p.x << " y = " << p.y << endl;
      return stream;
   }
   friend istream &operator>>(istream &stream, point &p){
      cout << " Enter x value: ";
      stream >> p.x;
      cout << " Enter y value: ";
      stream >> p.y;
      return stream;
   }
   float getx(){ return x;}
   float gety(){ return y;}
};
```

Before seeing how inheritance as such works we need to create a base class which can be inherited. The `point` class isn't really suitable since there are no other classes which could inherit the characteristics of a point. Stretching definitions a little I suppose we could have a class `coloured-point`, but that's probably as far as we could go.

So let's consider the `line` class. This can be defined as follows:

```
class line {
   point start, end;
public:
   line (point s, point e) { start = s; end = e; }
   ~line(){}
   float length();
};
float line::length(){
   float x = end.getx() - start.getx(),
   y = end.gety() - start.gety();
   return sqrt( x*x + y*y );
}
```

In this class we see that a line is constructed from the `point` class (contains object(s) of type `point`) but it is not inherited from the `point` class. However we can now derive further classes from the basic `line` class, such as `coloured_line` and `dashed_line`. There are quite a number of important points to discuss concerning this class (see Program 8.4). First of all notice that we have defined an enumerated type `colour` which we can use to create suitable variables. Since variables of type `colour` are enumerated types we cannot output them directly so we use a `switch` statement to display the line `colour`. Second, notice how the constructor functions are defined, e.g.

```
// constructor 3
coloured_line(point s, point e):line(s, e){
   line_colour = BLK; // BLACK s.x,s.y - e.x,e.y
}
```

In this case the constructor is defined with two parameters s and e of type `point` – the same two parameters are passed to the `line` constructor which follows after the colon. When an object of type `coloured_line` is instantiated the first thing that will happen is that the base class constructor function will be called (i.e. `line()`) after which the remainder of the appropriate derived class constructor function will be executed (in this case to set `line_colour` to `BLK`). In the cases when the default base constructor is to be called (e.g. constructors 1 and 2 of `coloured_line`) we can omit the reference to `line()` to give e.g.:

```
// constructor 2
coloured_line(colour c) { line_colour = c;   // c 0,0 - 0,0
}
```

In this case `line()` will be called automatically when an object is created using constructor 2 (remember our previous discussion earlier in this section when we began looking at inheritance).

We will now take a look at the operation of Program 8.4 (`LINE2.cpp`) which uses the three classes `point`, `line` and `coloured_line` which we have been discussing.

Program 8.4

```
//: LINE2.cpp
//. a point class used in constructing a line class and using
//. a coloured_line class to demonstrate inheritance

#include <iostream.h>
#include <conio.h>
#include <math.h>

class point {
protected:
   float x, y;      // x and y coordinates
public:
   point(){};       // constructor
   ~point(){};      // destructor
   point(float u, float v){ x = u; y = v;}
            // constructor with initialisation
   void setxy(float u, float v){ x = u; y = v;}
   void showxy(){ cout << " x = " << x << " y = " << y
                      << endl;
   }
   void readxy();
   float getx(){ return x;}
   float gety(){ return y;}
};

void point::readxy() {
   cout << " Enter x value: "; cin >> x;
   cout << " Enter y value: "; cin >> y;
}
// ...............................................................
class line{
protected:
   point start, end;
public:
   line(point s, point e){
      start = s; end = e;
   }
   line(){ start.setxy(0.0,0.0); end.setxy(0.0,0.0); }
   ~line(){};
   float length();
};

// base class - line

float line::length(){
   float endx = end.getx(), startx = start.getx();
   float endy = end.gety(), starty = start.gety();
```

```cpp
   if ((endx == startx) && (endy == starty))
      return 0.0;
   else
      return sqrt( (endx-startx)*(endx-startx) +
              (endy-starty)*(endy-starty));
}
// ..............................................................
// derived class
enum colour { BLK, WH, YEL, ORA, RD, GR, BLU };

class coloured_line : public line {
   colour line_colour;
public:
                  // constructor 1
   coloured_line() {
      line_colour = BLK;    // BLACK 0,0 - 0,0
   }
                  // constructor 2
   coloured_line(colour c) {
      line_colour = c;      // c 0,0 - 0,0
   }
                  // constructor 3
   coloured_line(point s, point e) : line(s, e) {
      line_colour = BLK;    // BLACK s.x,s.y - e.x,e.y
   }
                  // constructor 4
   coloured_line(colour c, point s, point e) : line(s, e) {
      line_colour = c;       // c s.x,s.y - e.x,e.y
   }
   ~coloured_line(){}      // destructor
   void set_colour(colour c){ line_colour = c;}
   void show_colour();
   void set_start(float sx, float sy) {
      start.setxy(sx, sy);
   }
   void set_end(float ex, float ey) {
      end.setxy(ex, ey);
   }
};

void coloured_line::show_colour(){
   cout << " col = ";
   switch(line_colour) {
      case BLK   : cout << " BLACK "; break;
      case WH    : cout << " WHITE "; break;
      case YEL   : cout << " YELLOW "; break;
      case ORA   : cout << " ORANGE "; break;
      case RD    : cout << " RED "; break;
      case GR    : cout << " GREEN "; break;
      case BLU   : cout << " BLUE "; break;
      default    : cout << " Invalid colour (" << line_colour << "
   }
   cout << endl;
}
// ..............................................................
void main(void){
   clrscr();
```

```
    point a(10, 10), b;          // create two points
    cout << " LINE2 " << endl;
    cout << " ===== " << endl;

    cout << " a : "; a.showxy();

    b.setxy(5, 10);              // give b new x and y values
    cout << " b : "; b.showxy();

    line l1(a, b);
    cout << " l1 : " << endl; // create a line joining a and b
    cout << " length = " << l1.length() << endl;

    coloured_line cl(a,b);       // create a coloured line

    cout << " cl : " << endl;
    cl.show_colour();
    cout << " length = " << cl.length() << endl;

    // create another coloured line

    point c(5.0, 8.0), d(7.0, 9.0); // create two more points
    coloured_line cl2(YEL,c,d);      // and a YELLOW coloured
                                     // line from c to d
    cout << " cl2 : " << endl;
    cl2.show_colour();
    cout << " length = " << cl2.length() << endl;

    // ... and finally a third coloured line

    coloured_line cl3;           // create a third coloured line

    cout << " cl3 : " << endl;
    cl3.show_colour();
    cout << " length = " << cl3.length() << endl;

    // now change the end points of cl3
    float x, y;

    cout << " cl3: " << endl << " Enter x and y coords " << endl;
    cout << " for start > ";
    cin >> x  >> y;
    cl3.set_start(x, y);

    cout << " for end > ";
    cin >> x >> y;
    cl3.set_end(x, y);

    cout << " length = " << cl3.length() << endl;

    cout << " Press any key to Quit ";
    getch();
}
```

We begin by constructing two point objects a and b and giving a the *x*, *y* co-ordinates of 10,10. We then set the *x* and *y* values of b to 5 and 10 respectively and then create a line object l1 with end points a and b. The length of l1 is then displayed using the member function of line `length()`. Next we create a coloured line `c1` joining the two points `a` and `b`.

Then two more points are created and initialised (`c` and `d`) and a coloured line `cl2` created joining them and initialised with the colour `YEL`.

Lastly a third coloured line is created (with no initialisation – `cl3`) after which the user is prompted to enter the *x* and *y* co-ordinates for the start and end points of the line.

Test run 8.2 shows a sample run using 1, 6 for the start *x, y* values of `cl3` and 5, 9 for the end point.

🖥 **Test run 8.2**
```
LINE2
=====
a :   x = 10 y = 10
b :   x = 5 y = 10
l1 :
length = 5
c1 :
col =   BLACK
length = 5
cl2 :
col =   YELLOW
length = 2.236068
cl3 :
col =   BLACK
length = 0
cl3:
Enter x and y coords
for start >  for end >  length = 5
Press any key to Quit
```

Let's now take a look at how the constructor functions operate for the `coloured_line` class. We can do this by modifying the four constructor functions of the `coloured_line` class so that a statement is output each time the function is called indicating which one it is, e.g. `cout << " constructor 1 called " << endl;`. Test run 8.3 show a sample run once these modifications are made.

The point to note here is that the constructors are called in the order 3, 4 and 1. Constructor 3 is the one with a start and end point as parameters, constructor 4 the one with a colour and start and end points as parameters and constructor 1 is the default constructor with no parameters. So when we create the coloured line `c1` (which joins the points `a` and `b`) constructor 3 is called, and so on.

It is possible to eliminate the need for constructors 1 and 2. How might this be done? Add another `coloured_line` object (`cl4`), which is initialised to `RD` say, to check that constructor 2 is called. Then work out how you might be able to eliminate the need for constructors 1 and 2 and try out your solution.

```
LINE2A
======
a :   x = 10 y = 10
b :   x = 5 y = 10
l1 :
length = 5
constructor 3 called
c1 :
col =  BLACK
length = 5
constructor 4 called
cl2 :
col =  YELLOW
length = 2.236068
constructor 1 called
cl3 :
col =  BLACK
length = 0
...
```

This can be done by giving constructor 4 default values for the colour and the start and end points. However in order to provide a start and end value of 0,0 we need to construct a zero point e.g. before the definition of the col-oured_line class we have:

```
const point zero(0.0, 0.0);
```

and then in coloured_line we have the constructor 4 modified to read:

```
coloured_line( colour c = BLK, point s = zero,
          point e = zero) : line( s, e) {
   line_colour = c;
}
```

We also have two member functions of coloured_line which set the start and end values. Since both of these sets of functions access start and end (which are members of line) they must be given the access status of protected within line. Try commenting out protected from the line class definition and see what happens.

You will find that neither start nor end are accessible by coloured_line – they are now private to line and therefore can only be used by member functions of line. So if we wish derived classes to have access to non-public members of the base class, through their own member functions, then these members must be given an access mode of protected.

When we look further at the relationship between the line class and the coloured_line class we see that the way these classes have developed means that we have functions to set and show the start and end points of col-oured_line objects but no such functions are available for objects of type line. It makes sense therefore to include these four functions in this latter class. Then any class derived from line will also possess the ability to set and show the start and end points of a line. This means that the only new members of coloured_line will be those directly related to the addition of colour to the line, which is as it should be!

Program 8.5 (LINE2H.cpp) illustrates the version which we have now arrived at.

Program 8.5

```
//: line2h.cpp
//.   a point class used in constructing a line class and using
//.   a coloured_line class to demonstrate inheritance
//.   this example creates a coloured line from an existing line
//.   also adds ability to display start and end points of a line
//.   this version changes start point of cl5


// comment out protected in line class definition
// and see what happens!
// set_start() and set_end() now member functions of line
// and can be accessed by coloured_line so no need for
// start and end to be protected - they can be private in line

#include <iostream.h>
#include <conio.h>
#include <math.h>
// ............................................................
class point {
//protected:
    float x, y;        // x and y coordinates
public:
    point(){};                  // constructor
    ~point(){};                 // destructor
    point(float u, float v){ x = u; y = v; }
        // constructor with
        // initialisation
    void setxy(float u, float v){
        x = u; y = v; }
        friend ostream &operator<<(ostream &stream, point &p){
            stream << " x = " << p.x << " y = " << p.y << endl;
            return stream;
    }
    friend istream &operator>>(istream &stream, point &p){
        cout << " Enter x value: ";
        stream >> p.x;
        cout << " Enter y value: ";
        stream >> p.y;
        return stream;
    }
    float getx(){ return x; }
    float gety(){ return y; }
};
// ............................................................
class line{
```

```cpp
//protected:
   point start, end;
public:
   line(point s, point e){
      start = s; end = e;
      cout << " line constructor 1 called " << endl;
   }
   line(){
      start.setxy(0.0,0.0); end.setxy(0.0,0.0);
      cout << " line constructor 2 called " << endl;
   }
   void show_start(){ cout << start; }
   void show_end(){cout << end; }
   float length();
   void set_start(float sx, float sy) {
      start.setxy(sx, sy);
   }
   void set_end(float ex, float ey) {
      end.setxy(ex, ey);
   }
};

float line::length(){
   float endx = end.getx(), startx = start.getx();
   float endy = end.gety(), starty = start.gety();

   if ((endx == startx) && (endy == starty))
      return 0.0;
   else
      return sqrt( (endx-startx)*(endx-startx) +
                   (endy-starty)*(endy-starty));
}
// ............................................................
// derived class

enum colour { BLK, WH, YEL, ORA, RD, GR, BLU };
const point zero(0.0, 0.0);
class coloured_line : public line {
   colour line_colour;
public:
   coloured_line(point s, point e):line(s, e){
      line_colour = BLK;              // BLACK s.x,s.y - e.x,e.y
   cout << " constructor 3 called " << endl;
   }

// constructor 4
   coloured_line(colour c = BLK, point s = zero,
            point e = zero) : line(s,e){
      line_colour = c;         // c s.x,s.y - e.x,e.y
      cout << " constructor 4 called " << endl;
   }

   coloured_line(colour c, line l) : line(l){
      line_colour = c;
      cout << " constructor 5 called " << endl;
   }
   void set_colour(colour c){ line_colour = c;}
   void show_colour();
```

```
    };

void coloured_line::show_colour(){
    cout << " col = ";
    switch(line_colour) {
        case BLK  : cout << " BLACK "; break;
        case WH   : cout << " WHITE "; break;
        case YEL  : cout << " YELLOW "; break;
        case ORA  : cout << " ORANGE "; break;
        case RD   : cout << " RED "; break;
        case GR   : cout << " GREEN "; break;
        case BLU  : cout << " BLUE "; break;
        default   : cout << " Invalid colour ("
                         << line_colour << ")";
    }
    cout << endl;
}
// ..............................................................
void main(){
    clrscr();

    point a(10, 10), b;          // create two points
    cout << " LINE2H " << endl;
    cout << " ====== " << endl;

    cout << " a : " << a;

    b.setxy(5, 10);              // give b new x and y values
    cout << " b : " << b;

    line l1(a, b);
    cout << " l1 : " << endl; // create a line joining a and b
    cout << " length = " << l1.length() << endl;

    coloured_line cl2;

    coloured_line cl3(RD);

    // create a coloured line from an existing line
    coloured_line cl5(WH, l1);

    cout << " cl5 : " << endl;
    cl5.show_colour();
    cout << " length = " << cl5.length() << endl;
    cout << " start: ";
    cl5.show_start();
    cout << " end: ";
    cl5.show_end();
    cl5.set_start(3, 2);
    cout << " ... after cl5.set_start(3,2); " << endl;
    cout << " start: ";
    cl5.show_start();

    cout << " Press any key to Quit ";

    getch();
}
```

Incidentally the process of rewriting the base class once a derived class has been developed is not unusual. Often we might come up with a class which it makes sense to break down into one (or more) base class(es).

The above discussion doesn't mean that there is no need to use `protected` in a base class – often it is sensible to make normally private data members protected. We need to do this in circumstances when the derived classes may need new methods which can access the base data members directly and whose methods might not be anticipated when the base class is developed.

8.2.4 The publication, book and magazine classes

As a further example of inheritance we will consider how to create a class which may be inherited by, for example, two further classes `book` and `magazine`. Consider first a book – some of the attributes might be as follows:

- Title;
- Author;
- Publisher;
- Year of publication;
- Place of publication;
- Selling price;
- Number of pages;

and a magazine might have the following attributes:

- Title;
- Editor;
- Publisher;
- Frequency of publication;
- Selling price.

We can create a common base class, called publication, which has the following attributes:

- Title;
- Publisher;
- Selling price.

This will require methods, in addition to the constructor and destructor methods, such as:

```
set_title()          get_title()
set_publisher()      get_publisher()
set_selling_price()  get_selling_price()
```

The constructor method (publication()) creates a publication object and initialises both the title and publisher attributes to a space through the use of the string function strcpy(). Similarly the function set_title() allows title to be given a value (pointed to by the parameter t) and initialises the selling price to 0. In this function we use strncpy() to ensure that no more than TITLE_LNGTH characters are copied into title. The set_publisher() methods has a similar structure and the set_selling_price() an even simpler one. Finally the three get_ methods simply return the desired attribute. Notice that the two functions which return strings need to be declared as pointers to char (e.g. char *get_title()).

The book class is declared in the normal way:

```
class book : public publication {
   ...
```

indicating that it is descended form the publication class. The additional attributes for this class are: author, year_of_publication, place_of_ publication and pages. Methods are then added to deal with these new attributes. Finally similar considerations apply to the magazine class.

Program 8.6 (PUB1.cpp) illustrates these classes – take a look at it now and try it out.

📋 **Program 8.6**

```
//: PUB1.cpp
//. illustrating inheritance
//. the publication, book and magazine classes
#include <conio.h>
#include <iostream.h>
#include <string.h>

const TITLE_LNGTH = 30;
const PUB_LNGTH = 30;

class publication {
   char title[TITLE_LNGTH];
   char publisher[PUB_LNGTH];
   float selling_price;
public:
   publication(){ strcpy(title, " ");
      strcpy(publisher, " ");
   }
   ~publication(){}
   void set_title(char *t){
      strncpy(title, t, TITLE_LNGTH);
      selling_price = 0.0;
   }
   char *get_title(){ return title; }
   void set_publisher( char *p){
      strncpy(publisher, p, PUB_LNGTH);
   }
```

```cpp
      char *get_publisher(){ return publisher; }
      void set_price(float price){ selling_price = price; }
      float get_price(){ return selling_price; }
};
// ...............................................................

const AUTHOR_LNGTH = 20;
const POP_LNGTH = 20;

class book : public publication {
   char author[AUTHOR_LNGTH];
   unsigned year_of_publication;
   char place_of_publication[POP_LNGTH];
   unsigned pages;
public:
   book(){ strcpy(author, " ");
      year_of_publication = 1455;
      // probable date of publication of first movable
      // metal type printed book - The Gutenberg Bible
      strcpy(place_of_publication, " ");
      pages = 0;
   }
   ~book(){};
   void set_author(char *a) {
      strncpy(author, a, AUTHOR_LNGTH);
   }
   char *get_author(){ return author; }
   void set_yop(unsigned y){ year_of_publication = y; }
   unsigned get_yop(){ return year_of_publication; }
   void set_pop(char *pop){
      strncpy(place_of_publication, pop, POP_LNGTH);
   }
   char *get_pop(){ return place_of_publication; }
   void set_pages(unsigned p){ pages = p; }
   unsigned get_pages(){ return pages; }
};
// ...............................................................
enum pubfreq { WEEKLY, FORTNIGHTLY, MONTHLY, QUARTERLY, OTHER,
                            NOT_KNOWN };
const ED_LNGTH = 20;

class magazine : public publication {
   char editor[ED_LNGTH];
   pubfreq frequency_of_publication;
public:
   magazine(){
      strcpy(editor, " ");
      frequency_of_publication = NOT_KNOWN;
   }
   ~magazine(){}
   void set_editor(char *ed) {
      strncpy(editor, ed, ED_LNGTH);
   }
   char *get_editor(){ return editor; }
   void set_fop( pubfreq f ){ frequency_of_publication = f; }
   pubfreq get_fop(){ return frequency_of_publication; }
   void display_fop();
};
```

```
void magazine::display_fop(){
   switch(frequency_of_publication) {
      case WEEKLY   :  cout << " Weekly "; break;
      case FORTNIGHTLY:  cout << " Fortnightly "; break;
      case MONTHLY :    cout << " Monthly "; break;
      case QUARTERLY :  cout << " Quarterly "; break;
      case OTHER    :    cout << " Other "; break;
      case NOT_KNOWN :  cout << " Unknown "; break;
   }
}
// .........................................................
void main(void) {
   clrscr();
   publication p1;

   cout << " PUB1 " << endl;
   cout << " ==== " << endl << endl;
   cout << "      TITLE : " << p1.get_title() << endl;
   cout << " PUBLISHER : " << p1.get_publisher() << endl;
   cout << " Enter the title : ";

   char t[TITLE_LNGTH];
   cin.getline(t,TITLE_LNGTH);
   p1.set_title(t);
   cout << "      TITLE : " << p1.get_title() << endl;
   char *publ = "Macmillan";
   p1.set_publisher(publ);
   cout << " PUBLISHER : " << p1.get_publisher() << endl;
   cout << " Now for a book ";
   book b1;

   b1.set_title("Gutenberg Bible");
   b1.set_pop("Mainz");
   b1.set_author("God!");
   b1.set_publisher("Johannes Gutenberg?");

   cout << endl << " The first book using movable metal type-"
                               << endl;
   cout << b1.get_title() << endl;
   cout << b1.get_author() << endl;
   cout << b1.get_publisher() << endl;
   cout << b1.get_pop() << endl;
   cout << b1.get_yop() << endl;

   cout << endl << " Finally a magazine " << endl;
   magazine m1;

   m1.set_title("EXE");
   m1.set_fop(MONTHLY);
   m1.set_publisher("Process Communications Ltd");

   cout << endl << " A magazine -" << endl;
   cout << m1.get_title() << endl;
   m1.display_fop(); cout << endl;
   cout << m1.get_publisher() << endl;
   cout << " Press any key to Quit ";
   getch();
}
```

8.2.5 *The quadrilateral, rectangle and trapezium classes*

As a final example of single inheritance we examine a class `quadrilateral` which can be used to derive other classes such as rectangle, square, trapezium, kite or rhombus. These derived classes can inherit the data members and member functions (attributes and methods) of `quadrilateral` but may also add additional ones or replace functions of the base class with more appropriate functions. We will be looking at all of these aspects in this section.

A quadrilateral is a general four-side plane figure which is defined by its four corner points. It has an area and a perimeter. Since the corners of this figure are defined by an *x*, *y* value we can again use the `point` class in our construction of this new one. It is important to remember that the `quadrilateral` class is not derived from the `point` class and therefore does not inherit the `point` attributes or methods, rather the `quadrilateral` class is constructed from the `point` class.

Our `quadrilateral` class will therefore consist of four points `p1`, `p2`, `p3` and `p4`; various constructor functions; a function to get the area; one to return the perimeter; and functions to set and get the points which make up the quadrilateral.

Before deriving the quadrilateral class there are a couple of issues worth considering. First, when we write the `set_corners()` function it would make sense to use four points as arguments to this function which in turn implies that we might require to assign one object of type `point` to another of the same type; in other words we require an assignment operator for use with points, so that we can write e.g.

```
p1 = pa;   // p1 and pa both point objects
```

Secondly, in calculating the perimeter we will need to compute the length of a line joining adjacent corners. Thus a function `distance()` would be another useful addition to the `point` class. These two additional functions can be written as follows:

```
point point::operator=(point p){
    x = p.x;   y = p.y;
    return *this;
}
double point::distance(point p){
    double xdist = x - p.x;
    double ydist = y - p.y;
    return sqrt((xdist * xdist) + (ydist * ydist));
}
```

We can now use these two `point` member functions as and when necessary in our `quadrilateral` class. Program 8.7 (`QUAD1.cpp`) illustrates this new class and computes the perimeter of the quadrilateral, we will discuss how the area function is constructed shortly.

Program 8.7

```cpp
//: QUAD1.cpp
//. a quadrilateral class used to demonstrate inheritance

#include <iostream.h>
#include <conio.h>
#include <math.h>
// ............................................................
// point class

class point {

protected:
    float x, y;        // x and y coordinates
public:
    point(){};                // constructor
    point(float u, float v){ x = u; y = v;}
            // constructor with initialisation
    void setxy(float u, float v){
        x = u; y = v;}
        friend ostream &operator<<(ostream &stream, point &p){
            stream << " x = " << p.x << " y = " << p.y << endl;
            return stream;
    }
    friend istream &operator >>(istream &stream, point &p){
        cout << " Enter x value: ";
        stream >> p.x;
        cout << " Enter y value: ";
        stream >> p.y;
        return stream;
    }
    point operator=(point p);  // overloaded assignment operator
    double distance(point p);
};

point point::operator=(point p){
    x = p.x;    y = p.y;
    return *this;
}

double point::distance(point p){
    double xdist = x - p.x;
    double ydist = y - p.y;
    return sqrt((xdist * xdist) + (ydist * ydist));
}

//............................................................

// quadrilteral class

class quadrilateral{
    point p1, p2, p3, p4;
public:
    quadrilateral(){};        // default constructor
    quadrilateral(point pa, point pb, point pc, point pd);
    ~quadrilateral(){};       // destructor
    void set_corners(point pa, point pb, point pc, point pd);
```

```
      void show_corners();
      double perimeter();
};

quadrilateral::quadrilateral(point pa, point pb,
                                        point pc, point pd) {
    p1 = pa;    p2 = pb;
    p3 = pc;    p4 = pd;
}

void quadrilateral::set_corners(point pa, point pb,
                                        point pc, point pd) {
    p1 = pa;    p2 = pb;
    p3 = pc;    p4 = pd;
}

void quadrilateral::show_corners(){
    cout << " corners are: " << endl;
    cout << " p1: " << p1;
    cout << " p2: " << p2;
    cout << " p3: " << p3;
    cout << " p4: " << p4;
}

double quadrilateral::perimeter(){
    double perim = 0.0;

    perim += p2.distance(p1);
    perim += p3.distance(p2);
    perim += p4.distance(p3);
    perim += p1.distance(p4);
    return perim;
}
// ......................................................
void main(){
    clrscr();

    point a(1, 1), b, c, d;
    cout << " QUAD1 " << endl;
    cout << " ===== " << endl;

    cout << " a : " << a;

    b.setxy(1, 5);
    cout << " b : " << b;
    c.setxy(5, 5);
    cout << " c : " << c;
    d.setxy(8, 2);
    cout << " d : " << d;

    quadrilateral q1;
    q1.set_corners(a, b, c, d);
    q1.show_corners();
    cout << endl << " perimeter = " << q1.perimeter() << endl;

    cout << " Press any key to quit " << endl;
    getch();
}
```

This program simply sets up four points (1,1), (1,5), (5,5) and 8,2) and computes the perimeter of the quadrilateral formed by them.

You should have no difficulty in understanding how this class is constructed, or how it behaves. Notice that the second of the two constructor functions and the set_corners() function both use the pointer assignment operator to simplify initialising the corners. Also show_corners() uses the showxy() member functions of point (but only via the objects p1, p2, etc) to display the *x* and *y* co-ordinates of each corner. Finally, as mentioned above, the perimeter() function uses the point member function distance() to find the distance between adjacent corners.

Now let's see how to compute the area of a quadrilateral. A quadrilateral is made up of two triangles with one side in common, so if we can find the area of these two triangles we can compute the area of the rectangle by simply adding these two areas. The area of a triangle in this instance is best computed using the formula based on the length of sides of the triangle since we can easily compute these using the distance() function. So if $s=(a+b+c)/2$, where *a*, *b* and *c* are the lengths of the sides of the triangle, then the area of the triangle is given by:

$$Area = \sqrt{s.(s-a).(s-b).(s-c)}$$

So in the quadrilateral class we can incorporate a public member function area() which uses a private function triangle_area() to compute the area of the quadrilateral's constituent triangles.

These two new functions are:

```
double quadrilateral::triangle_area(point pta, point ptb,
    point ptc){
    double s;      // semi-perimeter of triangle
    double a = pta.distance(ptb);    double b = ptb.distance(ptc);
    double c = ptc.distance(pta);
    s = (a + b + c)/2.0;
    return sqrt(s * (s-a) * (s-b) * (s-c));
}

double quadrilateral::area(){

    return triangle_area(p1, p2, p3)+triangle_area(p3, p4, p1);
}
```

Again you should have no difficulty in understanding how these functions work.

Now, finally, we have arrived at a position when we can introduce some inheritance. We can derive a rectangle class from the quadrilateral class – it has the same basic characteristics as a quadrilateral but with the additional feature that adjacent sides are at right angles.

The simplest way to create a `rectangle` class is to inherit all the functionality from `quadrilateral`:

```
// rectangle class
class rectangle : public quadrilateral{
public:
   rectangle(point rp1, point rp2, point rp3, point rp4) :
      quadrilateral(rp1,rp2,rp3,rp4){
   };
};
```

This just calls the `quadrilateral` constructor function and in the process assigns the private data members of `quadrilateral` p1, p2, p3 and p4 to rp1, rp2, rp3 and rp4. The functions `perimeter()` and `area()` can still be used by objects of type rectangle.

This is fine so long as we do not want to introduce new member functions of `rectangle` which require access to any of the corners p1, p2, p3 or p4 of the base class. How can we get around this problem? Well, the solution is to make the corners of the quadrilateral protected instead of private.

In order to check out the modified version of the `rectangle` class we can alter the constructor function so that it checks the diagonals of the rectangle and thus determine whether the figure is in fact a rectangle. In a rectangle the diagonals are equal so we can compare the length of the diagonals and if they are unequal return an error. Since we need to take account of rounding errors we will in fact check that the difference between the two is no greater than a small amount epsilon (e.g. 1×10^{-6}). The new version of the `rectangle` constructor function is therefore:

```
// rectangle class - second version
static const double epsilon = 1.0e-6;
class rectangle : public quadrilateral{
public:
   rectangle(point rp1, point rp2, point rp3, point rp4) :
      quadrilateral(rp1,rp2,rp3,rp4){
      if (fabs(p1.distance(p3) - p2.distance(p4))>epsilon) {
         cout << " This is not a rectangle!" <<  endl;
         exit(1);
      }
   };
};
```

There are a few other modification that we can make to this class which are to do with the special form of a rectangle and can allow us to use slightly simpler functions to compute the perimeter and the area. First of all we note that, as just mentioned, for a rectangle the diagonals are equal. It would be useful therefore to store the diagonal of any rectangle which is constructed. We therefore introduce a private attribute `diagonal` and give it a value when a rectangle is constructed. So we now have:

```
// rectangle class - third version
static const double epsilon = 1.0e-6;
class rectangle : public quadrilateral{
   double diagonal;
public:
   rectangle(point rp1, point rp2, point rp3, point rp4) :
      quadrilateral(rp1,rp2,rp3,rp4){
      if (fabs(p1.distance(p3) - p2.distance(p4))>epsilon) {
         cout << " This is not a rectangle!" << endl;
         exit(1);
      }
      diagonal = p1.distance(p3);
   };
};
```

Next, the perimeter of a rectangle is simply twice the sum of two adjacent sides of the rectangle. We can therefore write a more simpler but more specialised version of perimeter() to take account of this fact. Thus

```
double perimeter() { // of a rectangle
   return 2.0*(p1.distance(p2)+p2.distance(p3));
};
```

Similarly the area of a rectangle is just the product of the lengths of two adjacent sides:

```
double area(){      // of a rectangle
   return p1.distance(p2)*p2.distance(p3);
};
```

As a final example in this section on inheritance we introduce yet another type of quadrilateral, the trapezium. A trapezium is a quadrilateral with two, and only two, sides parallel. We require the constructor function to check the four points to see whether or not they form a trapezium. This requires one further function gradient() which will return the slope of the line joining two points, i.e. for the points x_1, y_1 and x_2, y_2 the gradient is $(y_2 - y_1)/(x_2 - x_1)$. So a suitable function might be:

```
double trapezium::gradient(point p1, point p2) {
   double xdiff = p1.getx()-p2.getx();
   double ydiff = p1.gety()-p2.gety();
   if (fabs(xdiff) <= epsilon )
      return -epsilon;
   else
   if (fabs(ydiff) <= epsilon)
      return epsilon;
   else
      return ydiff/xdiff;
}
```

where we have modified the point class so that the functions getx() and gety() are available.

The constructor function for trapezium therefore becomes:

```
// trapezium class
static const double epsilon = 1.0e-6;

class trapezium : public quadrilateral{
   double gradient(point p1, point p2);
public:
   trapezium(point tp1, point tp2, point tp3,
                    point tp4) :
   quadrilateral(tp1, tp2, tp3, tp4) {
      if (((gradient(p1, p2) == gradient(p4, p3)) &&
         (p1.distance(p2) != p3.distance(p4))) ||
         ((gradient(p2, p3) == gradient(p1, p4)) &&
         (p2.distance(p3) != p4.distance(p1))))
            cout << " Trapezium constructed ";
      else {
         cout << " This is not a trapezium!";
         exit(1);
      }
   }
};
```

The compound `if` statement checks for two parallel sides of unequal length but since either opposite pair of sides might be parallel we have to check each pair.

8.3   Multiple inheritance

The examples above have all used single inheritance, in that a number of derived classes have been derived from a single base class (in the latter examples, the `quadrilateral` class). In this section we introduce the idea of multiple inheritance, where a class is derived from two or more base classes.

A generic example is as follows:

```
class base1 {
protected:
   int i;
public:
   base1(){ i = 0; }
   base1(int i1){ i = i1;}
   ~base1(){}
   void showi(){ cout << " i = " << i;}
};

class base2 {
protected:
   float f;
public:
   base2(){ f = 0; }
   base2(int f1){ f = f1;}
```

```
    ~base2(){}
    void showf(){ cout << " f = " << f;}
};

class multinh : public base1, public base2 {
public:
    void set(int j, float x) { i = j; f = x;}
};
```

The derived class `multinh` has access to the public member functions of both
`base1` and `base2` as well as to their (protected) data members `i` and `f`. So, assuming that `m` is an object of type `multinh`, we can set `i` and `f` by means of the
`multinh set()` function:

```
    m.set(4, 8.5);
```

and display `i` and `f` through calls such as:

```
    m.showi();
    m.showf();
```

We will have another brief look at multiple inheritance a little later once we
have discussed virtual functions.

8.4   Virtual functions

Virtual functions are a central part of object-oriented programming and enable
the extensibility of inheritance to be fully exploited. We will introduce the use
of virtual functions by considering an example.

Suppose we have a number of classes relating to two-dimensional objects
(e.g. circle, square, triangle). We can also create a base class which holds the
information common to each of these objects (at the moment all these shapes
have in common is that they have a name!). The classes used for specific
shapes can then be derived from this base class (one for each of `circle`,
`square` and `triangle`) and which provide the detail for each class (e.g. ra-
dius, side and side1, side2, side3).

The base class `name`, might look something like this:

```
// base class
class name {
  protected:
   char *obj_name;
  public:
   name(char *o_name) { obj_name = o_name;} // constructor
   void display_info(){ cout << obj_name << endl; }
};
```

This class just contains a pointer to an object name (*obj_name), a simple constructor and a method to display the name (display_info()). Notice that, in Program 8.8, we have declared obj_name as protected rather than private – this is to ensure that derived classes can have access to this attribute.

We can then create derived classes as follows:

```
// now to create some derived classes
// circle
class circle : public name {
   int radius;
  public:
   circle( char *o_name, int rad):name(o_name),radius (rad){}
   void display_info(){
     cout << obj_name << endl;
     cout << " radius = " << radius << endl;
   }
};
```

Similar classes will also be created for the square and triangle.

In each of these derived classes additional data members will be added to specify the characteristics of that class and the display_info() method will be overloaded to enable these characteristics to be displayed.

📋 **Program 8.8**

```
//: EARLY1.cpp
//. illustrating the need for virtual functions and late binding
//. this program attempts to print information about some
//. simple geometrical objects.
#include <conio.h>
#include <iostream.h>

// base class "name" goes here

// now to create some derived classes
// "circle" class goes here
// "square"

class square : public name {
   int side;
  public:
   square( char *o_name, int s) : name(o_name), side(s){}
   void display_info(){
     cout << obj_name << endl;
     cout << " side = " << side << endl;
   }
};
// ...............................................................
// triangle
class triangle : public name {
   int side1, side2, side3;
  public:
   triangle( char *o_name, int s1, int s2, int s3) :
       name(o_name), side1(s1), side2(s2), side3(s3){}
```

```
      void display_info(){
         cout << obj_name << endl;
         cout << " side1 = " << side1 << endl;
         cout << " side2 = " << side2 << endl;
         cout << " side3 = " << side3 << endl;
      }
};
// ........................................................
void main(void) {
   circle c("circle", 2);
   square s("square", 4);
   triangle t("triangle", 3, 4, 5);

   clrscr();
   cout << " EARLY1 " << endl;
   cout << " ====== " << endl << endl;

   cout << " Static or Early binding " << endl;
   c.display_info();
   s.display_info();
   t.display_info();

   cout << " Press any key to Quit ";
   getch();
}
```

Test run 8.4 shows a sample run. It can be seen that it gives us what we require, namely information about each of the shapes created in the program.
So where does virtual come in? Suppose we wish to create a list of objects of various classes e.g. a mixture of circles, squares and triangles. We first of all create some circles, squares and triangles:

```
   circle c1("small circle", 1),
      c2("large circle", 1000);
   square s1("small square", 2),
      s2("medium square", 50);
   triangle t1("right angled",3, 4, 5);
```

💻 **Test run 8.4**

```
 EARLY1
 ======

 Static or Early binding
 circle
  radius = 2
 square
  side = 4
 triangle
  side1 = 3
  side2 = 4
  side3 = 5
 Press any key to Quit
```

Inheritance 275

We then create an array of pointers to such objects as follows:

```
name *geom_shapes[] = {    &c1, &c2, &s1, &s2, &t1};
```

The information about each object in the list can then be displayed using a loop – notice how `sizeof()` is used to count the number of objects pointed to:

```
int n = sizeof(geom_shapes)/sizeof(geom_shapes[0]);
for(int i = 0; i < n; i++)
   geom_shapes[i]->display_info();
```

Program 8.9 gives an attempt to display the details of the objects in the array (EARLY2). Test run 8.5 gives a sample run.

Program 8.9

```
//: EARLY2.cpp
//. illustrating the need for virtual functions and late binding
//. this program attempts to print information about some
//. simple geometrical objects.

#include <conio.h>
#include <iostream.h>
// ...........................................................
// base class name goes here

//now to create some derived classes
// circle class definition goes here

// square class definition goes here

// triangle class definition goes here
// ...........................................................
void main(void) {
   circle c1("small circle", 1), c2("large circle", 1000);
   square s1("small square", 2), s2("medium square", 50);
   triangle t1("right angled", 3, 4, 5);

   name *geom_shapes[] = {
      &c1, &c2, &s1, &s2, &t1
   };

   clrscr();
   cout << " EARLY2 " << endl;
   cout << " ====== " << endl << endl;
   cout << " An array of pointers to geometrical shapes"
                           << endl;
   cout << " - still using early binding :" << endl;

   int n = sizeof(geom_shapes)/sizeof(geom_shapes[0]);
   for (int i = 0; i < n; i++)
      geom_shapes[i]->display_info();

   cout << " Press any key to Quit ";
   getch();
}
```

```
EARLY2
======

an array of pointers to geometrical shapes
 - still using early binding:
small circle
large circle
small square
medium square
right angled
 Press any key to Quit
```

The problem with this is that we have no information about any of the objects except their names. What we also wanted was, for the circles, for example, their radii, for the squares the lengths of their sides and so on. What has in fact happened is that the base method (`display_info()`) has been called in each case instead of the method appropriate for the particular object being pointed to. Whereas before, in Program 8.8 (`EARLY1.cpp`), the compiler knew which object was in use, in this program all we have is an array of pointers to objects of type `name`, so the compiler has no way of knowing which type of geometrical object is being pointed to, which is where virtual functions come in. Modify the Program 8.9 (`EARLY2.cpp`) by adding the keyword `virtual` in front of the definition of `display_info()` in the `name` class:

```
virtual void display_info(){ cout << obj_name << endl; }
```

Now try this version out and see what you get. (A better name for this program would be `LATE2` – see the discussion which follows for an explanation!) Test run 8.6 shows a sample run.

```
LATE2
=====

an array of pointers to geometrical shapes
 - this time using dynamic or late binding :
small circle
 radius = 1
large circle
 radius = 1000
small square
 side = 2
medium square
 side = 50
right angled triangle
 side1 = 3
 side2 = 4
 side3 = 5
 Press any key to Quit
```

This time it works as intended so that we get the additional information concerning the size of the objects in the list. We have now implemented 'late binding' or 'dynamic binding' which means that the correct methods are identified at run time rather than at compile time when 'early binding' or 'static binding' is appropriate.

So how does this work? Because we have declared an array of pointers to objects belonging to the class `name`, whenever a method defined in `name` is called the normal response would be to call that method. However since the method `display_info()` in `name` is declared as virtual the method associated with the class which is being pointed to (`circle`, `square` or `triangle`) is called instead.

When a function is declared as `virtual` the possibility remains open that a function with the same name can be defined in any descendant class. However the definition which is used to override the original definition must have an identical parameter list – e.g. if there are no parameters in the base virtual function then there must be none in the descendant one, of if the base parameter is an `int`, then the descendant parameter must be an `int`, etc. This shows that virtual functions are not really overloaded functions, since with overloaded functions it is necessary for either the number, or type, of parameters to differ. If a virtual function is re-defined which has different parameters and/or numbers of parameters then the base virtual function may still be used if the need arises.

A second important point is that the virtual nature of functions is inherited. Thus if the base function is `virtual` then any function matching that one in any first, second, or *n*th generation of descendant classes will also be `virtual`.

Finally it is not necessary to re-state that a function is virtual in a descendant class, as the above point also suggests. However if you wish to make it clear that an inherited function is `virtual` then this is still allowed. So, for example, in our previous example where we had the virtual function

```
virtual void display_info();
```

in the name class, we could also have defined this function as virtual in the circle `class`:

```
virtual void display_info(){ ... } // for circle
```

8.5 Pure virtual functions

There is one further aspect of virtual functions which you should be aware of. This concerns the idea of pure virtual functions and introduces us to the concept of abstract classes. A pure virtual function is one declared like this:

```
virtual type function_name() = 0;
```

which seems to suggest that the function is assigned the value 0, which is another way of saying that this function has no body and therefore when the compiler cannot create an object specified by the class of which `function_name()` is a member. When a pure virtual function is declared two conditions are being imposed. First no objects can be created directly from this class – it becomes an abstract class (or abstract base class). In order for any objects to be created this class must be used as a base for some other class or classes. Second any derived class must redefine the 'pure virtual function' in order to ensure that the derived class is converted into a 'concrete' class which can be used to instantiate objects.

An example of an abstract base class and a class derived from it is illustrated by the Program 8.10.

If you comment out the definition for `display_info()` in one of the derived classes and re-compile you will find that a compilation error will result. This illustrates that every class derived from the base class must contain a method with the same name as the pure virtual method in the base class. Since derived classes inherit the virtuality of a method this needs to be overridden in order for the new class to be able to instantiate objects.

It is worth noting at this stage that there is no restriction on the number of pure virtual functions which a class may have. The presence of at least one such function will turn the class into an abstract (base) class. If other pure virtual functions are also declared in that class then these must also be overridden in any descendent classes – if any of the functions are not re-declared then the derived class will also be an abstract class and therefore incapable of instantiating objects.

Having looked at how to construct pure virtual functions and thus abstract base classes and investigated the use in a simple example, the question arises 'when might we use pure virtual functions?'. Perhaps a better question is 'When do we need abstract classes?' since the reason behind declaring a pure virtual function is to create an abstract class. The answer to this question is when there is (are) method(s) which cannot be defined in the base class (remember that a pure virtual function has no body) but which must be available to objects of the derived class.

Program 8.10

```
//: LATE6.cpp
//. introducing a pure virtual function into name
//    This program creates an array of pointers to name (called
//    shape) and then allows the user to enter their choice of
//    goemetrical shapes.
//    The presence of display_info() in name as a 'pure virtual
//    function' means that derived classes must provide
//    their own display_info() method(s).
```

```
#include <conio.h>
#include <iostream.h>
// .................................................
// abstract base class
class name {
  protected:
  char *obj_name;
  public:
  name(char *o_name) { obj_name = o_name;}   // constructor
  virtual void display_info() = 0;   // a 'pure virtual function'
  ~name(){}                          // destructor
};
// .................................................
//now to create some derived classes
// 'circle' class definition goes here

// 'square' class definition goes here

// 'triangle' class definition goes here
// .................................................
void main(void) {

  clrscr();
  cout << " LATE6 " << endl;
  cout << " ===== " << endl << endl;

  cout << " Another way of creating dynamic objects" << endl;
  cout << " ... and illustrating late binding " << endl   << endl;
  // create an array of pointers to shape
  name *shape[10];

  cout << " Select some shapes " << endl;
  cout << " SHAPE MENU " << endl;
  cout << " ========== " << endl << endl;

  cout << " 1. Circle "   << endl << endl;
  cout << " 2. Square "   << endl << endl;
  cout << " 3. Triangle " << endl << endl;
  cout << " 4. QUIT "     << endl << endl;
  int i = 0, n, option;
  float r, s, s1, s2, s3;
  do{
    cin >> option;
    switch (option) {
      case 1: cout << " Enter radius : ";
        cin >> r;
        shape[i++] = new circle("circle", r);
        break;
      case 2: cout << " Enter length of side : ";
        cin >> s;
        shape[i++] = new square("square", s);
        break;
      case 3: cout << " Enter side lengths "
                   << endl;
        cout << " Side 1: "; cin >> s1;
        cout << " Side 2: "; cin >> s2;
        cout << " Side 3: "; cin >> s3;
```

```
                shape[i++] = new
                triangle("triangle", s1, s2, s3);
                break;
           case 4: ;// quit
      }
   } while (option != 4);
   n = i;
   cout << " The shapes you enetered were: " << endl;
   for (i = 0; i<n; i++)
      shape[i]-> display_info();
   cout << " Press any key to Quit ";
   getch();
}
```

8.6   Destructors and single inheritance

When using inheritance it is important to understand how destructors work
and when a destructor is called. You will remember from earlier discussions
concerning destructors (Section 5.10) that when an object goes out of scope
the destructor for that class (if there is one) is called. In this section we extend
our earlier discussion by taking a look at the general question 'What happens
with destructors in the case of inheritance?' and the more specific topic of
virtual destructors.

A simple illustration of when destructors (and constructors) are called
when inheritance is involved can be given by considering the base class name
and the square, circle and triangle classes which we have already been
looking at. We begin by first modifying each of the classes involved so that a
message is displayed whenever the constructor and destructor methods are
called. So for the name class we now have:

```
// base class
class name {
  protected:
  char *obj_name;
  public:
  name(char *o_name) { obj_name = o_name;      // constructor
          cout << " name constructor called " << endl;
  }
  ~name(){ cout << " name destructor called " << endl; }
  virtual void display_info(){ cout << obj_name << endl; }
};
```

Note that we are using the latest version of these classes with the display_
info() method specified as a virtual function in the base class. Similar modifications to the constructor and destructor methods are made for the other
three classes. Program 8.11 then creates two static objects: a circle and a triangle, followed by a couple of dynamic objects: a circle and a square.

```
//: INHDESC.cpp
//. destructors and inheritance
//  base, circle, square and triangle class definitions go here
// ....................................................................
void main(void) {
    clrscr();
    cout << " INHDESC " << endl;
    cout << " ======= " << endl << endl;
    cout << " ... illustrating late binding, " << endl;
    cout << " ... constructor and destructor calls " << endl;
    cout << " First some static objects: " << endl << endl;

// start a new block - to see when the destructors are called
    {
        circle c("circle", 2);
        triangle t("triangle", 3, 4, 5);

        c.display_info();
        t.display_info();
    }
    cout << " Press any key to Continue ";
    getch();
    clrscr();

    cout << " Now for some dynamic objects: " << endl;

    // create a pointer to shape
    name *shape;

    // now instantiate a circle
    shape = new circle("circle", 2.5);
    shape -> display_info();
    delete shape;                      // dangerous!

    // ... and now create a square pointed to by shape
    shape = new square("square", 4.0);
    shape -> display_info();
    delete shape;
    cout << " Press any key to Quit ";
    getch();
}
```

Notice that, in order to check on destructor calls, we enclose the c and t static objects in braces – the various destructors will then be called on exit from that block. Test run 8.7 shows a sample run.

If you take a close look at this output you will see that the constructor calls (as you would expect) and the destructor calls (as you might expect) work fine. However it is worth looking at the detail in these calls. When the circle object c is instantiated the first constructor which is called is the name constructor followed by the circle constructor. Then, when this object goes out of scope, the destructors are called in reverse order – circle followed by name. So there are no problems, or surprises here.

```
INHDESC
=======
... illustrating late binding,
... constructor and destructor calls
First some static objects:

name constructor called
circle constructor called
name constructor called
triangle constructor called
circle
 radius = 2
triangle
 side1 = 3
 side2 = 4
 side3 = 5
 triangle destructor called
 name destructor called
 circle destructor called
 name destructor called
 Press any key to Continue
Now for some dynamic objects:
 name constructor called
 circle constructor called
circle
 radius = 2
 name destructor called
 name constructor called
 square constructor called
square
 side = 4
 name destructor called
 Press any key to Quit
```

But what about the dynamic objects? Again there are no problems with the constructor calls, these are exactly as we have come to expect. However when we look at which destructors are called we see that only the name destructor method is used – there is no evidence in the 'dynamic section' of the program of either the circle or square destructor methods being used. Why is this? The reason is do to with the way in which methods are bound to dynamic objects. For the same reason that the show_name() method was made a virtual function in name, the name destructor also needs to be made virtual. In the present program we create a pointer to an object of type name (called shape) and then get this to point to a circle. After displaying the shape's details this is then deleted using the keyword delete:

```
name *shape;
// now instantiate a circle
shape = new circle("circle", 2.5);
shape -> display_info();
delete shape;              // dangerous!
```

As the comment points out, and as we have discovered, this is dangerous. Although the pointer to name is destroyed the circle is still lying around somewhere (or at least the bits not deleted when the ~name() method is called). If we add virtual before the ~name() method and recompile and run the program, then the output is as Test run 8.8.

With this modification we now obtain the correct processing of dynamic objects. This illustrates that it is important when considering the design of classes first if they are likely to be inherited by other classes and second if objects are likely to be created dynamically. If the answer to both of these questions is 'yes' then the destructor method in the base class should be made virtual as should any other methods which are likely to be replaced by, more appropriate, descendant class methods.

🖥️ **Test run 8.8**

```
INHDESC1
========

    ... this part the same as before

Now for some dynamic objects:
name constructor called
circle constructor called
circle
 radius = 2
 circle destructor called
 name destructor called
 name constructor called
 square constructor called
square
 side = 4
 square destructor called
 name destructor called
 Press any key to Quit
```

8.7   Multiple inheritance – another look

Earlier we promised that we would return to the topic of multiple inheritance and now that we have covered the issues of virtual functions we can do just that. If you read other literature on object-oriented programming, or analysis and design, you will discover that there are two points of view concerning multiple inheritance. One is that it need never be used and that the need for it reflects a flaw in the analysis and design stages of the problem. The second is that it can be a useful tool if used with care. Certainly you should not try to use multiple inheritance unless there is a good reason for it. One example when it could be argued that it is advantageous is in the case of windows in a standard windows environment. In such cases a window can contain other windows which themselves can contain yet other windows. A `window` class is best described in terms of inheritance from three classes:

- A `screen_object` class which includes items like height, width, colour and methods such as `move()`, `change_height()` and `change_width()`.
- A `text` class which provides the details of how the text is to appear in the window and providing basic editing facilities.
- A `tree` class which models the hierarchical structure of the group of windows – e.g. sub window, parent – and methods for adding and removing windows.

We will only spend a short time looking at multiple inheritance – and this mostly in pointing out problems that you may encounter! First, consider two classes `date` and `time` each of which have similar methods such as `set()`, `get()` and `show()`. Now suppose we wish to combine these two classes by creating a `clock` class which inherits both the date and time classes. Program 8.12 is a simplified version of a program which uses just such a combination. Test run 8.9 gives a sample run.

Suppose however that there was no `show()` method in the `clock` class. It should be obvious that the attempt to call `c.show()` will fail, not because there is no `show()` method, but because an ambiguity arises in which of the base class `show()` method to use. Comment out the show definition in the `clock` class and see what error message you get.

In this case we can easily overcome the problem by explicitly calling either the `date` or `time` `show()` method, e.g.

```
c.date::show();
c.time::show();
```

Another ambiguity arises when two classes inherit the same base class and these two classes are combined to form yet another class – thus giving a diamond shaped structure to the inheritance diagram. As an illustration we return to the `name`, `circle` and `square` classes discussed earlier. Suppose we construct another class `odd_shape` which inherits both the `circle` and `square` classes. Take a look at Program 8.13 below before reading on. Test run 8.10 shows a sample run.

```
//: CLOCK.cpp
//. example of multiple inheritance using date and time classes

#include <conio.h>
#include <iostream.h>
// ..........................................................
// simple date class
class date{
protected:
    char day;
    int month;
    int year;
public:
    date(){}
    date(char d, int m, int y){ day = d; month = m; year = y;}
    ~date(){}
    void set(char d, int m, int y){ day = d; month = m;    year = y
    void get(char &d, int&m, int &y){ d = day;m = month;   y = year
    void show(){ cout << (int)day <<" / " << month << " / " << year
};
// ..........................................................
// simple time class
class time {
protected:
    int hr, min, sec;
public:
    time(){ hr = min = sec = 0; }
    time(int h, int m, int s){ hr = h; min = m; sec = s;}
    ~time(){}
    void set(int h, int m, int s){ hr = h; min = m; sec = s;}
    void get(int &h, int &m, int &s){ h = hr; m = min;
                          s = sec;}
    void show(){ cout << hr << " : " << min << " : " << sec;}
};
// ..........................................................
// a clock class, inheriting both date and time
class clock : public date, public time {
public:
    clock(): date(), time(){}
    clock( char d, int m, int y, int h, int mi, int s) :
        date(d, m, y), time(h, mi, s){}
    void set(char d, int m, int y, int h, int mi, int s){
        day = d; month = m; year = y;
        hr = h; min = m; sec = s;
    }
    void show() { time::show(); cout << endl;
          date::show(); cout << endl;
    }
};
// ..........................................................
void main(void) {

    clock c;

    clrscr();
    cout << " CLOCK " << endl;
```

```
    cout << " ===== " << endl << endl;

    c.set(4, 12, 1996, 9, 15, 0);

    c.show();

    cout << " Press any key to Quit ";
    getch();
}
```

🖳 **Test run 8.9**
```
CLOCK
=====

9 : 15 : 0
4 / 12 / 1996
Press any key to Quit
```

📋 **Program 8.13**
```
//: MULTINH3.cpp
//. this program illustrates how in multiple inheritance
//. two instances of a base object may be created.

#include <conio.h>
#include <iostream.h>

// base class
class name {
  protected:
   char *obj_name;
  public:
   name(char *o_name) { obj_name = o_name;
     cout << "name constructed" << endl;
   }  // constructor
   virtual void display_info() = 0;
                // a 'pure virtual function'
};
// ............................................................
// circle
class circle : public name {
   int radius;
   public:
   circle( char *o_name, int rad) : name(o_name),
                     radius (rad){
     cout << "circle constructed" << endl;
   }
   void display_info(){
     cout << obj_name << endl;
     cout << " radius = " << radius << endl;
   }
   void change_name(char *n_name){ obj_name = n_name; }
};
// ............................................................
// square
```

```
class square : public name {
  int side;
  public:
   square( char *o_name, int s) : name(o_name), side(s){
     cout << "square constructed" << endl;
   }
   void display_info(){
     cout << obj_name << endl;
     cout << " side = " << side << endl;
   }
   void change_name(char *n_name){ obj_name = n_name;}
};
// ............................................................
// odd_shape
class odd_shape:public circle, public square{
  public:
   odd_shape( char *o_name, int s): circle(o_name, s),
                      square(o_name, s){
     cout << "odd_shape constructed" << endl;
   }
   void display_info(){
     circle::display_info();
     square::display_info();
   }
};
// ............................................................
void main(void) {

   clrscr();
   cout << " MULTINH3 " << endl;
   cout << " ======== " << endl << endl;

   cout << " Multiple inheritance with a common base class"
                      << endl;
   odd_shape o("circle & square",5);

   o.display_info();
   // 1st attempt
   //o.obj_name = "new_name";       // ambiguous

/* // 2nd attempt
   cout << " DIRECT access to obj_name: " << endl;
   o.circle::obj_name = "circle";
   o.square::obj_name = "square";
   o.display_info();
*/
   // 3rd attempt
   cout << " INDIRECT access - via change_name() methods: "
                      << endl;
   o.circle::change_name("circle");
   o.square::change_name("square");
   o.display_info();

   cout << " Press any key to Quit ";
   getch();
}
```

```
MULTINH3
========

Multiple inheritance with a common base class
name constructed
circle constructed
name constructed
square constructed
odd_shape constructed
circle & square
 radius = 5
circle & square
 side = 5
 INDIRECT access - via change_name() methods:
circle
 radius = 5
square
 side = 5
Press any key to Quit
```

First of all notice that the name constructor is called once for each of the two derived classes `circle` and `square` – indicated by the 'name constructed' message. This proves that there are two instances of the `name` class. Second take another look at the program and examine the three attempts at changing the name of the `circle` and `square` objects. The first attempt, via `o.obj_name = "new_name"`; fails because of the ambiguity of `obj_name` between the `circle` and `square` objects. The second attempt fails because `obj_name` is a protected member of `name`, not a public one, making `obj_name` public would allow direct access to be obtained via the scope resolution operator and the appropriate class name. The third attempt uses the two member functions of the circle and square classes respectively (i.e. `change_name()`).

In this particular example we do in fact require two `name` objects to be created – one for the circle and one for the square, but what if we only wanted one object of the `name` class to be created? This can be achieved by yet another use of the `virtual` keyword. The `circle` and `square` class definitions should be changed to read as follows:

```
class square : virtual public name { ... };
class circle : virtual public name { ... };
```

where the ... indicate that the rest of the class body remains the same. With this addition the `name` class is declared as a virtual base class thus allowing only one instance of the base class to be created.

8.8 Summary

This chapter should have enabled you to get your teeth into C++ and given you more understanding of how object-oriented programming can be used. As usual you should try out the Exercises given below to check that you have understood this chapter.

Topics covered:

- Single inheritance – base and descendant classes.
- The use of private, protected and public in inheritance.
- Multiple inheritance.
- Virtual functions.
- Pure virtual functions.

8.9 Exercises

As in previous chapters selected solutions are provided in Appendix A, so if you need a helping hand take a look.

8.9.1 Modify the `point.h` class so that it contains a new gradient function of the form `double gradient(point p);`. This can then be used with any points – not just by objects of the `trapezium` class (Section 8.2.5) – write suitable test programs to try out your function.

8.9.2 Write member functions of `coloured_line` to enable a coloured line to be generated from a line which already exists.

8.9.3 Write member functions of `coloured_line` to allow the x and y co-ordinates of start and end to be displayed.

8.9.4 Incorporate the modifications to the `rectangle` class discussed in Section 8.2.5 and test them out.

8.9.5

a) A square is a special form of a rectangle with all sides equal. Derive a class `square`, based on the `rectangle` class, containing just one constructor function and try it out.

b) The perimeter of a square can be computed by multiplying the length of any side by four, and the area is just the square of any side. Now add these two functions to your `square` class and test them.

8.9.6 Design and code a class hierarchy to simulate an `autoBankAccount` facility. The base class should use attributes `amount` and `pin_number` and methods:

`withdraw()`, `deposit()`, `balance()`, `activate()`, `validate()` and `change_pin_number()`.

Three classes are to inherit this base class `bankAssistant` – can only inherit `activate()` and `change_pin_number()`; `ownBank` – which allows all operations except `activate()` and `change_pin_number()`; `otherBank` – which only allows `validate()` and `withdraw()`.

The function descriptions are as follows:

`int withdraw()`

allows user to withdraw any amount in the set 10, 20 30, 50 100, 200, 300 provided the balance doesn't go below 0.

`void deposit()`

allows user to deposit any integer amount.

`void balance()`

displays the current balance.

`void activate(&pin)`

must be called by `bankAssistant` before any transactions can take place – it also sets the initial value of `pin_number` (to pin).

`void validate()`

to be used whenever a user wishes to access her account.

`void change_pin_number(&pin)`

used by `bankAssistant` to alter the pin number.

Container Classes and Templates

9.1 Introduction

This chapter deals with a common use of classes – as *containers* for other classes. We begin by looking at a simple list class and develop this so that it can be used with any collection of objects. This leads on to the concept of *template classes* which, in later implementations of C++, enable structures such as generic lists or generic bounded arrays to be constructed. Another use of templates is as generic functions and in Section 9.7 we look at a simple template function example. Finally we touch very briefly on the idea of exception handling in C++.

9.2 Container classes – a worked example

In this section we take a look at one important use of classes in C++, namely to represent container classes. A container class is a class that is designed to hold something. The important thing about such classes is that what they hold is irrelevant – at least at the design change. So a container class might be a stack, a queue, or a graph. The class would contain all the necessary methods to deal with objects contained in the class. So, for example a stack might have push(), pop(), top() and count(), to add an object to the stack, remove one from the stack, return a copy of the object currently on top of the stack and count the number of objects in the stack. A template class can therefore be created which can be used to hold any other class. So we could create a generic stack class which could be used whenever we require to implement a stack, no matter what we want to use the stack for.

As a 'gentle' introduction to this topic we will take a look at a simple list class to hold a variable number of integers. A list is made of nodes each of which contains in its simplest form a data item and a pointer to the next node. A typical list will have a head (a pointer to the first node in the list) and a tail (pointing to the last node in the list). In this particular implementation, whenever a new list is declared a single empty node is created and the head and tail both point to this single node. When an item is added to the list the data is inserted into the current last node and a new empty node created. An alternative method would only use a head pointer and the tail of the list would be indicated by a NULL pointer.

In addition to the head and tail pointers (head and tail), a third pointer is also required which is used to point to the current node. Finally we have an integer count which is used to keep track of the number of (occupied) nodes in the list.

The operations required on this simple list are create a node, construct a list, destroy a list, add a node and associated data, read an item from the list and move to the front of the list. Additional operations which are useful are ones to check if the node being accessed is the last node and to check the node count. Program 9.1 illustrates the basic elements for such a class and a simple program to try it out.

Program 9.1

```cpp
//: INTLIST.cpp
//. a simple list class - creating a list of ints
#include <conio.h>
#include <iostream.h>
#include <process.h>
#include <string.h>
// definition of a node for the list
struct node{
   int i;
   node *next;
};
// list class
class list {
   node *head,            // points to first node
      *tail,              // points to last node
      *this_node;         // points to current node
   node *create_node();
   int count;             // number of nodes
 public:
   list();
   ~list();
   void add(int val);
   void front(){ this_node = head; }  // move to start of list
   int get();
   int nodeOK(){ return (this_node != tail); }
   int no_nodes(){ return count; }
};
// private method used when creating the list or adding a node
node *list::create_node() {
   node *new_node;
   new_node = new node; // 0 if unable to allocate storage
   if (new_node == 0) {
      cout << " Out of Memory " << endl;
      exit(1);   // crude, but will do for now!
   }
   return new_node;
}
```

```
// constructor
list::list() {        // empty list; head & tail the same
   head = tail = create_node();
   count = 0;
}
// destructor
list::~list() {
   node *p;
   while (head != tail){
      p = head;
      head = head->next;
      delete p;
   }
   delete head;
}

// add data to the end of the list
void list::add(int val) {
   tail->i = val;             // put 'val' in current last node
   tail = tail->next = create_node();// create a new last
                 // node and update tail pointer
   count++;
}

// return the value stored in 'this_node'
int list::get() {
   int val = this_node->i; // return value in this_node
   this_node = this_node->next; // move to next node
   return val;
}
// ....................................................................
void main(void) {
   int n;

   list l;

   clrscr();
   cout << " INTLIST " << endl;
   cout << " ======= " << endl << endl;

   cout << endl << " Enter some +ve integers
                 (end with -ve value): " << endl;
   cout << " > ";
   cin >> n;
   while (n > -1) {
      l.add(n);
      cout << " > ";
      cin >> n;
   }
   l.front();
   cout << " You entered : " << endl;
   while(l.nodeOK())
      cout << l.get() << " ";
   cout << endl;
   cout << " No of integers = " << l.no_nodes() << endl;
   cout << " Press ENTER to Quit ";
   cin.get();
}
```

You will notice that in this example we have used a simple structure (struct node {...};) to define the nature of the nodes which are to make up the list. If we wish to create a new program to deal with a list of characters then it is a reasonably simple matter to modify the program to do this. Any reference to the data item in a node, or passed to or from a node, will need to be changed from an int to a char. So the struct becomes:

```
// definition of a node for the list (of chars)
struct node{
    char c;
    node *next;
};
```

Then, in the list class itself we need to modify the add() and get() methods. :

```
// list class
    ...
    void add(char val);
    ...
    char get();
    ...
};

// add data to the end of the list
void list::add(char val) {
    tail->c = val;              // put 'val' in current last node
    tail = tail->next = create_node();// create a new last
                   // node and update tail pointer
    count++;
}

// return the value stored in 'this_node'
char list::get() {
    char val = this_node->c;   // return value in this_node
    this_node = this_node->next; // move to next node
    return val;
}
```

Finally, the main() function requires rather more major modifications, including a cosmetic, but nevertheless useful important change to the identifier used for data entry (from n to ch):

```
void main(void) {
    char ch;
    list l;

    clrscr();
    cout << " CHARLIST " << endl;
    cout << " ======== " << endl << endl;
    cout << endl << "Enter some characters (end with .):" << endl;
    cout << " > ";
    cin >> ch;
    while (ch != '.') {
        l.add(ch);
```

```
       cout << " > ";
       cin >> ch;
   }

   l.front();
   cout << " You entered : " << endl;
   while(l.nodeOK())
       cout << l.get() << " ";
   cout << endl;
   cout << " No of chars = " << l.no_nodes() << endl;
   cout << " Press any key to Quit ";
   getch();
}
```

Now the new program works fine for `chars` and the modifications weren't too
horrendous. However each time we want to use the list for a different data
type we need to go through a similar routine of modification, not only of the
main program, as we would expect, but also of the list class itself. Also the
changes are scattered throughout this class making it time consuming and
prone to error – we could easily miss a change or make a change in the wrong
place. So how can we improve matters? The first step is to make the node
`structure` into a class. However we can't simply change `struct` to `class` –
try it out and see for yourself. Making such a change immediately means that
the contents of the node, in this case `char c;` and `node *next;` become private, and therefore inaccessible to the `list` class. We could of course make
them public but that is a long way round into returning the `class` to a `struct`
– remember a `struct` is essentially a class with all members public!

What making the node into a class suggests is that there should be methods
in this class to handle the detailed access to the node elements. What operations are required? First of all we need to get the pointer to the next node and
also set that pointer – when adding a node, for example. We also need to access the data item (in this case the `char`), so again we need a `get` and `set`
method for this class member. Taking on board these changes our `node` class
now takes this form:

```
// definition of a node for the list
// This contains the methods necessary to access a node:
//    get and change the contents
//    and get and set the pointer to the next node
class node{
   char item;
   node *next;
public:
   node(){}
   ~node(){}
   node *get_next(){ return next; }
   node *set_next(node *new_node){ next = new_node;}
   char get_item(){ return item; }
   void set_item(char new_item){ item = new_item; }
};
```

We have added a default constructor method and a destructor method and changed the name of the data attribute to a more generalised one – i.e. item. These methods are all very simple and as you can see can be written inline. We have now got a fair degree of encapsulation for our new node class, which as we have seen is an important concept in object-oriented programming (and not just object-oriented programming). The attributes of the class can only be accessed through the public methods supplied by the class.

Now to the list class, what changes need to be made in that? Obviously whenever any structure pointer operations are used they will be replaced by the appropriate access method from the node class. Take a look at the new version given below – the changes are indicated in bold type.

```
// list class
class list {
    node *head,           // points to first node
        *tail,       // points to last node
        *this_node;   // points to current node
    node *create_node();
    int count;            // number of nodes
  public:
    list();
    ~list();
    void add(char val);
    void front(){ this_node = head; }   // move to start of list
    char get();
    int nodeOK(){ return (this_node != tail); }
    int no_nodes(){ return count; }
};
// private method used when creating the list or adding a node
node *list::create_node() {
    node *p;
    new_node = new node;
    if (new_node == 0) {
        cout << " Out of Memory " << endl; exit(1);
    }
    return new_node;
}
list::list() {
    head = tail = create_node();
    count = 0;
}
list::~list() {
    node *p;
    while (head != tail){
        p = head;
        head = head->get_next();
        delete p;
    }
    delete head;
}

// add data to the end of the list
void list::add(char val) {
    tail->set_item(val); // put 'val' in current last node
```

```
      tail = tail->set_next(create_node());   // create a new
                           // last node and update tail pointer
      count++;
}
// return the value stored in 'this_node'
char list::get() {
   char val = this_node->get_item();
   this_node = this_node->get_next();
   return val;
}
```

As you might expect all the changes involve replacing the references to the node attributes (previously c and next) by the appropriate set or get methods. The main program requires no further modification.

The list class is certainly a little more generalised but if we want to use it for lists other than chars we still need to modify every reference to the data attribute of the node class as well as write a new node class to incorporate these changes. This suggests that it would make sense to wrap-up (encapsulate) the data attribute of the node by creating yet another class for this. If carried out correctly we would then only need to create different item_type classes for them to be used by the node class and the list class. Once we create this class we will find that some changes need to be made to the other two classes as well but we will end up with a more useful implementation.

So what do we require? First of all we need methods to allow the item to be assigned a value. It is useful to provide both a constructor method, to allow initialisation, and a set() method to allow an uninitialised item to be assigned a value or to change an existing value. We also need a get() method which will return an object of item_type. Finally we will need a show() method to display the contents of the object. Notice that all of these methods take over the detailed management of the object – for example only the item_type class (and the objects created from it) 'know' how to display the item and no other class need or should 'know' how to do this – another example of the importance of encapsulation. So, incorporating these ideas, our item_type class looks like this:

📖 **Header file (Reference Program 9.2a)**
```
//: ITEMTYPE.h
//. definition of an item to be contained in node
#include <iostream.h>
class item_type{
   float f;   int   n;
public:
   item_type(){}
   item_type(float fi, int i){f = fi; n = i;}
   ~item_type(){}
   void set(float fi, int i){f = fi; n = i;}
   item_type get(){ return *this;}
   void show(){cout << f << " " << n << endl; }
};
```

For illustrative purposes this class has been written to hold two elements – a float (f) and an int (n) – however it is a reasonably straightforward matter to modify it to contain other combinations of data (see, for example, the exercises at the end of the chapter).

So much for the new class, now for the other two classes. First let's look at the changes that have been made to the node class:

📖 **Header file (Reference Program 9.2b)**

```
//: NODE.h
//. a node definition, for use with a list, or ...
// This contains the methods necessary to access a node:
//    get and change the contents
//    and get and set the pointer to the next node
class node{
   item_type item;
   node *next;
public:
   node(){}
   ~node(){}
   node *get_next(){ return next; }
   node *set_next(node *new_node){ next = new_node;}
   item_type get_item(){ return item; }
   void set_item(item_type new_item){ item = new_item; }
   void show(){item.show();}
};
```

A close inspection of the above code will reveal that the main changes to the previous version involve the replacement of all the references to the specific data type char by the generic data type item_type. One additional method has been added to allow the node to display an item. This method also allows the list class to be able to display data items as we shall see shortly. So finally we come to the new version of the list class itself. As you would, hopefully, expect the only changes required are to the two methods which involve the data items being set or retrieved (i.e. add() and get()). Two additional methods have been incorporated in this version to enable the data to be displayed (show() and next_node()). For completeness we give the new list class below:

📖 **Header file (Reference Program 9.2c)**

```
//: LIST.h
//. list class - using the node and item_type classes
#include <iostream.h>
#include <process.h>
class list {
   node *head,         // points to first node
      *tail,        // points to last node
      *this_node;  // points to current node
   node *create_node();
   int count;          // number of nodes
```

```
  public:
    list();
    ~list();
    void add(item_type val);
    void front(){ this_node = head; }   // move to start of list
    item_type get();
    int nodeOK(){ return (this_node != tail); }
    int no_nodes(){ return count; }
    void show(){this_node->show();}
    void next_node(){this_node = this_node->get_next();}
};

// private method used when creating the list or adding a node
node *list::create_node() {
    node *p;
    p = new node;
    if (p == 0) {
        cout << " Out of Memory " << endl; exit(1);
    }
    return p;
}

list::list() {
    head = tail = create_node();
    count = 0;
}

list::~list() {
    node *p;
    while (head != tail){
        p = head;
        head = head->get_next();
        delete p;
    }
    delete head;
}

// add data to the end of the list
void list::add(item_type val) {
    tail->set_item(val);       // put 'val' in current last node
    tail = tail->set_next(create_node());  // create a new last
                // node and update tail pointer
    count++;
}

// return the value stored in 'this_node'
item_type list::get() {
    item_type val = this_node->get_item();
    this_node = this_node->get_next();

    return val;

}
```

A program to demonstrate these new classes is given in Program 9.2d.

```
//: ITEMLIST.CPP
//. program to test the item_type, node and list classes
void main(void) {

    list l;
    item_type n1(3.4, 123),  n2(-9.47, 456);
    clrscr();
    cout << " ITEMLIST " << endl;
    cout << " ======== " << endl << endl;

    l.add(n1);
    l.add(n2);

    l.front();
    cout << " List : " << endl;
    while(l.nodeOK()){
        l.show();
        l.next_node();
    }
    cout << endl;
    cout << " No of nodes = " << l.no_nodes() << endl;
    cout << " Press any key to Quit ";
    getch();
}
```

If you try this program out using the classes we have just developed and incorporating the relevant header files (itemtype.h, node.h, list.h, conio.h and iostream.h) then you should obtain the output in Test run 9.1.

We are now almost at the end of our discussion of this list example. However there is still one other consideration which is worth dwelling on for a moment or two – namely data entry. At present the program needs to 'know' exactly what form the item_type has in order for any data to be entered via any external device, for example via the keyboard. In this particular example it is not difficult to set up a data entry procedure in the main program – we will need to prompt the user for a float followed by an int, store them in an item_type object and then add this object to the list. With a more complex item_type this would become tedious and cumbersome. Before reading on think about which would be the best class to handle such complications.

Test run 9.1

```
ITEMLIST
========

List :
3.4 123
-9.47 456

No of nodes = 2
Press any key to Quit
```

If you have followed our discussion so far then you will readily agree that the item_type class should handle all the details regarding data entry. This then creates a tight encapsulation of these objects, ideally dealing with any data entry errors. The main program should then simply call the relevant methods (possible in some form of control loop) and any problems concerning data entry will be devolved to the item_type objects themselves.

As a final example then, we consider an item_type which is used to store a string and an unsigned int. To complicate matters a little, and in order to illustrate some basic error trapping, we want the name to consist of two, or more, parts separated by a space, or spaces and the unsigned int member will be used to represent a year, for example year of birth.

Program 9.2

```
//: LISTPOET.cpp
//. a simple list class - names and years of birth
#include <conio.h>
#include <iostream.h>
#include <process.h>
#include <string.h>
#include <iostream.h>
#include <iomanip.h>
#include <stdlib.h>
#include <ctype.h>

// definition of item to be contained in node
const SIZE = 20;

class item_type{
    char name[SIZE];
    unsigned    year;
public:
    item_type(){}
    item_type(char *nme, unsigned db);
    ~item_type(){}
    void set(char *nme, unsigned db);
    item_type get(){ return *this;}
    void show();
    int enter();
};

item_type::item_type(char *nme, unsigned db){
    strncpy(name, nme, SIZE);
    name[SIZE-1] = '\0';
    year = db;
}
void item_type::set(char *nme, unsigned db){
    strncpy(name, nme, SIZE);
    name[SIZE-1] = '\0';
    year = db;
}
void item_type::show(){
    cout.setf(ios::left);
    cout << setw(20) << name << " ";
```

```
      cout << resetiosflags(ios::left)
          << setw(5) << year << endl;
}
// read information from keyboard
int item_type::enter(){
    char s1[82], s2[82];        // to hold data entered
    int i;                       // to hold an integer for year

    cout << " Name: ";
    while(isspace(cin.peek()))
       cin.get();
    cin.getline(s1, 82);
    if (!stricmp(s1, "STOP")) return 0;   // input complete

    cout << "  YoB: ";

    do{                          // simple validation for year
       cin.getline(s2, 82);
       i = atoi(s2);
       if (i < 0){
          cout << " Invalid Year, please re-enter " << endl;
          cout << "  YoB: ";
       }
    } while (i < 0);

    set(s1, i);

    return 1;
}
// ...........................................................
// node class definition goes here
// ...........................................................
// list class definition goes here
// ...........................................................
void main(void) {
    list l;
    item_type n1("John Milton", 1608),
         n2("T. S. Eliot", 1888),
         n3("Wilfred Owen", 1893);
    clrscr();
    cout << " LISTPOET " << endl;
    cout << " ======== " << endl << endl;
    l.add(n1);
    l.add(n2);
    l.add(n3);

    cout << "        Poet            Born " << endl;
    cout << "-------------------------" << endl;

    l.front();
    while(l.nodeOK()){
       l.show();
       l.next_node();
    }
    cout << endl;

    cout << " No. of Poets = " << l.no_nodes() << endl;
    cout << " Press ENTER to continue ";
```

```
cin.get();
list 12;
cout<<"Now enter your favourite Poets & their Dates of Birth "
                                          << endl;
cout << " - to stop enter STOP for name" << endl;

while(12.enter()) ;  // read details from keyboard until
                     // STOP entered
clrscr();
cout << "         Poet           Born " << endl;
cout << "-------------------------" << endl;

12.front();
while(12.nodeOK()){
   12.show();
   12.next_node();
}
cout << endl;
cout << " No. of Poets = " << 12.no_nodes() << endl;
cout << " Press ENTER to Quit ";
cin.get();
}
```

There are a couple of points worth noting in the above listing. First notice
how in the constructor function and the set function for item_type the last
character in the name is set to '\0'. Since we have no way of knowing how
long the string is that is passed to either of these functions, or indeed whether
they are correctly terminated it is wise to ensure that it is terminated correctly
inside these functions. An additional null terminator will do no harm – without one the consequences could be disastrous.

Secondly note how the show() function has been written. This uses some
of the formatting techniques mentioned in Chapter 4 in order to produce a reasonable layout for the names and years of birth; the names are left justified in
a field width of 20 and the years of birth are right justified in a field width of
5.

Thirdly take a look at the enter() function which controls the input of
information from the keyboard. There is some primitive data validation in this
routine, but there is room for improvement – see the Exercise at the end of the
Chapter for suggestions. We use two strings of 82 characters to read the data
from the keyboard. Perhaps this is overkill but it means that a line of text can
be entered without any ill effects. The function includes obvious details such
as providing prompts for input and a basic check on the value of the integer
entered. There are also some other constructs to help with error trapping. First
the buffer is checked for any spurious white spaces and if any are found these
are discarded; in this instance we use the peek() and get() functions for this
purpose. Next the getline() function is used to read characters into the variable s1 (a maximum of 82 or until ENTER is pressed). This is then compared
with the terminating string (STOP) using the stricmp() function. Notice that
strcicmp() returns 0 if the strings match (the i indicates that case should be

ignored) and so `!stricmp()` is TRUE when the strings match, not `stricmp()`. The year is entered again by reading in a line of characters to provide better error checking. Once data has been entered this is converted to a (possibly signed) integer (`i`) which is checked and if negative a request is made for re-entry of the year. Once a valid year has been entered the `set()` method is used to initialise the name and year attributes.

The main program holds no surprises and simply displays some examples and then request the user to enter some names and dates of their own. Note that the list and node classes remain as in the previous program. Therefore, in order to use this list class for another `item_type` all that is required is to write a new `item_type` class (or more likely modify the existing one) and write a suitable main program.

Although this fairly simple example has taken some time to explain you should find it instructive in the way in which the classes were developed. In fact the majority of this design should have been done, and would normally be done, at a much earlier stage rather than in this ad hoc fashion which we have used here. However the purpose of going through this process was to illustrate how a class, or set of classes, might evolve. This example illustrates how classes can be used as containers. We have here a container class `list` which holds a number of nodes. Each `node` object contains an `item_type` object which, as long as that class contains the methods given here which are relevant for its own particular structure, can be used with the node and therefore list class. We could also write stack or queue classes which used the `node` class and an array class which used the `item_type` class directly.

With the earlier releases of C++ container classes and/or multiple inheritance were the only ways in which such structures as these we have been discussing could be implemented. Now, with the later releases of C++ we have the additional option of using templates. So, to conclude this chapter we provide, in the next section, a brief discussion of templates (and template functions).

9.3 Template classes

We begin our consideration of templates by looking at the syntax of template class definitions and declarations. The definition of a template class takes the following general form:

```
template<class T>
class className{
    ...
    T identifier;
```

```
    T *pointer;
    ...
    className();
    void function1(int n, T x);
    T get(){ return identifier;}};
    T *function2();
};
template<class T>
className<T>::className(){
    ...
}
template<class T>
void className<T>::function1(int n, T x){
    ...
}
template<class T>
T * className<T>::function2(){
    ...
}
```

The first point to notice is that the class definition and each function definition outside the class definition are preceded by `template<class T>` in order to identify which routines are part of the template class. The identifier `T` can be any valid identifier but it is usual simply to use `T` for this purpose. If more than one template is being constructed then `TN`, `TS` etc. can be used or longer, more descriptive names if it is thought necessary. Within the class itself `T` is used in place of a normal data type (built in or user defined). Outside the class definition the function definitions, in addition to being preceded by `template<class T>` as already mentioned, have the usual `className` identifier replaced with the combination `className<T>`.

When a template is used to instantiate objects the following form is used:

```
className<type> identifier_list;
```

where type is the data type used to replace the `T` in the className template definition. So we might have:

```
queue<int> n1, n2; // two queues of ints
queue<vehicle> toll_bridge;
            // a queue consisting of objects of a vehicle class

queue<person> waiting_room;  // a queue of people class
```

Although the above may look complicated enough the syntax of template definitions and declarations can become more complicated, but we will not worry about these aspects at the moment. We will begin by looking at a common example of the use of templates in order to introduce the basic syntax, that of an array which include simple checking on the indexes used.

A very simple array class, containing some primitive bound checking, is given in Program 9.3.

Program 9.3

```
//:   TEMPLARR.CPP
//.   a simple illustration of templates - using an array

#include <iostream.h>
#include <conio.h>
#include <process.h>

// Template class

template <class T>
class array{
   T *data;       // can use T here to identify the type
   int size;
public:
   array(int sz);
   ~array(){ delete [] data; }
   T & operator[](int i);   // can use T here as well
};

template <class T>// need this line before each definition
array<T>::array(int sz){
   data = new T [sz];     // T used here to specify type
   if (!data){
      cout << " **** ARRAY CLASS **** " << endl;
      cout << " Unable to allocate storage " << endl;
      cout << " for array: size = " << sz << endl;
      exit(1);
   }
   size = sz;
}

template <class T>
T & array<T>::operator[](int i){   // and here for return type
   if(i >= 0 && i < size)
      return data[i];
   cout << " **** ARRAY CLASS **** " << endl;
   cout << " Array out of bounds (0 - " << size << " )\n";
   cout << " ...... index = " << i << endl;
   exit(1);
}
// ...............................................................
void main(){
   array<int>   iarray(10);   // declare an integer array
   array<float> farray(5);    // and a float array
   int i;

   clrscr();
   cout << " TEMPLARR " << endl;
   cout << " ======== " << endl << endl;
   cout << " First an array of ints: " << endl;

   for (i = 0; i < 10; i++){
      iarray[i] = 2*i+1;    // an array of some odd nos.
      cout << iarray[i] << " ";
   }
   cout << endl << endl;
```

```
cout << " Now for some floats " << endl;
cout << " Please enter 5 floats: " << endl;
for (i = 0; i < 5; i++){
  cout << " > ";
  cin >> farray[i];
}

cout << " You entered: " << endl;

for (i = 0; i < 5; i++)
  cout << farray[i];
cout << endl;

cin.get();
cout << " Press ENTER to continue " << endl;
cin.get();

cout << " testing for bound checking " << endl;
// because of the bound checking this will abort the program
cout << " farray[5] = " << farray[5] << endl;
}
```

The above code should present no difficulties for you. The constructor function, in addition to allocating storage for the array, tests for successful allocation. If a negative value for sz is used or a value which is too large is used then the program terminates with a suitable error message. The overloaded [] operator also includes a crude method of checking the array index against the array bounds. However this is better than having the program crash as it might otherwise do. There are a number of alternative methods of trapping errors such as these and we will mention some of them briefly in a moment.

The syntax for the template class is reasonably straightforward in this example. If you remember the following rules you cannot go far wrong:

i.   Write you prospective template class first of all for a specific type and test it thoroughly.
ii. Add template <class T> before the template class definition and any function definitions not defined inline.
iii. If there are any functions defined outside the class definition then insert <T> between the class name and the scope resolution operator (::).
iv. Replace all references to the original specific type by T – be careful here to only replace the occurrences which actually refer to the class type (e.g. if the original class was tested using an int then it is extremely unlikely that replace all occurrences of int will be the correct strategy, for example a counter used in a for() loop should not be changed to T). For this reason it is better to use char or float as the original specific type.
v.   Now declare an object using the original specific type and test the class using the same data as previously used.

Once the template class has been successfully tested it can be used with other classes – provided of course that they have the necessary overloaded operators used by the template class. Thus if the template class assumes that the << operator is overloaded then you must ensure that any class that is used by the template class also has this operator overloaded. As an example, we can use the item_type class with our array template class, to create an array of philosphers and their years of birth (Program 9.4).

📋 **Program 9.4**

```
//:   TEMPLAR1.CPP
//.   template example using an array of item_type

#include <iostream.h>
#include <conio.h>
#include <process.h>

#include "itemtype.h" // contains item_type class definition
#include "arrtempl.h"// contains array template class def'n
// ...................................................
void main(){
   array<item_type>   philosophers(10);
   item_type          philosopher;

   int i = 0, nphilosophers;

   clrscr();
   cout << " TEMPLAR1 " << endl;
   cout << " ======== " << endl << endl;

   cout << " Enter some philosophers & their Dates of Birth "
                      << endl;
   cout << " - to stop enter STOP for name" << endl;

   while(philosopher.enter())// read details from keyboard
                // until STOP entered
      philosophers[i++] = philosopher;

   nphilosophers = i-1;

   clrscr();
   cout << "      Philosopher      Born " << endl;
   cout << "-------------------------" << endl;

   for (i = 0; i <= nphilosophers; i++)
      cout << philosophers[i];
   cout << endl;

   cout << " Press ENTER to Quit ";
   cin.get();
}
```

This program deliberately doesn't check the range of i in the data entry loop so that range checking has the possibility of coming into play. Obviously a better program would attempt to prevent out of bounds before reaching the stage of aborting a program. How might you modify the while loop to achieve this?

This program works fine so long as we deal with philosophers born on or after 1 AD! But what about the Greeks? Plato, Socrates and Aristotle all lived, and died, before then. We can make a simple modification to the item_type class which need have no affect on the array class. One solution is to add a new attribute to this class, say era, which can be an enumerated type having the values BC or AD. The enter() method for item_type can be modified to accept negative years or positive years. Negative years implies BC and positive ones AD. Apart from some minor changes to the information displayed on the screen no changes need be made to the above program. In the program that follows however we have made the obvious change of using a new file and a new class for this extended class (class name_yr_era in namesera.cpp).

📋 **Program 9.5**

```
//:    TEMPLAR2.CPP
//.    templates - an array of name_yr_era stored in namesera

#include <iostream.h>
#include <conio.h>
#include <process.h>

// ..............................................................
#include "namesera.h"// contains name_yr_era class definition
#include "arrtempl.h" // contains array template definition
// ..............................................................
void main(){

    array<name_yr_era> philosophers(4);
    name_yr_era philosopher;

    // .... as above for TEMPLAR1

    cout << " Enter some philosophers & their Dates of Birth "
                        << endl;
    cout << " for years BC type in -ve year (e.g. -450 = 450 BC"
                        <<endl;
    cout << " - to stop enter STOP for name" << endl;

    // .... as above for TEMPLAR1

}
```

The changes to the item_type affect the constructor, set(), enter(), show() and the overloaded << operator function, together with the addition of the enumerated type era to hold BC or AD and the corresponding attribute e in the class definition. So our new version of item_type (renamed name_yr_era) becomes:

📖 **Header file (Reference Program 9.6)**

```
//: NAMESERA.H
//. name_yr_era Template file

#include <conio.h>
#include <iostream.h>
#include <process.h>
#include <string.h>
#include <iostream.h>
#include <iomanip.h>
#include <stdlib.h>
#include <ctype.h>

// name_yr_era class
const SIZE = 20;
enum era {BC, AD};

class name_yr_era{
   char name[SIZE];
   unsigned   year;
   era        e;
public:
   name_yr_era(){}
   name_yr_era(char *nme, unsigned db, era el);
   ~name_yr_era(){}
   void set(char *nme, unsigned db, era el);
   name_yr_era get(){ return *this;}
   void show();
   int enter();
   friend ostream& operator<<(ostream& s, name_yr_era item);
};

name_yr_era::name_yr_era(char *nme, unsigned db, era el){
   strncpy(name, nme, SIZE);
   name[SIZE-1] = '\0';
   year = db;
   e = el;
}
void name_yr_era::set(char *nme, unsigned db, era el){
   strncpy(name, nme, SIZE);
   name[SIZE-1] = '\0';
   year = db;
   e = el;
}
void name_yr_era::show(){
   cout.setf(ios::left);
   cout << setw(20) << name << " ";
   cout << resetiosflags(ios::left)
        << setw(5) << year << " "
        << (e == BC ? "B.C." : "A.D.") << endl;
}
// read information from keyboard
int name_yr_era::enter(){
   char s1[82], s2[82];    // to hold data entered
   int i;                  // to hold an integer for year
   era el;                 // temp storage for the era
   cout << " Name: ";
```

```
         while(isspace(cin.peek()))
            cin.get();

         cin.getline(s1, 82);
         if (!stricmp(s1, "STOP"))
            return 0;

         cout << "  YoB: ";
         do{
            cin.getline(s2, 82);
            i = atoi(s2);
            if (i < 0){   // set e attribute
               e1 = BC;
               i = -i; // and ensure year will be positive
            } else
               e1 = AD;
         } while (i < 0);

         set(s1, i, e1);
         return 1;
      }

ostream& operator<<(ostream& s, name_yr_era item){
   s.setf(ios::left);
   s << setw(20) << item.name << " ";
   s << resetiosflags(ios::left)
         << setw(5) << item.year << " "
            << (item.e == BC ? "B.C." : "A.D.") << endl;
   return s;
}
```

There should be no problems with understanding the changes that have been
incorporated in the above code. Firstly the enumerated type era is defined and
then used to declare an additional attribute e inside the class. Secondly the
constructor and set() functions have an extra parameter to accommodate the
era. Next, the enter() function has been modified so that negative numbers
are accepted and used to set the era to BC. It's important here to ensure that
the year itself has a positive value (remember it is an unsigned variable) so we
simply reverse the sign of i in the relevant place in the if statement. Finally, in
both the show() and operator<<() functions, the output statement is modified with the addition of:

(e == BC ? "B.C." : "A.D.") <<   and (item.e == BC ? "B.C." :
"A.D.") << respectively, to enable the era to be displayed. Notice also that in
the overloaded operator<<() function we return s – the stream objects accepted as an argument – this is necessary so that items can be included anywhere in a cout type expression, e.g. cout << " Philosopher " << i <<
philosophers[i] << endl;

   Test run 9.2 shows a test run with these modifications and some suitable
input data.

```
     Philosopher              Born
----------------------------------
Socrates                  469 B.C.
Plato                     427 B.C.
Aristotle                 384 B.C.
St Thomas Aquinas        1225 A.D.

     Press ENTER to Quit
```

Earlier we said that the error trapping mechanism employed in the array template class is rather crude and that other options are available. We mention briefly two options now. The first method incorporates the `assert` macro available in C and C++ through the header file `assert.h`. The two functions which carry out some form of error trapping – the constructor and `operator[]` functions – can be used to demonstrate the use of `assert`. This macro takes an expression as an argument which if it is true (i.e. evaluates to a non-zero value) then no action is taken and processing continues as normal. However, if the assertion fails – the expression evaluates to 0 – then the program terminates with an error message written to the standard error file `stderr` – normally the screen. The new versions of these two functions are given below:

```
#include <assert.h>
template <class T>
array<T>::array(int sz){
   data = new T[sz];
   assert(data); // unable to allocate storage
   size = sz;
}

template <class T>
T & array<T>::operator[](int i){
   assert(i >= 0 && i < size);
   return data[i];
}
```

Examples of the output obtained on error conditions are:

```
Assertion failed: data, file ..\CPPPROGS\TEMPLAR3.CPP, line 25
Abnormal program termination
```

in the case of an error in specifying the size of the array, and

```
Assertion    failed:    i    >=    0    &&    i    <    size,    file
..\CPPPROGS\TEMPLAR3.CPP, line 31
Abnormal program termination
```

The output you obtain may differ in detail from the above examples but the same type of information will be provided by assert.

9.4   Exception handling

The other method of error trapping which we allude to very briefly involves the idea of *exception handling*. This has been included in the draft ANSI/ISO standard for C++ and is now widely available in C++ implementations. Exception handling is much more comprehensive than the simple methods used above, either via exit() or assert(), and allows the programmer to control what happens when errors (exceptions) occur. Essentially exception handling uses the three keywords try, throw and catch. try is used to label a block within which if errors occur these can be detected and recovered from, outside a try block exceptions or errors cannot be dealt with. The catch handler has to follow immediately the close of the try block and if more than one catch handler are required then they follow on in subsequent blocks. Finally the throw keyword is used in the try block, or a function nested within the block, to transfer to an appropriate catch handler when an error condition or exception occurs. As an example we illustrate how exception handling might work with the two functions used in the Program 9.3.

The functions will look something like this:

```
template <class T>
array<T>::array(int sz){
   data = new T[sz];
   if(!data)
      throw 0;   // unable to allocate storage
   size = sz;
}
template <class T>
T & array<T>::operator[](int i){
   if(i >= 0 && i < size)
      return data[i];
   else
      throw 1;   // index outside array bounds
}
```

Then within the main program we might have the following:

```
...
void main(void){
try{
   array<float> f1(5);   // a float array

   ...

   cout << " testing for bound checking " << endl;

   cout << " f2[-1] = " << f2[-1] << endl;
   }
// catch any errors
catch(int error_code){
   switch(error_code){
```

```
    case 0:
        cout << " Unable to allocate storage " << endl;
        cout << " for array: size = " << sz << endl;
        break;
    case 1:
        cout << " Array out of bounds (0 - " << size << " )\n";
        cout << " ...... index = " << i << endl;
        break;
    }
}
```

In practice we wouldn't just duplicate the messages contained in the earlier versions of these function but attempt to fix the problem either by requesting further user input or by setting default values – for example, setting the upper bound of the array to a predefined value. A more complete discussion of this topic is beyond the scope of this book, but if you are interested then check your implementation and its accompanying documentation to see how exemption handling is implemented.

9.5   The list class – as a template

Earlier in this chapter we looked at a `list` class which we used to store the names of poets and their years of birth (see Program 9.3, LISTPOET.cpp). This list made use of two other classes; a `node` class and an `item_type` class. Suppose we want to use this `list` class for objects which belong to a class other than `item_type`. In its current form we need to do one of two things to achieve this. One option is to change all references in both the `node` and `list` classes to our new class. Another is to modify the contents, the attributes and where necessary the methods, of the `item_type` class. Neither of these alternatives is very attractive. For each new class we need to make a number of changes, all of which are time consuming and prone to error. The obvious solution is to use a template for both the `list` and `node` classes so that any class (built-in or user-defined) can be used as an object in the list.

So let's look at how this might be achieved. The first consideration concerns the nature of some of the methods in the `list` and `node` classes. These classes weren't originally designed with the object of making them into generic classes, so there are some features which are undesirable and some that are missing! Consider first of all the `show()` function in the `node` class. This calls a similar function for an `item_type` object. But think for a moment about what objects we might wish to store in a node. Apart from some of our own design we might well wish to construct a list of `int`s, or `char`s, or ... any of the built-in types. None of these types will have a `show()` method, so if we convert the `node` class into a template and try to use one of the standard data types as an object in the node (and ultimately the list) it won't work. The `show()` method in `item_type` is really another name for the << operator. So a small change to the `show()` method in the `node` class, to produce:

```
void show(){ cout << item; }
```

will now allow any object with an overloaded << operator to be used with the this class. Of course we will need to ensure that any user-defined types have such an overloaded operator and so for example we will need to write such a function for our `item_type` class – but we will deal with that later.

Now to the `list` class. In this class we have a similar problem only this time with input. Currently we have an `enter()` method which allows objects belonging to the `item_type` class to be entered from the keyboard. We still require such a method (or at least the functionality of such a method) but again we want to be able to enter built-in data types as well as other user-defined data types. The `list::enter()` method calls an `item_type::enter()` method to read in data and this is really where the problem lies. Since `list` has no idea what type of data is to be entered we can easily remove this method from the `list` class and write replacement code in the main program to check the data entered and add it to the list until a suitable terminating value is entered.

With these changes we can convert the `node` and `list` classes into templates which can be used with any data types. The modified classes are given below.

📖 Header file (Reference Program 9.7)

```
//: LISTTEMP.h
//. a simple list class - using templates
// ..............................................................
// definition of a node for the list
// This contains the methods necessary to access a node:
//    get and change the contents
//    and get and set the pointer to the next node
template <class T>
class node{
   T item;
   node *next;
public:
   node(){}
   ~node(){}
   node *get_next(){ return next; }
   node *set_next(node *new_node){ next = new_node;}
   T get_item(){ return item; }
   void set_item(T new_item){ item = new_item; }
   void show(){cout << item;}
};
// ..............................................................
// list class
template <class T>
class list {
   node<T> *head,        // points to first node
```

```
              *tail,    // points to last node
              *this_node;  // points to current node
   node<T> *create_node();
   int count;              // number of nodes
 public:
   list();
   ~list();
   void add(T val);
   void front(){ this_node = head; }  // move to start of list
   T get();
   int nodeOK(){ return (this_node != tail); }
   int no_nodes(){ return count; }
   void show(){this_node->show();}
   void next_node(){this_node = this_node->get_next();}
};
// private method used when creating the list or adding a node
template <class T>
node<T> *list<T>::create_node() {
   node<T> *new_node;
   new_node = new node<T>;
   if (new_node == 0) {
      cout << " Out of Memory " << endl; exit(1);
   }
   return new_node;
}

template <class T>
list<T>::list() {
   head = tail = create_node();
   count = 0;
}
template <class T>
list<T>::~list() {
   node<T> *p;
   while (head != tail){
      p = head;
      head = head->get_next();
      delete p;
   }
   delete head;
}

// add data to the end of the list
template <class T>
void list<T>::add(T val) {
   tail->set_item(val);         // put 'val' in current last node
   tail = tail->set_next(create_node());  // create a new last
                                //  node and update tail pointer
   count++;
}
// return the value stored in 'this_node'
template <class T>
T list<T>::get() {
   T val = this_node->get_item();
   this_node = this_node->get_next();
   return val;
}
```

The majority of the changes incorporated in the above code involve usimg the template syntax as necessary and the template identifier T whenever item_type is referenced in the original. These together with the other changes mentioned above enable a simple list class of ints to be created using a program such as in Program 9.8.

📄 **Program 9.8**

```
//: TEMPINT.CPP
//. a Template list class - illustrating use with an int

#include <conio.h>
#include <iostream.h>
#include <process.h>
// ............................................................
// definition of node and list classes go here
// ............................................................
void main(void) {
   list<int> ilist;
   int n;

   clrscr();
   cout << " TEMPINT " << endl;
   cout << " ======= " << endl << endl;

   cout << " Please enter 5 ints " << endl;

   for(int i = 0; i < 5; i++){
      cout << " > ";
      cin >> n;
      ilist.add(n);
   }

   cout << endl << " Numbers were: ";
   ilist.front();
   while(ilist.nodeOK()){
      ilist.show();
      cout << " ";
      ilist.next_node();
   }
   cout << " Press ENTER to Quit ";
   cin.get();
}
```

So there is no difficulty about using built-in types with this list class – try it and see – Exercise 9.9.2 at the end of this chapter make some suggestions.

We said above that some modifications were also needed to the item_type class so that it will work with our new template classes. We now look at what these modifications involve. Both are very straightforward and basically involve replacing the enter() and show() function names with the appropriate syntax for declaring and defining the overloaded >> and << operators for use with istream and ostream respectively. The function declarations (prototypes) in the item_type class definition now become:

```
friend istream& operator>>(istream& s, item_type &item);
friend ostream& operator<<(ostream& s, item_type item);
```

with the corresponding changes made to the `enter()` and `show()` methods to give:

```
// read information from keyboard using >>
istream& operator>>(istream& s, item_type &item){
   char s1[82], s2[82];    // to hold data entered
   int i;           // to hold an integer for year

   cout << " Name: ";

   while(isspace(cin.peek()))
      cin.get();

   cin.getline(s1, 82);
   if (!stricmp(s1, "STOP")){
      item.set(s1, 0);
      return s;
   }
   cout << "  YoB: ";

   do{                  // simple validation for year
      cin.getline(s2, 82);
      i = atoi(s2);
      if (i < 0){
         cout << " Invalid Year, please re-enter "
                     << endl;
         cout << "  YoB: ";
      }
   } while (i < 0);
   item.set(s1, i);
   return s;
}
// output to screen
ostream& operator<<(ostream& s, item_type item){
   cout.setf(ios::left);
   cout << setw(20) << item.name << " ";
   cout << resetiosflags(ios::left)<<setw(5) <<item.year << endl;
   return s;
}
```

If you compare these functions closely with the original `enter()` and `show()` functions you will notice some small changes in the functions' bodies. First of all both functions return the stream argument `s` on exit, for the reason mentioned in our discussion of the `name_yr_era` class. Secondly, because of the fact that the `>>` function returns `s` we need another mechanism for checking the end of input since we can no longer return 0 to indicate the end of input and 1 otherwise. In the solution used here we simply ensure that when 'stop' is entered the `name` attribute of the `item_type` argument is set to STOP (with the `year` set to 0). This value can then be checked in any input loop used in the main program.

9.6 Template classes and parameters

In the array template discussed earlier we had the following class definition:

```
// Template class
template <class T>
class array{
   T *data;      // can use T here to identify the type
   int size;
public:
   array(int sz);      ~array(){ delete [] data; }
   T & operator[](int i);   // can use T here as well
};
```

This meant that to create an dynamic array object we used the form:

```
array<name_yr_era> philosophers(4);
```

This example can be used to introduce an alternative method which uses more than one parameter in a template class definition and in the corresponding object instantiation. We can define our template array class like this:

```
// Template class using array size as a parameter
template <class T, int sz>
class array{
   T *data;      // can use T here to identify the type
   int size;
public:
   array();   ~array(){ delete [] data; }
   T & operator[](int i);   // can use T here as well
};
```

Then whenever we wish to create an array object we simply include the size of the array in the angle brackets along with the data type:

```
array<name_yr_era, 4> philosophers;
```

One point to remember when creating templates such as these is that wherever the < > occur the same number of parameters must be include, as for the initial template <class > definition. So for example the constructor method for the array template looks like this:

```
template <class T, int sz>
array<T, sz>::array(){
   data = new T[sz];
   if (!data){
      cout << " **** ARRAY CLASS **** " << endl;
      cout << " Unable to allocate storage " << endl;
      cout << " for array: size = " << sz << endl;
      exit(1);
   }
   size = sz;
}
```

9.7 Template functions

The last section is this chapter provides a short introduction to template functions. We have seen that `template` classes can be used to create generic classes for use with a variety of objects. Occasionally it is useful to provide generic functions which can be used with any objects. The most common use of such functions concern implementing `max()` and `min()` functions to compare two values and return the maximum and minimum. These can be used to emulate and replace the corresponding macros. Other common uses involve swap functions and sorting and searching algorithms. So, for example, we could use a fast binary search algorithm in the design of a search template function which could be used with objects of any desired class. The simplest example involves writing a `swap()` function. In C++ we can write a function which swaps two `int`s as follows:

```
void swap(int &i1, int &i2){
   int temp = i1;
   i1 = i2;
   i2 = i1;
}
```

Similar functions can also be written for `float`s, `double`s, etc. For example:

```
void swap(double &d1, double &d2){
   double temp = d1;
   d1 = d2;
   d2 = d1;
}
```

We can even write such a function for a user-defined type, e.g.

```
void swap(item_type &it1, item_type &it2){
   int temp = it1;
   it1 = it2;
   it2 = it1;
}
```

Each version of the swap function (each *overloaded* version) contains almost identical code – the only essential difference is the data types which are being used. This is where `template` functions come in. A `template` function to replace all the above `swap()` functions looks, not unexpectedly, like this:

```
template <class T>
void swap(T &i1, T &i2){
   T temp = i1;
   i1 = i2;
   i2 = i1;
}
```

where the function definition is preceded by the usual `template <class T>` expression and all specific data types are replaced by T. To use this `template` function with a particular data type is very simple (see Program 9.9). Test run 9.3 shows a sample run.

📋 **Program 9.9**

```
//: TEMPLFUN.CPP
//. illustration of template functions - a swap() function
#include <iostream.h>
#include <conio.h>
// swap template function definitiongoes here,
// or include the appropriate header file containing it
void main(){
    int n = 8, m = 12;

    clrscr();
    cout << " TEMPLFUN " << endl;
    cout << " ======== " << endl << endl;

    cout << " A couple of ints ... " << endl;
    cout << " n = " << n << " m = " << m << endl;
    swap(n, m);
    cout << " After swapping: ";
    cout << " n = " << n << " m = " << m << endl;

    double d = 12.78, e = -15.8883;

    cout << " Now two doubles ... " << endl;
    cout << " d = " << d << " e = " << e << endl;
    swap(d, e);
    cout << " After swapping: ";
    cout << " d = " << d << " e = " << e << endl;
    cin.get();
}
```

🖥 **Test run 9.3**

```
TEMPLFUN
========

A couple of ints ...
n = 8 m = 12
After swapping:  n = 12 m = 8
Now two doubles ...
d = 12.78 e = -15.8883
After swapping:  d = -15.8883 e = 12.78
```

Normally we would not use the `swap()` function in such a primitive way as the above, for example it would probably be used as part of a sort routine, which might also be written as a template. In such cases we would be using statements such as `if (i1 > i2) swap(i1, i2);` or `if (i1 < i2) swap(i1, i2);` to enable data to be sorted into ascending or descending order. If we used the swap function to sort any of the built-in types then everything would work fine. But what about user-defined classes, can you see any problems with these? The important point here is that if we use such expressions with our own classes then we must either overload the < and > operators to deal with the comparison of objects belonging to our class or we compare attributes of the objects, not the objects themselves. This last method makes sense since sorting is likely to be based on numerical or alphabetical order. So, for example with the `names_yr_era` class we can sort our philosophers into alphabetical order by comparing the names of philosophers objects. Like this:

```
if (stricmp(p1.get_name(), p2.get_name()) > 0)
    swap(p1, p2);
```

which uses the built-in function `stricmp()` together with a user-defined function `get_name()`, or, like this:

```
if (p1.get_name() > p2. get_name())
    swap(p1, p2);
```

which makes use of an overloaded > operator for use with strings which must be provided by the `names_yr_era` designer.

9.8   Summary

In this chapter we looked at the topic of container classes and then how template classes can be used to create generic container classes.

Topics covered:

- Container classes.
- Linear linked lists.
- Template classes.
- Template functions.
- Exception handling.

9.9   Exercises

9.9.1   Make the modifications discussed in the text to enable the INLIST program (Program 9.1) to be used for a list of chars.

9.9.2 The various versions of the `list` class discussed in the text could be improved by adding another method – `display()` – which can be used to display all the elements in the list. For example `poets. display();` will display all the poets in the `poets` list. Write a function to perform this task and try it out. (A good one to start with could be based on the code given in Program 9.2d.)

9.9.3 Write other versions of the `item_type` class (Program 9.2a) to enable the following data to be stored. Then write suitable programs to test them out.

a) An element class to hold the name of a chemical element (char array of 15), its Atomic Number (use `unsigned int`), its chemical symbol (char array of 4) and its atomic weight (a float). Use the following data to check you final program:

Hydrogen,	1,	H,	1.008
Oxygen,	8,	O,	16
Aluminum,	13,	Al,	26.97
Chromium,	24,	Cr,	52.01
Iron,	26,	Fe,	55.84
Silver,	47,	Ag,	107.88
Uranium,	92,	U,	238.17

b) A weather class to hold details of weather reports from cities around the world. The attributes for this class are: Name of city, weather type, minimum temperature (in C) and maximum temperature. Write methods such that the city is always written with its first letter in uppercase and all subsequent letters in lower case. Use an enumerated type for the weather type with the following enumerators C, F, S, Dr, R, Sn, Sl, Sh, Th, Fg, M, to represent different weather conditions (Cloudy, Fair, Sunny, Drizzle, Snow, Sleet, Showers, Thunder, Fog, Mist). Add one further enumerator to the above list 'na' to indicate that no report is available. Test your program by using suitable data – all quality newspapers contain daily information.

9.9.4 Modify the `weather` class so that it contains a date. Use the date class discussed earlier – see also Appendix A. Modify the previous program, or write a new one, to test out this class.

What other solution is there to obtaining a combined `date` and `weather` class which does not involve modifying the `weather` class?

Try this other solution out.

9.9.5   The item_type class in Program 9.3 could be improved by making some modifications to the enter() method so that, for example, a more rigorous check is made on the year – such as it must be no later than 15 years before the present year. Investigate the built-in date routines and find a function which enables you to obtain the system year, then use this in the enter() method to check the date. As a further useful exercise you could write a private method which carries out the necessary date checking functions.

9.9.6   Write a stack class, based on the list class (e.g. Program 9.2c), which uses the node and item_type classes discussed in the text (e.g. Programs 9.2b and 9.2a). The stack class contains the operations push(item_type val) to add an item to the top of the stack; pop(item_type &val) to remove an item from the top of the stack; display() to display all the items in the stack; and get_no_items() to return the number of items in the stack in addition to the necessary constructor and destructor functions.

9.9.7   Make the changes mentioned in the text to the item_type class so that it can be used with the template, node and list classes and write a program to try it out.

9.9.8   Modify the template array class so that the array size is included as a parameter. Remember to modify the constructor header.

A | Date Class

Program A.1

```
//        dateops.cpp
//        The date class and example program

#include <iostream.h>
#include <conio.h>
#include <string.h>

#define TRUE 1
#define FALSE 0
// ........................................................
static int days_in_month[] = {
    31, 28, 31, 30, 31, 30, 31, 31, 30, 31, 30, 31
};

static char *months[] = {
    "January",     "February",    "March",      "April",
    "May",         "June",        "July",       "August",
    "September",   "October",     "November",   "December"
};

class date {
    int date_set;      // date_set = TRUE if date has valid value,
                       // otherwise FALSE
    int day;
    int mm;       //      range 1 - 12
    int year;          //  must be complete i.e. 1996 = 1996 not 96)

    long day_num(date dt);    // private member functions
    int isleap(int y);

public:
    date() { date_set = FALSE;}      // constructor - used to
         // initialise date_set so that unset dates
                       // can be trapped
                       // overloaded constructor
    date(int d, int m, int y){ day = d; mm = m;
                                    year = y; date_set = TRUE;}
    void set(int d, int m, int y);
    void next();
    void prev();
    void print_long_date();

    void operator=(date &dt);

    date operator+(int n);    // add n days e.g. d1 + n
    friend date operator+(int n, date &dt); // e.g. n + d1

    long operator-(date dt);    // no. days between two dates
    date operator-(int n);      // subtract n days from a date
    date operator++();          // prefix ++
    date operator++(int);       // postfix ++
    date operator--();          // prefix --
    date operator--(int);       // postfix --
    date operator+=(int n);     // d1 = d1 + n
    date operator-=(int n);     // da = d1 - n
```

326

```
        // comparison operators for date
    int operator<(date &dt);
    int operator>(date &dt);
    int operator<=(date &dt);
    int operator>=(date &dt);
    int operator==(date &dt);
    int operator!=(date &dt);
        // overloaded << and >>
    friend ostream &operator<<(ostream &stream, date dt);
    friend istream &operator>>(istream &stream, date &dt);
};
// ..........................................................
void main(void) {

    date d1, d2(23,10,1996);
    date christmas(25,12,1996);

    clrscr();
    cout << " DATEOPS " << endl;
    cout << " ======= " << endl;
    cout << " Illustrating some overloaded operators using dates" << endl
              << endl;
    cout << " d2 : " << d2;

    d1 = d2;
    cout << " After d1 = d2 ..." << endl;
    cout << " d1 : " << d1;

    d1.set(14,9,1996);
    cout << " After d1.set(14,9,1996) ..." << endl;
    cout << " d1 : " << d1;

    d1--;
    cout << " After d1-- ..." << endl;
    cout << " d1 : " << d1;

    date d3;
    cout << endl << " Now enter a date - " << endl;
    cin >> d3;
    cout << " d3 : " << d3 << endl;

    cout << " Days between d3 and d1 = " << d3-d1 << endl;

    if (d3 > christmas)  // use overloaded > to compare dates
       cout << " Sorry - Christmas is over " << endl;
    else if (d3 < christmas)    // ... and <
       cout << christmas - d3 << " days to Christmas 1996" << endl;
    else
       cout << " HAPPY CHRISTMAS! " << endl;

    date today;        // new object

    cout << endl << " Now enter today's date - " << endl;
    cin >> today;
    cout << " today : " << today << endl;
    cout << " In 60 days time it will be " << 60+today << endl;
    cout << " or ";
    (60+today).print_long_date();

    cout << " Press any key to Quit " << endl;
    getch();
}
// ..........................................................
// date class - function definitions
void date::set(int d, int m, int y) {
    day = d;
```

```
        mm = m;
        year = y;
        date_set = TRUE;
    }

    //      get next day
    //      leap years catered for

    void date::next(){

        if (!date_set) {
            cout << endl << " *** Invalid date sent to NEXT() *** " << endl;
            return;
        }

        int d_in_m[12];

        for(int m = 0; m < 12; m++)
            d_in_m[m] = days_in_month[m];
        if (isleap(year))
            d_in_m[1]++;

        day++;

        if (day > d_in_m[mm-1]) {
            mm++;
            if (mm > 12) {
                mm = 1;
                year++;
            }
            day = 1;
        }
    }
    // ..............................................................
    // display date in long form
    //      i.e. using 'January' etc.

    void date::print_long_date() {
        cout << day << " " << months[mm-1] << " " << year << endl;
    }
    // ..............................................................
    // get previous date
    // leap years catered for

    void date::prev(){

        if (!date_set) {
            cout << endl << " *** Invalid date sent to PREV() *** " << endl;
            return;
        }

        int d_in_m[12];

        for(int m = 0; m < 12; m++)
            d_in_m[m] = days_in_month[m];
        if (isleap(year))
            d_in_m[1]++;

        day--;
        if ( day < 1) {
            mm--;
            if (mm < 1) {
                mm = 12;
                year--;
            }
            day = d_in_m[mm-1];
```

```
      }
}
// ..................................................................
//      overloaded assignment operator

void date::operator=(date &dt) {
   day = dt.day;
   mm = dt.mm;
   year = dt.year;
}
// ..................................................................
//      add n days to a date
//      e.g. d1 + 5

date date::operator+(int n) {
   int d_in_m[12];

   for(int m = 0; m < 12; m++)
      d_in_m[m] = days_in_month[m];
   if (isleap(year))
      d_in_m[1]++;

   date dt = *this;
   n += dt.day;


   while( n > d_in_m[dt.mm-1]) {
      n -= d_in_m[dt.mm-1];
      if (++dt.mm == 13) {
         dt.mm = 1;
         dt.year++;
      }
   }
   dt.day = n;
   return dt;
}

//      add n days to a date
//      e.g. 5 + d1
//      note - this uses the previous operator

date operator+(int n, date &dt) {
   return dt + n;
}

//      overloaded minus
//      allows two dates to be subtracted
//      e.g. d1 - d2
//      d1 must be >= d12

long date::operator-(date dt) {
   if (day_num(*this) >= day_num(dt))
      return day_num(*this) - day_num(dt);
   else
   {
      cout << " first date must be >= second date " << endl;
      return -1;
   }
}
// ..................................................................
//      decrement date - prefix
date date::operator--() {
   if (!date_set) {
      cout << endl << " *** Attempt to decrement an invalid date *** "
                                   << endl;
      return *this;
```

```
        }

    int d_in_m[12];

    for(int m = 0; m < 12; m++)
        d_in_m[m] = days_in_month[m];
    if (isleap(year))
        d_in_m[1]++;

    day--;
    if ( day < 1) {
        mm--;
        if (mm < 1) {
            mm = 12;
            year--;
        }
        day = d_in_m[mm-1];
    }
    return *this;
}

//          decrement date - postfix

date date::operator--(int) {

    if (!date_set) {
        cout << endl << " *** Attempt to decrement an invalid date *** "
                            << endl;
        return *this;
    }
    int d_in_m[12];

    for(int m = 0; m < 12; m++)
        d_in_m[m] = days_in_month[m];
    if (isleap(year))
        d_in_m[1]++;

    date dt = *this;
    day--;
    if ( day < 1) {
        mm--;
        if (mm < 1) {
            mm = 12;
            year--;
        }
        day = d_in_m[mm-1];
    }
    return dt;
}
// ..................................................
//      overloaded left shift
//      allows cout to be used directly with a date
//      e.g. cout << d1;

ostream &operator<<(ostream &stream, date dt) {
    stream << dt.day << " / " << dt.mm << " / " << dt.year;
    return stream;
}

//      overloaded right shift
//      allows cin to be used to input date info.
//      e.g. cin >> d1;

istream &operator>>(istream &stream, date &dt) {
    unsigned short century;
```

```
      cout << "      Enter day : ";
      stream >> dt.day;
      cout << "    Enter month : ";
      stream >> dt.mm;
      cout << "      Enter year : ";
      stream >> dt.year;
      if (dt.year < 100) {
         cout << " Enter century : ";
         stream >> century;
         dt.year += (century-1)*100;
      }
      cout << endl;
      return stream;
}
// .............................................................
//      convert date to a day number
//      day 0 is 1/1/0 A.D.
//      note - this assumes that y is the actual year (e.g 1996 not 96)

long date::day_num(date dt) {
   long d;
   int y;

   y = dt.year-1;

   d = 365 * (long) y + (y / 4) - (y / 100) + (y / 400);
   for (int m = 1; m < dt.mm; m++)
      d += days_in_month[m];

   d += dt.day;
   if (isleap(dt.year))
      if (dt.mm > 2)
         d++;
      else
      if (dt.mm == 2)
         if (dt.day == 29)
            d++;

   return d;
}
// .............................................................
//      test for leap year
//      y must be real year e.g. 1996 not 96)

int date::isleap(int y) {
   if ((y % 4) == 0) {
      if (( y % 100) != 0)
         return TRUE;
      else
      if ((y % 400) == 0)
         return TRUE;
      else
         return FALSE;
   }
   else
      return FALSE;
}
// .............................................................
// overloaded comparison operators
// <, >, <=, >=, == and !=
// note type must be long  (i.e. long int)

int date::operator<(date &dt)
{
   if (day_num(*this) < day_num(dt))
      return TRUE;
```

```
      else
         return FALSE;
   }


   int date::operator>(date &dt)
   {
      if (day_num(*this) > day_num(dt))
         return TRUE;
      else
         return FALSE;
   }

   int date::operator<=(date &dt)
   {
      if (day_num(*this) <= day_num(dt))
         return TRUE;
      else
         return FALSE;
   }

   int date::operator>=(date &dt)
   {
      if (day_num(*this) >= day_num(dt))
         return TRUE;
      else
         return FALSE;
   }

   int date::operator==(date &dt)
   {
      if (day_num(*this) == day_num(dt))
         return TRUE;
      else
         return FALSE;
   }

   int date::operator!=(date &dt)
   {
      if (day_num(*this) != day_num(dt))
         return TRUE;
      else
         return FALSE;
   }
   // ..........................................................
```

B. C++ Tokens

What follows is a complete list of operators, punctuators and preprocessor tokens as defined in the draft ANSI/ISO standard for C++. Where two tokens appear on the same line they must be used as a pair.

B.1 Comments

/* */   (Opening) forward slash asterisk and (closing) asterisk forward slash – standard C style for comments which is also available in C++.

//   Double forward slash – used to indicate (C++ specific) comment all that follows is ignored until the next line.

B.2 Separators

{ }   (Opening) and (closing) braces – used to indicated beginning and end of a compound statement.

[ ]   (Opening) and (closing) brackets – enclosing array subscripts, both single and multi–dimensional.

( )   (Opening) and (closing) parentheses – used to group expressions, to indicate function calls, to indicate function parameters and to enclose conditional expressions.

,   Comma – used to separate function arguments and as an operator in comma expressions.

;   Semicolon – used to indicate the end of a statement. Can be used on its own to indicate an empty statement is only used after } in structure or class declarations.

:   Colon used to indicate a labelled statement – also used as an operator, see below.

. . .   Ellipsis, consists three full stops with no white spaces separating them. Used to indicate a variable number of arguments, or arguments with varying types in function prototypes.

B.3 Preprocessor operators

The hash sign (also called pound in US terminology!) – used to indicate a preprocessor directive.

`##`	Double hash – used to perform token replacement during the preprocessor scanning stage of compilation.

B.4 Operators

`<: :>`	
`<% %>`	
`%:`	
`%:%:`	
`new`	Used for dynamic memory allocation.
`delete`	Used to release memory allocated previously by new.
`?`	Used only as part of the conditional operator (*exp1* ? *exp2* : *exp3*) which is equivalent to `if` (*exp1*) *exp2*; `else` *exp3*;.
`::`	The scope resolution operator – used to control the scope and access of class attributes and methods.
`.`	Dot operator – used to provide direct selection of a member of a structure (`struct`, `union` or `class`).
`.*`	Used to dereference a pointer to a class member.
`+`	Plus sign – a binary operator, used to indicate addition. Can also be used as a unary operator with an arithmetic expression to force integral promotion.
`−`	Minus sign – as a binary operator used to indicate subtraction – as a unary operator used to change sign of its operand.
`*`	Asterisk – as a binary operator used to indicate multiplication – as a unary operator used to indicate indirection.
`/`	(Forward) slash – used on its own to indicate division.
`%`	Percent sign – modulo operator, used in arithmetic expressions to calculate the remainder after integer division.
`^`	Circumflex (or caret) – bitwise exclusive or exclusive-OR.
`&`	Ampersand – as a binary operator used for bitwise AND; as a unary operator used as the address operator and to indicate a reference variable.
`|`	A binary operator used to indicate bitwise (inclusive) OR.
`~`	Tilde – a unary operator used to compute the bitwise complement of its operand.
`!`	A unary operator used as logical NOT.
`=`	Assignment operator.
`<`	Relational less than operator.
`>`	Relational greater than operator.
`< >`	(Opening) and (closing) angle brackets used with the #include preprocessor directive to delimit header file names. Used in templates to delimit a template argument list (often just <T>).
`+=`	Add and assign.
`−=`	Subtract and assign.
`*=`	Multiply and assign.
`/=`	Divide and assign.
`%=`	Modulo and assign.

`^=`	Bitwise XOR and assign.
`&=`	Bitwise AND and assign.
`|=`	Bitwise OR and assign.
`<<`	Left shift operator – binary operator used to shift bits left a given number of places. Overloaded in C++ to move data onto an output stream.
`>>`	Right shift operator – binary operator used to shift bits right a given number of places. Overloaded in C++ to move data from input stream to program variables.
`<<=`	Left shift and assign.
`>>=`	Right shift and assign.
`==`	Equal to.
`!=`	Not equal to.
`<=`	Less than or equal to.
`>=`	Greater than or equal to.
`&&`	Logical AND.
`||`	Logical OR.
`++`	Increment operator (prefix or postfix).
`--`	Decrement operator (prefix or postfix).
`,`	Comma operator – when used in a comma expression (e.g. i = 2, i + 6) the result is an lvalue equal to the value of the right–most operand (e.g. i + 6, or 8).
`->*`	Dereference pointer to a pointer to a class member (cf. .* above).
`->`	Structure or union pointer operator – used for indirect selection (str_ptr->member is equivalent to the expression (*str_ptr).member).

The following operators have been included in the ANSI/ISO C++ standard as equivalents to the corresponding operators indicated above.

`and`	`&&`	(Logical AND)
`and_eq`	`&=`	(Bitwise AND and assign)
`bitand`	`&`	(Bitwise AND)
`bitor`	`|`	(Bitwise OR)
`compl`	`~`	(Bitwise – 1's – complement)
`not`	`!`	(Logical NOT)
`not_eq`	`!=`	(Not equal to)
`or`	`||`	(Logical OR)
`or_eq`	`|=`	(Bitwise OR and assign)
`xor`	`^`	(Bitwise exclusive OR)
`xor_eq`	`^=`	(Bitwise exclusive OR and assign)

C Solution to Selected Exercises

Solutions to selected exercises and all of the source code in the book can be downloaded from the WWW page:

```
http://www.svc.org.uk/cplus/cplusinfo.htm
```

or from the Macmillan site at:

```
http://www.macmillan-press.co.uk/mastering
```

Otherwise, by email, from the author with:

```
arthurc@ed-coll.ac.uk
```

or from the editor with:

```
w.buchanan@napier.ac.uk
```

The solutions and source code can also be requested by post, along with a floppy disk and a stamped addressed envelope, from:

Suzannah Tipple,
Macmillan Press Ltd,
Houndsmill,
Basingstoke,
Hampshire.
UK.
RG21 6XS.

Index

Inline functions, 171, 172, 220
    macros, 172
    use of, 171
Insertion operator, 209, 210
Instances, 135–137, 146, 155, 157, 162, 194, 226, 287, 289
Int pointer, 79, 84, 86, 88, 89, 92, 105
Integer division, 169
Intention, 19
ISO/ANSI, 5, 6, 31, 40
Istream member functions, 123, 134

Julian, 221

Keywords, 5, 6, 21, 32, 101, 135, 136, 138, 243, 245, 314

Least significant bit, 38
Linked lists, 323
Logical negation, 13
Lowercase, 7, 172

Main program function, 1, 4
Memory, 11, 14, 49, 57, 58, 62, 75, 78, 82, 84, 88, 101–110, 116, 149–152, 198, 200, 204, 205, 234, 236, 237, 239, 241
Menu-driven, 33
Metric, 175–179, 200, 217–219, 224
Millennium, 206
Most significant bit, 38
Multi-dimensional arrays, 100
Multiple declarations, 166
Multiple inheritance, 243, 244, 252, 272, 273, 284–287, 305

Name constructor, 281–284, 289
Negative integers, 159
Nested if statements, 18
New and delete, 101
Newline, 3
Non-member and non-friend operator overloading, 190, 220

Object-oriented programming, 135, 138, 142, 168, 219, 243, 273, 284, 290, 297
Objects, 6, 34, 43, 58, 116, 136–140, 142, 147, 149, 151–153, 155, 156, 158, 162–164, 167, 168, 173, 182, 190, 195, 199, 200, 203–205, 213, 215, 221, 223, 226–228, 230–232, 234, 237–244, 246, 247, 249, 251, 258, 269, 270, 273–279, 281–284, 289, 290, 292, 298, 302, 306,

312, 315, 316, 321, 323
Octal, 4, 9, 10, 32, 117–120
Operand, 13, 23, 122, 185, 186, 211
Operator
    overloading, 164, 182, 219
    precedence and associativity, 30, 32
Overloadable operators, 183
Overloading
    +, 186, 211
    +=, 185, 219
    =, 204, 208
    auto-increment operator, 192
    constructor, 145, 168, 195, 207, 228, 245, 248, 250
    function, 143, 145, 161, 194, 220, 241, 278
    functions with different parameter types, 168, 170
    left shift operator <<, 209
    operator declarations, 191
    operator definitions, 191
    postfix--, 208
    unary operators, 191, 220

Parameter
    list, 36, 92, 165, 194, 204, 209, 278
    types, 168
Pascal, 4, 16, 58, 65, 158
Penny farthings, 244
Philosophers object, 323
Pint, 76–78, 81, 83, 86–88, 111, 113, 176–179
Pneumatic, 244
Point class, 174, 180, 252–254, 259, 266, 267, 271
Point objects, 256, 266
Pointers, 75–112, 230, 242
    arithmatic, 83, 84, 88, 97, 112, 113, 231, 239
    comparing points, 85, 112
    expression, 79, 112
    how point arthmetic works, 83
    initialisation, 82
    notation, 110
    objects, 230, 242
    their uses, 75
    to a function, 76, 233, 234
    void pointers, 89
Polymorphism, 168, 219
Postfix, 220
Precedence, 30, 31, 106, 182
Pre-processor, 59, 172
Printer, 115